WRESTLING WITH THE ANGEL

INSURRECTIONS: CRITICAL STUDIES
IN RELIGION, POLITICS, AND CULTURE

INSURRECTIONS: CRITICAL STUDIES IN RELIGION, POLITICS, AND CULTURE

Slavoj Žižek, Clayton Crockett, Creston Davis, Jeffrey W. Robbins, Editors

The intersection of religion, politics, and culture is one of the most discussed areas in theory today. It also has the deepest and most wide-ranging impact on the world. Insurrections: Critical Studies in Religion, Politics, and Culture will bring the tools of philosophy and critical theory to the political implications of the religious turn. The series will address a range of religious traditions and political viewpoints in the United States, Europe, and other parts of the world. Without advocating any specific religious or theological stance, the series aims nonetheless to be faithful to the radical emancipatory potential of religion.

For a list of titles in this series, see page 301

TRACY McNULTY

WRESTLING WITH
THE ANGEL

Experiments in Symbolic Life

Columbia University Press / New York

Columbia University Press
Publishers Since 1893
New York   Chichester, West Sussex
cup.columbia.edu
Copyright © 2014 Columbia University Press
All rights reserved

Library of Congress Cataloging-in-Publication Data

McNulty, Tracy.
   Wrestling with the angel: experiments in symbolic life / Tracy McNulty.
      pages cm. — (Insurrections: critical studies in religion, politics,
and culture)
   Includes bibliographical references and index.
ISBN 978-0-231-16118-3 (cloth)—ISBN 978-0-231-16119-0
(pbk.)—ISBN 978-0-231-53760-5 (e-book)
   1. Lacan, Jacques, 1901–1981.   2. Psychoanalysis.   I. Title.

BF173.M35846 2014
128—dc23

                                                    2013042826

Cover design: Noah Arlow

To Brad and Devin

CONTENTS

CODA: TOWARD AN AESTHETICS OF SYMBOLIC LIFE

ACKNOWLEDGMENTS

A CONFERENCE ON "Saint Paul and Modernity" organized by Ken Reinhard offered the opportunity to begin formulating the central argument of the book, while the conference I coorganized with Jason Frank on "Taking Exception to the Exception" allowed me to work on Walter Benjamin as well as to begin thinking about questions of written law in the context of political theory. Jeffrey Librett's conference on "Political Theology and the Question of the Border" allowed me to extend that argument to Schmitt and to think about its relation to psychoanalysis, while the conference Peter Goodrich organized at Cardozo Law School on "Alain Badiou: Law and Event" gave me an opportunity to work on the legal writings of Pierre Legendre as well as Badiou. I thank Elizabeth Weed for her invitation to address the topic of "psychoanalysis and social change" for a special issue of *differences*, which provided fodder for this book as well as projects yet to come.

Juliet Flower MacCannell is my teacher, mentor, and friend of more than twenty years, as well as the most immediate source of inspiration for this project. Like just about everything I've written, this book is inspired and influenced by her work in ways that exceed citation. Jason Frank inspired me to take the plunge into political theory, and our hundreds of conversations on the topic of this book and on so many others have shaped my thinking on all aspects of the argument, but especially the discussion of the written law. Willy Apollon, Danielle Bergeron, and Lucie Cantin prompted my interest in the enabling function of constraints with their groundbreaking work in the psychoanalytic treatment of psychosis and their reflections on the transference and the analytic act; I thank them for many years of rewarding collaboration, and for reminding me constantly that psychoanalysis can be a creative force for social change. Camille Robcis's questions and demands for a more vital and relevant account of the symbolic in an early seminar on Lacan played an important role in my decision to write this book, while Shanna Carlson, Carissa Sims, and Daniel Wilson have challenged and enlarged my understanding of the symbolic with their work on gender, femininity, and logic. Peter Hallward's work on political philosophy and popular will has suggested new horizons that I have only begun to explore here, and I look forward to taking further in the sequel to this book.

My comrades in the Psychoanalysis Reading Group—Heidi Arsenault, Karen Benezra, Andrew Bielski, Matteo Calla, Shanna Carlson, Rebecca Colesworthy, Paul Flaig, Diana Hamilton, Fernanda Negrete, Carissa Sims, and Daniel Wilson—have been a tremendous source of intellectual stimulation and camaraderie for many years now, and inspire me daily with their passion for psychoanalysis and the originality and interest of their work. Alexis Briley, Morgane Cadieu, and Cary Howie are kindred spirits in their love of constraints, obstacles, and the claustrophilia of tight spaces, whose insights and suggestions for further reading have provided inspiration at critical stages in this project. The students in my seminars "Political Theology," "Rethinking the Symbolic," "Creativity and Constraints," and "Psychoanalysis and Sexual Difference" helped me to develop and refine the argument of this book. In addition to those already mentioned, I would like to thank Tal Gluck, Alex Haber, Martin Hagglund, Susan Hall, Ryan Jackson, Emily Kane, Megan Kruer, Ariana Marmora, Klas Molde, Adeline Rother, Avery Slater, Jack Stetter, and Yael Wender for their questions, comments, and suggestions.

The questions of Alain Badiou, Petar Bojanic, Ellen Burt, Peter Gilgen, Peter Goodrich, Luke Fraser, Bonnie Honig, Julia Lupton, Bernie Meyler, Susan Buck-Morss, Ken Reinhard, Neil Saccamano, Kam Shapiro, Geoff

Waite, and Slavoj Žižek on the talks and conference papers that led to the formulation of this book have been extremely helpful in revising or refining its argument; I hope I've managed to address at least a few of their concerns and questions.

The comments of Alexis Briley, Morgane Cadieu, Jason Frank, Peter Hallward, Dominiek Hoens, Adrian Johnston, Jeffrey Librett, Juliet Mac-Cannell, Eleanor Kaufman, Richard Klein, and Elizabeth Weed on earlier drafts of this material have been indispensable in helping me to shape my ideas. I owe a huge debt of gratitude to Adrian Johnston and Elizabeth Weed in particular, who read so much of this manuscript so many times in the process of reviewing it for the press and who have been extraordinarily generous in sharing their comments, suggestions, and criticisms. I thank Adrian specifically for being friend enough to also be an enemy when the circumstances warrant it.

A generous fellowship from Robert and Helen Appel supported a semester of research in London in the early stages of writing, while the many department chairs I've worked with in rapid succession over the past few years—Walter Cohen, Jonathan Culler, Richard Klein, Kathleen Perry Long, and Tim Campbell—supported the project by providing research and travel funds that helped with various aspects of the manuscript's preparation.

Thanks to Wendy Lochner at Columbia University Press for taking an interest in the project and shepherding it through the review process, to Christine Dunbar for her lively correspondence and much-needed assistance with the preparation of the manuscript, and to Robert Demke for his careful copyediting.

Finally, I am grateful to Devin Zukovic for sharing the first four years of his life with this book, and to Brad Zukovic for sharing his life with me. This book is dedicated to them.

Chapter 2, "Demanding the Impossible: Desire and Social Change," was published in *differences* 20, no. 1 (Spring 2008): 1–39; portions of chapter 3, "Wrestling with the Angel," were published under the same title in *Umbr(a)* (2005): 73–84; chapter 4 was first published as "The Gap in the Law and the Border-Breaching Function of the Exception" in *Konturen* 1 (2008), http://

konturen.uoregon.edu/volume1.html; chapter 6 appeared in *Cardozo Law Review* 29, no. 5 (April 2008): 2209–2238, in a special issue devoted to the work of Alain Badiou; a fuller version of chapter 6 was published as "The Commandment Against the Law: Writing and Divine Justice in Walter Benjamin's 'Critique of Violence,'" *diacritics* 37, nos. 2–3 (Spring 2008): 34–60; portions of chapter 7 were published under the title "Enabling Constraints: Toward an Aesthetics of Symbolic Life" in *Umbr(a)* (2010): 35–63.

WRESTLING WITH THE ANGEL

INTRODUCTION

Enabling Constraints

HERE IS WHAT CONCERNS ME: a growing sense that despite the varied and important ways in which contemporary social and political theory has attempted to understand and defend the cause of freedom, the latter is too often defined solely in negative terms, as a freedom *from* limits or constraints: oppressive norms, restrictive or prejudicial laws, the reified accretions of the status quo that make it resistant to change.

When Georg Cantor defined mathematics as a practice of "freedom realized through constraints,"[1] he gave expression to something that is all too often overlooked today: that the pursuit of subjective freedom may be enabled—and not impeded—by the struggle with limits, obstacles, and constraints. This claim belongs to a storied genealogy of philosophical, legal, religious, and aesthetic reflection on the enabling function of constraints, which this book seeks both to recall and to restore to its rightful place as a crucial contribution to debates about what it means to be free, and how the subject's freedom—or what I prefer to call its desire—can be solicited and sustained as a source of creativity, innovation, and social and political change.

We generally have no difficulty affirming the importance of constraints in practices like mathematics, music, or poetry, or more broadly in the sphere of education. In each of these domains, some kind of constrained practice takes the place of—or at least precedes—intuition, improvisation, or insight. We develop a capacity for musical improvisation by learning the standards, appeal to fixed poetic forms like the sonnet to give expression to singular experiences or to articulate a new aesthetic program, and gain access to advanced mathematics only by disabling intuitive representations through the rigorous literalism of proofs and equations. And while the educative process is highly constrained, even strictly regimented, we recognize that education is not merely a matter of internalizing rules and norms, but about learning to be free and to make the most of that freedom.

In the social and legal spheres, however, this enabling dimension of constraint is often overlooked. While we may recognize the need to limit criminal behavior or compel citizens to take responsibility for their actions, we tend not to view political or legal constraints as facilitating subjective freedom. More often than not, we see laws and limits as *limiting*, as circumscribing our freedom or subordinating it to the interests of the group or nation rather than sustaining or supporting it. This is due in part, I suspect, to the lack of any widely recognized distinction between rule and constraint, or between the prescriptions or prohibitions of positive law and the structural (or even psychical) function of limits and obstacles.

Such a distinction is crucial to the philosophy of Immanuel Kant, on the other hand, whose conception of morality calls upon the subject to forego the props and supports of positive law and to devise moral maxims that are neither modeled upon nor subordinated to prescriptive rules or prohibitions. As such, it might be understood as a rejection of any constrained lawfulness. Importantly, however, Kant shows that the receding of law as traditionally understood must correspond to a renewed investment in constraints. In his *Critique of Practical Reason*, he defines the will as the power of rational beings "to determine their causality by the presentation of rules" (rules that they themselves author), and thus as a capacity to "perform actions according to principles."[2] In the judgments human beings make about the lawfulness of their actions, he specifies that "their reason, incorruptible and self-constrained, . . . always holds the will's maxim in an action up to the pure will, i.e., to itself inasmuch as it regards itself as practical a priori." The moral feeling of duty is therefore linked to the exercise of an "inner but intellectual constraint," and not to a submissive posture with respect to an external authority. This is why law (understood as a capacity for self-legislation, or for giving oneself the law) and free will are for Kant inseparable.

Kant's understanding of morality underscores something we can easily overlook: that the struggle with constraints does not simply produce a more legitimate (or even more just) result, but enables and supports the exercise of freedom—freedom from authority, from norms of conduct, and even from ideals and values (precisely those features, that is, with which the concept of law is so often collapsed). Understood in this manner, the moral maxim introduces a distinction between two fundamentally different understandings of law: as the representation of an authority or normal state of affairs (and thus as an inflexible rule, order, or sign of power) and as a practice of struggling with constraints that not only does not entail submission to authority, but actively precludes it.

The novelty of Kant's approach emerges in comparison with a writer whose position might seem to be very close, the apostle Paul. Like Kant, Paul eschews the props and supports of positive law, which stand in the way of true freedom (or grace) because they bind us to the mortal body that is the object of the law's prohibitions, and thus to "what is." The law has its place, of course, but only as a "tutor" or "guardian," which advises and guides us until we reach maturity and are able to access the spirit of the law directly, without passing through its letter. The law's dimension as constraint or limit must therefore fall away in favor of another understanding of law, which consists in full identification with its source or the internalization of its spirit. Paul gives expression to a dominant way of thinking about constraints, as essentially linked to training or education. In contrast, Kant shows that the struggle with constraints is not a matter of training or preparing for an eventual freedom or for an act to come, but a free act in and of itself. (In the same way, a great poet like Mallarmé shows that the most radical poetic innovations are defined not merely by throwing off existing conventions or the constraints of genre, meter, or rhyme, but by their renewal of the possibilities and full potential of poetic constraint.) Hence while Paul and Kant both see as inevitable the decline of law traditionally understood,

Kant differs from his predecessor in arguing that this shift must correspond to a renewed engagement with constraints, and specifically in an attention to the lettered or formal character of constraint that precludes any facile surrender to (or identification with) the "spirit" of law.

The *Critique of Judgment* complements and completes this argument by emphasizing that the "self-constraint" of reason is itself supported by the struggle with external or formal constraints, but precisely on the condition that the latter are apprehended as enabling constraints or barriers, and not as mere rules. In a discussion of the second commandment of the Hebrew Decalogue—which bans the manufacture of images, and by extension the imaginary function that reduces the imagination to what can be represented—Kant argues that the commandment allows for a "negative exhibition of the infinite" that constrains the imagination, prevents it from rising to the level of "fanaticism," and thereby enables it to do another kind of work, that at stake in sublime aesthetic judgments.

Many of the examples I will discuss deal with different aspects of law (and especially written law), which is so often posited as antithetical to freedom and free will. To look at legal constraints alongside formal constraints (poetry, math, art, psychoanalysis) is, I hope, to see the function of rules and constraints in a different light. What they share is an investment in the difference between the *letter* as constraint and the *law* as a prescriptive rule or representation of a law-making authority. Although the two are often collapsed (as in the letters of Paul, whose polemic against the written law is an important point of reference in my argument) they nonetheless remain fundamentally distinct, as Kant, among others, shows us. And just as literal (and even literary) constraints allow us to understand something crucial about law, their juxtaposition with the juridical and moral contexts in turn allows us to appreciate the subjective and even social stakes of literary, mathematical, or psychoanalytic constraints, or their capacity to support *subjective* freedom (and even free will) and not merely creative or intellectual freedom.

This claim is central to the work of the experimental literary collective Oulipo, whose members are dedicated to a textual practice defined by voluntary submission to formal and literal constraints (traditional fixed poetic forms like the sonnet or haiku, but also the literal constraints implied in written forms such as metagrams, palindromes, and lipograms). George Perec, for example, writes of the "liberating potential of rigorous formal constraint," advancing that "the suppression of the letter, of the typographical sign, of the basic prop, is a purer, more objective, more decisive operation, something like *constraint degree zero*, after which everything becomes possible."[3] At stake are not only new literary possibilities, however, but latent possibilities within the writer as a subject. In the words of Oulipian Marcel Bénabou, "it is not only the virtualities of language that are revealed by constraint, but also the virtualities of [he] who accepts to submit himself to constraint."[4] The constraint gives rise not only to a poetics of the literary text, therefore, but to what might be termed a *poetics of subjectivity*. It supports the emergence of a virtual subject, a subject solicited and sustained by the struggle with the creative constraints implied in a practice of the letter.

Oulipians' most important contribution to the field of aesthetics may be the claim that constraints enable freedom by defending against *inspiration*. For Raymond Queneau, "the inspiration that consists in blind obedience to every impulse is in reality a sort of slavery. The classical playwright who writes his tragedy observing a certain number of familiar rules is freer than the poet who writes that which comes into his head and who is the slave of other rules of which he is ignorant."[5] The stakes of this claim can be understood by contrast with Surrealism, whose understanding of freedom it specifically rejects. Surrealist André Breton, for example, gives voice to a very traditional and widespread view according to which freedom is necessarily freedom *from* the law, freedom from constraints of all kinds: social norms and conventions, moral inhibitions, and even the rules and conventions of genre, all of which are conceived as inhibiting the free reign of the imagination. Strikingly, however, this "freedom from" goes hand in hand with a marginalization of the subject, and in particular of the subject's volition or will. The poet is understood as nothing more than the passive receptacle of an inspiration that breaks in on his consciousness, in the form of gratuitous phrases that come "knocking at the window."[6] To this involuntary or "automatic" submission to inspiration, the Oulipians oppose the voluntary submission to constraint as enabling a different relation to freedom, not as a freedom *from* obstacles or limits but as a freedom *to* that foregrounds the activity of the will.

In some beautiful pages that resonate with the words of Cantor, philosopher and playwright Alain Badiou proclaims that "mathematics is the necessary exercise through which is forged a subject adequate to the transformations he will be forced to undergo."[7] What he affirms in mathematics is not its timeless ideality or pure intelligibility, therefore, but its subject: the subject from whose desire it originated, and the subject whose freedom it enables. When Kant claims in his *Critique of Pure Reason* that the transformations that made mathematics a science "must have been due to a revolution brought about by the happy thought of a single man," he emphasizes the singular desire at its origin and the self-constrained nature of the method to which it gave rise: "A new light flashed upon the mind of the first man (be he Thales or some other) who first demonstrated the properties of the isosceles triangle. The true method, so he found, was not to inspect what he discerned either in the figure, or in the bare concept of it, . . . but to bring out what was necessarily implied in the concepts that he himself formed a priori and had put into the figure in the construction by which he presented it to himself."[8] And of Spinoza's *Ethics*, Badiou writes that "it would be no exaggeration to say that, for Spinoza, mathematics governs the historial destiny of knowledge, and hence the economy of freedom, or beatitude. Without mathematics, humanity languishes in the night of superstition, which can be summarized by the maxim: there is something we cannot think."[9] These examples attest to what Badiou calls the "concrete universalism of a trajectory of thought,"[10] a trajectory sustained by constraints that enable and sustain the subject in its struggle against subjugating forms of representation that limit reason or will to what can be imagined, and hence to the ontotheology of the image. Hence the distinctly political valence of mathematics in Badiou's his own work. In allowing for the "nomination" or calculation of an event that cannot be inscribed within the order of sense or captured in a representation, mathematical ontology promises to refound the political on a nonimaginary basis.

These brief examples enumerate just a few of the constrained practices with which this book will be concerned, to which subsequent chapters will add many more. Foremost among these are the constraints that structure the experience of psychoanalysis, which allow the subject who submits to them to declare its freedom from the norms and ideals that prop up the ego, and to assume responsibility for its unconscious desire. The function of formal, written constraints in the work of Oulipo resonates powerfully with psychoanalysis, where "the subject who accepts to submit himself to constraint" actually offers a very precise definition of the analysand under transference. This subject is "virtual" in that the subject of the unconscious is a pure hypothesis that cannot be verified empirically. It is witnessed only in speech, in those discontinuities and slips of the tongue that interrupt the discourse of the ego. The subject of psychoanalysis is thus a subject that can be known or constructed only on the condition that it be called forth under the constraint of the transference and made the object of a possible construction.

IN PRAISE OF SYMBOLIC FICTIONS

One aim of this project (which I will emphasize in this introduction, as well as in the next chapter) is to argue for a fuller and more felicitous understanding of the psychoanalytic concept of the symbolic, examining both its importance within psychoanalytic theory and practice and the resources it might offer for an examination of the social link and the political sphere. I was driven to write this book partly in response to a persistent difficulty I have encountered in teaching psychoanalysis and cultural theory. While Jacques Lacan's distinction between the registers of the real, the imaginary, and the symbolic has become part of the lingua franca of the human sciences, it is often at the cost of obscuring the properly psychoanalytic stakes of these terms. The symbolic in particular makes little sense to many readers, especially in its relation to desire, and for good reason.

There are two familiar accounts of the symbolic out there, neither of which is very compelling. The first understands the symbolic as a normative order, assimilated to cultural values and ideals and the primarily patriarchal institutions and practices that sustain them: religious law, the institutions of marriage and inheritance, the mechanisms of kinship exchange, the nuclear family. We generally get this view of the symbolic from its critics, especially in the areas of gender studies and progressive political thought, who justifiably object to the purported "necessity" of such institutions and the refusal of their historical character.[11] While this account does not encapsulate the psychoanalytic stakes of the symbolic, it is not a figment of these critics' imaginations, either. There is no denying that some social analysis grounded in an account of the symbolic is also socially conservative, even reactionary, and invokes the supposed authority of "the symbolic order" to pronounce judgment on nonnormative forms of kinship and social organization (notably gay marriages and nontraditional families) or to rationalize calls for "stability" or order (in the case of political conflicts or popular mobilizations). Even when this normative judgment is not present, invocations of the symbolic often appear to be structurally conservative, resistant to historicization, and devoid of any reference to creativity, innovation, or renewal. When the literature speaks of the need to "submit to the symbolic order," it is hard not to hear either an invocation of moral duty or a note of resignation, a positing of the symbolic as one of those unpleasant realities of human existence, as inevitable as death and taxes.

What the antinormative critique of the symbolic shares with its most conservative applications, however, is a tendency to equate the symbolic with patriarchal institutions and norms, and to thereby overlook the tremendous resources it offers for envisioning new forms and practices. While one invokes the authority of "tradition" to claim that these contents and norms are fundamental and unchanging, the other seeks to critique, enlarge, or dismantle them in the name of newer, generally more progressive configurations. But while the normative account falsely reduces the symbolic to specific contents, what its critics generally offer up as an alternative is a predicate-driven understanding of the subject (in terms of gender, class, or ethnicity, for example) that forecloses any real understanding of the subject (of language, of the unconscious, of desire) as distinct from the ego or social actor. It substitutes one set of contents for another or seeks to enlarge the field of possibilities, but leaves the contents model unquestioned. Both approaches leave us with no other way to think about the social link than as a domain structured by values and ideals (what Freud termed the "ego ideals"), whether constant and eternal or endlessly changing. They thus consign the social to the field of the imaginary.

Alternately, the symbolic is presented as a blind, mechanistic automatism having nothing to do with identities, values, or cultural contents. In the work of Slavoj Žižek, for example, the symbolic is frequently metaphorized as an impersonal and ignorant bureaucracy, incapable of acknowledging the subject who appeals to it for recognition or recompense.[12] Like Michel Foucault's celebrated analysis of the "panopticon,"[13] Žižek's work makes a crucial contribution to social and political theory by showing the locus of the authoritative Other supposed by the normative account to be completely empty, underscoring instead the purely structural character of the symbolic. While such an interpretation is undeniably both richer and more accurate (psychoanalytically speaking) than the one that assimilates the symbolic to normative codes, the broader critical reception of Žižek's work often turns this account into something of a caricature by reducing the symbolic to an automatism whose function is above all alienating and dehumanizing, or at best comical or parodic. In a slightly different vein, Alain Badiou's influential work affirms the symbolic, but only on the condition that it be defined through recourse to mathematics. As illuminating as this approach can be, it tends to jettison an essential component of the symbolic in abandoning all reference to the social relation. To stop at these ultrastructural definitions is to lose something essential, namely, the idea that the symbolic sustains life in common by supporting the conditions of credibility of social coexistence and constraining our subjective desires to find a public expression.

Many familiar accounts of the symbolic share the assumption that it is fundamentally at odds with subjective freedom. They tend to conceive of the constraint imposed by the need to pass through the locus of the Other as alienating, inhibitive, or exclusionary, and therefore characterize constraints or limits in terms that are generally negative, or at best neutral. They hold symbolic limits to be *limiting*, in the sense of constricting the subject's freedom. It is hardly surprising, then, that some of the most influential contemporary work in social and political theory champions what are essentially "imaginary" or "real" solutions, very much to the exclusion of the symbolic and everything it implies. Both of the accounts mentioned above tend to contribute to an understanding of the real as what is excluded from the social, and thus to collapse the symbolic with hegemonic representations.[14] The antinormative approach tends to eschew limits and constraints altogether, aligning them with exclusionary norms and traditions. To the limits implied in a symbolic logic of difference, it opposes a logic of diversity: against the finitude of a lacking field, it affirms a potentially infinite number of possible sites and positions. Certain theories of the political, on the other hand, identify the symbolic with a reified "existing order" that can be transformed only through the eruption of an "event," an explosive encounter with an inassimilable real that alone offers hope for the arrival of the new. Both, in other words, tend to emphasize the "order" in the symbolic order and to identify constraints and limits with the maintaining of that order.

While there is some truth in each of these approaches, they also need further nuancing. In the account that aligns the symbolic with social institutions and practices, I affirm the idea that desire has to be negotiated in public, that it answers to constraints and limits that are necessarily intersubjective (the constraint implied in having to pass through the field of the Other or language) even if they cannot be reduced to the embrace of specific norms or contents. I clearly share with the antinormative view a demand that the symbolic not simply become an evacuated, abstracted new name for intolerance and ostracism. Finally, authors like Žižek and Badiou have very interesting things to say about what Badiou calls the "necessary exercises" enabling subjective or political transformations, which are very much in the spirit of what I am trying to do, even if this more delicate work is sometimes overwhelmed by the loud emphasis on breaks and ruptures.[15] I propose that the problem of the "constraint" is a meeting ground where these different accounts can meet up with one another and be put to the test of experimentation. To borrow the words of Gilles Deleuze from an important early essay on structuralism, my view is that the symbolic "only has value to the extent that it animates new works which are those of today, as if the symbolic were the source, inseparably, of living interpretation and creation."[16] What I hope to demonstrate is that possibilities for genuine creativity, invention, and novelty can and do emerge immanently within practices of symbolization: that the symbolic, as Lacan puts it, "is at the heart of creating."[17]

A point often missed by his critics is that Lacan historicizes the question of the symbolic and sees the modern era as one in which its efficacy is regularly doubted, dismissed, or taken to task. A notable exception is the work of Juliet Flower MacCannell, who emphasizes that "what is new in Lacan's reading of Law and the Drives is his perception that the symbolic tactics civilization employs to open and close its self-inflicted wounds (the wounds that make us human) are no longer compelling fictions."[18] Unlike some of his more conservative adherents, Lacan had no interest in propping up the paternalistic forms of social life that he clearly and consistently diagnosed as in a state of decline, whether for better or for worse. But while for some the declining relevance of patriarchal "fictions" is reason to scrap the symbolic altogether, MacCannell—like Lacan himself—takes the opposite tack: what is required is a *renewal* of the symbolic, which must be made to "do the job it is supposed to do—the job of embracing and sustaining the most contradictory and conflicting of dreams and desires."[19] MacCannell's work is refreshing in that it takes for granted that the "old" symbolic forms are no longer compelling, but nevertheless does not give up on the need for such fictions altogether. What she affirms is precisely the structural function of limits and constraints, which have a creative or productive dimension that cannot be reduced to the function of prohibitions and rules.

In a psychoanalytic study of Adolf Eichmann, MacCannell locates in the genocidal program of the Third Reich the insistence of a "will-to-jouissance"—a superegoic imperative to "enjoy" the obscene object of the drive—that is enabled by the failure of traditional symbolic laws. For Mac-Cannell, Eichmann is symptomatic of an era in which "more 'balanced' modes of symbolic temporizing have taken a back seat" and are replaced by "a direct, 'imbalanced' relation to Drive. . . . Under Holocaust, nuclear and global catastrophic threats, the will-to-jouissance insists with immediate virulence."[20] Increasingly, she argues, modern civilization confronts the danger—but also the temptation—of a "jouissance not restricted by the word, by the ethical framing of excess and lack." As so-called symbolic or paternal laws fade from the picture, fantasy fills the void by proposing objects to organize or structure the drive in their place. Fantasy grounds our contemporary culture by "invert[ing] the logical (symbolic) structuring of necessary lack in us as the Other's *bliss* or fulfillment [*jouissance*]." In Eichmann's grudging surrender to Hitler's genocidal imperative—the descent into what he describes as a "death whirl"—MacCannell sees an abdication of his own desire as a subject in an attempt to appease the unspoken will of the Führer.

MacCannell's essay also provides an important insight into the symbolic's function. She observes that while Eichmann always submitted to the authority of rules and orders, he also "felt compelled to 'go beyond' the written law, the norms of constraint, beyond the limit. He was the instrument of a will-to-jouissance not necessarily his own." In opposing *rule* and *constraint*, MacCannell draws an implicit distinction between the rule in its imaginary function as a representation of a law-making authority (Hitler, in this case) and the properly symbolic dimension of limits and constraints. Eichmann attempts to bypass this symbolic dimension, identifying his own will with the law's *source*. She sees Eichmann as a subject who has decided to forgo the protections offered by the symbolic, making himself the mere agent of the Other's will or enjoyment. What Eichmann therefore refuses is not so much the limits the symbolic imposes on his actions (the restrictions that are a feature of all rules and laws), but the barrier it erects between his own desire as a subject and the demands of another person, and thus the demarcation of his own subjectivity as something more than an object or instrument of another's will. In opposing a limit to the Other's jouissance, the symbolic is a support for the subject's desire and not simply a source of privation. With this reading, MacCannell makes what I consider to be a crucial claim, largely absent from most treatments of the symbolic: that the subject's desire—and thus its freedom—is enabled and not impeded by symbolic limits and constraints.

What, then, is the structure of a symbolic fiction, and how is it different from a value, norm, or ideal, or from the many genealogical or ideological narratives that a collectivity tells itself?

I maintain that the symbolic is an absolutely crucial dimension of social coexistence, but one that is neither reducible to social norms and ideals (specific contents or values) nor something that can be assumed to be functioning in a necessary and inexorable way. As a dimension of human existence that is introduced by language—and thus inescapably "other" with respect to the laws of nature—the symbolic is an undeniable fact of human existence. The same cannot be said of the forms and practices that represent and sustain it, however. In designating these laws, structures, and practices as "fictions," Lacan makes clear that the symbolic is a dimension of social life that must be created and maintained, and that may also be displaced, eradicated, or rendered dysfunctional. The symbolic fictions that structure and support the social tie are therefore historicizable, emerging at specific times and in particular contexts and losing their efficacy when circumstances change. They are fragile and ephemeral, needing to be renewed and reinvented if they are not to become outmoded or ridiculous.

My objective here is therefore not to call for a return to traditional symbolic laws (laws that are clearly on the wane one way or the other, and not worth resurrecting in some nostalgic or reactionary mode), but to reflect on the relationship between the symbolic in its most elementary or structural form and the function of constraints and limits. My hypothesis is that the interdependence of desire and constraint may express the essence of the symbolic as Lacan conceives it, which is obscured when the symbolic is reduced to the function of rules and laws, and especially the "paternal" laws and prohibitions with which it is so often identified. Our tendency to conflate them—and therefore to dismiss as irrelevant or outdated the first along with the second—means that we risk not only misunderstanding the function and necessity of the symbolic where the subject of desire is concerned, but also collapsing it with the purely imaginary function of rules and norms as representations of societal ideals.

Lacan offers an important minimal definition of the symbolic when he muses that the written commandments of the Mosaic law may be nothing other than "the very laws of speech." This is because the condition of speech is "distance between the subject and *das Ding*," the object posited by the unconscious fantasy as a source of unbearable enjoyment or jouissance.[21] In distancing the Thing, the signifier opens up a space where the subject can live. As the "laws of speech," the commandments are not merely the laws of privation or lack. The symbolic is something other than the primordial subjection to the signifier that Lacan calls castration and that entails a lack of the object that would satisfy the drive and a perversion of the natural aims of the organism. This is an unavoidable experience for every speaking being, whether or not he finds symbolic laws to be credible or well founded. The symbolic, in contrast, is also a creative support for the subject of desire.

The "laws of speech" to which Lacan refers are the laws at work in the unconscious itself, which elucidates a dimension of the symbolic not reducible to the function of law as traditionally understood. Freud's work with hysterics makes clear that even in a world where traditional, "paternal" laws really are compelling fictions, at least for some, a given subject always encounters the symbolic in a way that is irreducibly specific and that may or may not find an analogy or echo in the paternal law that forbids access to the object that would satisfy desire. In other words, the fact that a society accepts as "compelling fictions" a given set of laws does not mean that the individual subject is any less obliged to come up with a way of managing lack and excess in her own body and her own psychic economy. This is the fundamental problem Freud encounters in his writings on femininity: how does a woman assume castration, if not by confronting the incest prohibition and passing through the Oedipus complex? She is not subject to the societal norms and prohibitions that model the masculine subject's relation to lack, yet she is confronted all the same with the inevitability of castration and the necessity of passing through the field of language to evoke and to manage the effects of the drive on her body.

The answer is to be found not in the sphere of social norms and obligations, but in the practice of psychoanalysis itself. With the invention of the transference, Freud solicits the unconscious to construct a knowledge about the subject's encounter with a real that allows for a "treatment" of the drive and its effects on the organism, as well as the possibility of redirecting the drive toward new aims. At stake is a passage through the field of the Other that, in reactivating the originary encounter with castration and allowing it to be constructed, also opens up a space for the subject of desire. In modeling and supporting the subject's relation to castration, the elaboration of the signifying chain allows it to become a source of creativity and invention, and not merely a tragedy or catastrophe that generates fantasmatic solutions. It in turn sheds light on the function of more "traditional" symbolic forms, including societal norms and prohibitions, which under certain conditions function not merely as representations or as institutional articulations of castration, but as structures that allow it to be tolerated and even affirmed, and in some cases to become the basis for creative work (the sublimations constitutive of culture itself).

Psychoanalysis is a practice that attempts to isolate the conditions under which such a space or structure can be created and sustained. One way to understand this project is as an attempt to find analogies for the analytic experience in the social, political, and artistic spheres, or to consider these domains from the perspective of the analytic experience. My aim is therefore not to use psychoanalysis as an interpretive grid through which to examine social and political phenomena, but to think about how the analytic procedure works, what it reveals about the creative function of limits and constraints, and how that perspective might illuminate procedures and institutions whose function we tend to take for granted, or, even worse, to reduce to something static and "dead."

This book examines the role of constraints in sustaining what I call the "experimental" dimension of the symbolic, both within traditional laws and institutions and in other, very different contexts. My focus is on articulations of the symbolic that take a creative form or enable a creative practice, and that therefore provide a structure in which the subject can renew or reactivate its encounter with the lack in the Other—or castration—in a way that allows the subject to exercise its freedom and give expression to its desire. I contend that at base all cultural articulations of the symbolic have an "experimental" dimension, even if they subsequently take on a normative character. The "becoming normative" of a symbolic form is not the telos that determines its function or value, however. "Experiment" implies an *experience*, something the subject undergoes; the emphasis is therefore upon the experience or the trajectory itself, and not the static "fact" of the symbolic or the laws or institutions that might represent its function.

Allow me to illustrate my point with three examples taken from the work of authors whose thinking has influenced my own, and that I view as emblematic not only of this "experimental" practice, but of the urgent task of transforming and renewing the symbolic forms that support the social link in a given historical context: Lucie Cantin's analysis of the religious practices and institutional reforms of the Spanish mystic Teresa of Ávila, the political philosophy of Jacques Rancière, and the work of contemporary French photographer Sophie Calle as read by Juliet Flower MacCannell.

A SPACE FOR THE UNFOLDING OF AN EXPERIENCE: THE MYSTICAL PRACTICES OF TERESA OF ÁVILA

I will begin with Teresa, a sixteenth-century nun and prominent figure of the Catholic Counter-Reformation who became a target of the Spanish Inquisition. Her experience of the limitations of the official "symbolic order" of her day leads her not merely to refuse its rigidity and outmodedness, but to attempt to reform and renew the symbolic by devising new institutions and creative practices. The fact of being a woman is crucial to her experience. Women have arguably never been addressed *as subjects* by traditional articulations of the symbolic, for which they are at best objects to be regulated or controlled (as in the mechanisms of kinship exchange that Claude Lévi-Strauss views as the structural consequence of the incest prohibition). For this very reason, however, women are uniquely poised to teach us something about symbolic life "after" the patriarchy, when traditional authorities no longer appear as credible guarantors for the social order. From a feminine perspective this appears not as a "loss" of ground, but as the exposure of a groundlessness that is a structural condition of the symbolic, and that must also be embraced as essential and unavoidable. Far from being a purely masculine or phallocratic preoccupation, Teresa shows that the task of transforming and renewing the symbolic is—and must be— an urgent project for women.

Teresa is known for two reasons: for her mystical visions and the meditational texts to which they give rise, and for her work as a religious reformer. The two are intimately linked. Like other female "seers" of her era, Teresa was subject to miraculous visions accompanied by spiritual revelations, profound bodily transformations, and absent states. Unlike most of them, however, Teresa was driven to give outward and practical expression to her ecstatic (and uniquely feminine) experience of losing herself in God.

Teresa felt a strong spiritual vocation as a young girl, and took vows to enter the Carmelite order at the age of sixteen. Even after entering the convent, however, she was unable to overcome what she later called her "vanity," her compulsive need to please others and to be celebrated and admired as an object of love or esteem. Despite reassurances from the members of her community, she knew that her dependence on the attention and approval of others compromised her spiritual life and put her on the path of sin. Although she readily prays, confesses her sins, and undertakes mortification of the flesh, Teresa finds that the practices of contemplation and penance prescribed by the Church have no effect upon her, and are unable to limit what she feels working her over from within. Always in fragile health, she begins to suffer from dramatic physical symptoms and life-threatening illnesses, at one point entering a coma that causes her to be pronounced dead, and from which she is preserved only by the vigilance of her loving father, who refuses to allow her burial.

Early in her sickness, Teresa begins to have visions and ecstatic experiences that she feels to be of divine origin. She experiences religious ecstasy through the use of the devotional text *Third Spiritual Alphabet*, which provides direction in inner contemplation and examinations of conscience. Through these ecstatic experiences, Teresa comes to a feeling of complete union with God, and determines that he requires her absolute submission. Her visions continue almost uninterrupted for two years. Their apex is an extended vision of being pierced through her heart by a seraph's arrow (the subject of Bernini's famous sculpture of the saint), which provokes an exquisite pain that sets her afire with love for God, an experience Teresa returns to again and again in her later mystical writings. Initially, however, these visions present themselves as unspeakable, incommunicable, and purely ecstatic, absenting her from the community and the world around her. Despite her blameless life and devotion to her spiritual vocation, those in her milieu question whether her newfound knowledge is of diabolical origin.

In a rich reading of Teresa's life and practice, psychoanalyst Lucie Cantin suggests that her deadly physical symptoms and spiritual visions are both indices of the fact that something in her body fails to be expressed in the order of the signifier, and therefore seeks another issue.[22] She offers that both are manifestations of what Lacan calls a "jouissance beyond the phallus," which differs from the jouissance lost to language (a loss symbolized by the phallus, as the organ whose enjoyment is limited by the subject's entry into law or speech) in being a jouissance that the signifier is unable to limit or to treat. At stake in both her symptoms and her mystical ecstasy is thus an experience of the signifier's inadequacy: though perceived the first time as a crisis that provokes symptoms, it is perceived the second time as an excess or "beyond" that is a source of exquisite rapture as well as a unique knowledge about the Other called God. Yet it is still a "knowledge that does not know itself" (Freud's early definition of the unconscious), a knowledge that cannot be transmitted.

Cantin compares Teresa's situation to that of the feminine subject entering analysis, who is confronted with the unbound jouissance of the drive that is ravaging her body in the form of symptoms, about which she is unable to say anything. Unlike phallic jouissance—the enjoyment of the organ that, in being marked as a "jouissance to lose," is articulated to the social order and in meaning—feminine jouissance risks being perceived only in the mode of the diabolical (as something to be exorcised or suppressed), or else being deprived altogether of linguistic or social expression; it then remains outside of speech, with no public dimension or sublimating potential. Cantin notes that from a young age Teresa is intensely concerned with her honor and the importance of her word and readily seeks out confession. But while these symbolic indices are important and bear witness to Teresa's ethics with respect to speech and the word, they are also unable to inscribe or contain what is working her over from within. The same is true of the traditional laws of lack and renunciation that structure the order's practice. Although Teresa is perfectly willing to submit to the laws of the Church, to renounce worldly pleasures, and to perform penance for her sins, none of these protocols is adequate to limit or control her experience of the drive. This accounts for the conflict she will experience for more than twenty years as she seeks a form for the "excess" that is ravaging her body, and for which she will long find no other means of expression than the symptom. Although clearly articulated to the signifier and the Law, she is still dealing with something in herself that cannot be inscribed in the field of the signifier, and that therefore exceeds the framework defined by Meaning and the Law. . . . With respect to the Catholic Church, she remains caught in an "experience": a knowledge that, without really opposing Church doctrine, nonetheless cannot be inscribed within it.

(77)

Eventually Teresa finds in submission to constraints a subjective practice that allows her to give a form to her experience. Instead of surrendering completely to this wordless jouissance, she attempts to channel it through prayer and meditation. Finding that the practice of contemplation prescribed by the Church has no effect upon her, she develops another approach to prayer and meditation that consists in focusing on the presence of Christ and thus in channeling and directing the sensations that her experience of the Other leaves upon her body. But it is only years later, in collaboration with her spiritual advisor, that Teresa will finally manage to inscribe her experiences within the symbolic and to transmit them in a form that others can receive.

Teresa's confessor is convinced that her visions are of divine origin and encourages her in her devotions. Yet he also demands that she commit them to speech. At her confessor's prompting, Teresa begins to compose a written account of her mystical experiences addressed to officials of the Church. In imposing this constraint, her confessor requires her to find a way to articulate her experience to the law of the symbolic (represented here by official Church doctrine), and to thereby submit the account of her mystical experiences to the requirement that her words be receivable by others. This demand constitutes the beginning of a truly *constrained* work that is analogous in many respects to the experience of an analysis. "There is no doubt," writes Cantin, "that Teresa of Ávila experiences jouissance. What is equally certain, however, is that she *knows nothing about it*. This is what her confessor seeks to remedy in giving the order to write. The requirement that she write about her spiritual state, writings destined to directors and confessors who will then judge them, helps to preserve her from madness" (82). Her confessor's intention is therefore not for Teresa to be diagnosed by others as an object of learned knowledge or spiritual doctrine, but for her to come to self-knowledge by elaborating in words what has hitherto been expressed only through a symptom or experience.

Her trajectory therefore closely parallels that of the feminine subject under transference, who seeks the signifiers that might provide another path for what is at work in her body (67). In both cases, the desire to know becomes the basis for an ethics that consists in attempting to find a form for what falls outside the order of the sayable. Teresa's earlier recourse to devotional texts, like her experience of being saved from death by her father's love, shows that she seeks support within the field of the signifier even as she is caught up in an experience that exceeds it. The signifiers of the Other allow her to limit this jouissance and render it no longer deadly (in the case of her father's love) and to channel and direct it through the experience of meditation. In submitting to the constraint that she write about her *own* experiences, however, Teresa is compelled to find words for this "other jouissance" itself, her ecstatic (and uniquely feminine) experience of the absent Other she calls "God." For Cantin, Teresa's ethics consists in "saying everything, hiding nothing, never renouncing the attempt to put into words— to make pass through the signifier—what nonetheless cannot be inscribed there" (78).

She contrasts Teresa's experience with that of the seventeenth-century French nun Jeanne des Anges, who was mother superior at the convent of Loudun at the time of the mass "demonic possession" for which it would become famous. A frivolous and vain young woman, Jeanne chafs at the constraints imposed upon her by the religious life, for which she feels no particular vocation; after taking her orders, she indulges without restraint in what she later calls "great libertinage" with her fellow nuns and the order's male confessors, and routinely lies about her conduct to advance her own interests and eventually to secure her position as mother superior. After years of this unregulated conduct, Jeanne begins to experience dramatic bodily symptoms and to be visited by vulgar dreams that cause her to rave loudly at night. These experiences culminate with her being "entered" by demons of lust and uncleanliness, which take possession of her body and cause her to convulse, blaspheme, and make sexual advances on the priests who examine her. Eventually sixteen of the nuns under her charge report similar signs of possession, leading Church officials to organize dramatic public exorcisms that take place before thousands of spectators. When examined by her superiors, Jeanne accuses the handsome priest Urbain Grandier of sorcery, insisting that it was he who allowed the demons to enter the nuns when he tossed a bouquet of roses over the convent wall, a crime for which he is subsequently convicted and burned at the stake. After the exorcism, Jeanne's spiritual advisor requires her to make confession and to submit to a lengthy process of introspection, not unlike that undertaken by Teresa. But while this process results in greater self-awareness and some acknowledgment of the part she played in her "possession," Cantin suggests that Jeanne, unlike Teresa, never assumes full responsibility for her symptoms. Instead she remains firm in her conviction that another is causing the agitation in her body, provoking in her something for which she does not have to answer.

The differences between them are further apparent in the nature of the conversion that follows. Jeanne reports that Saint Joseph appeared to her as a corporeal presence, leaving drops of "holy unction" on her nightgown that persisted after her return to consciousness as clearly visible stains upon the garment. Strikingly, however, Saint Joseph takes the place of the demons of lust that "possessed" her, without any qualitative transformation in her relation to this eroticized capture. After this experience, Jeanne embarks upon a new career that consists primarily in being paraded about as an object of fascination, attaining fame and notoriety—and even royal favor—by exhibiting the marks and stigmata of her possession and exorcism and the garment stained with the miraculous drops.

As Michel de Certeau observes in his important study of Loudun, Jeanne lived in a world where feminine jouissance was able to find public or social expression through the experience of possession.[23] This became an acceptable way to indulge in what was fundamentally a symptom, a refusal of responsibility that nonetheless found a certain form of social validation. The possessed, in presenting her symptom to the exorcist for treatment, could make another person responsible for what was happening to her while simultaneously finding a narcissistic satisfaction in being exhibited and celebrated as a spectacular and even miraculous object. She could therefore continue to enjoy the fantasy encoded in the symptom while demanding that another person take responsibility for its obscene or deadly effects. In thus defining its "outside," Cantin remarks that the diabolical possession also shored up the authority of the Church by allowing the priest-exorcist to function as the "Master," taking control of and treating this excess, and thereby sustaining the belief in a possible treatment of jouissance (67).

In contrast, Teresa finds in submission to constraints a subjective practice that allows her to be something other than an object of fascination, a performance of unregulated jouissance, or a showcase for the symptom. The positions of Jeanne and Teresa are therefore "radically different in their relation to a nonphallic jouissance: the first remains the prisoner of the ravaging work of the drive and the desperate quest for an object that would limit jouissance, while the second, through its relation to a lacking other that structures the space of desire, finds a way to metaphorize its impossible quest" (67). The point is not that these constraints "made" her take responsibility for her symptoms or ecstatic experiences, but rather that they supported her in her desire and determination to take responsibility, not by submitting to the rules or protocols of an institution, but by relying upon her own ethics as a speaking subject. Teresa's trajectory attests to the difference between a subject of desire and an object taken in charge by another, as well as to the symbolic mediation this difference supposes: a subject is alone with her experience of the drives and her responsibility and must act in the absence of any Other (whether a man, a God, or a demon) who might be blamed for her troubles or called upon for help.

"Alone" does not mean "without Other," however. This is where the role of constraints comes in and reveals the difference between an imaginary and a symbolic relation to the Other. Instead of invoking an Other who might be held responsible for her experience or asked to manage its effects, Teresa's quest involves what Cantin describes as a "passage through the Other," a passage through the signifiers of language and the absent locus of speech. It therefore elucidates something fundamental about the ethics of the feminine subject, for whom it is sometimes especially difficult to accept the ground-lessness of language and the inconsistency of the Other she addresses. Cantin observes that what often appears as a woman's contestation of the law, or as a mistrust of others' words, is perhaps more fundamentally what allows her to repress "the unbearable fact of the Other's inconsistency and the absence of any foundation for speech and language" (76). If Jeanne's conversion merely substitutes one consistent Other for another, Teresa's involves a confrontation with the Other in its inconsistency: the lacking Other that is the cause of her desire and of a jouissance that is different from the jouissance at stake in the symptom. Although it too is a jouissance "beyond the phallus," this "other jouissance" differs from the former in being directly related to the assumption of the Other's inconsistency. In Cantin's words,

> The other jouissance, the one to which the mystic bears witness and that Lacan designates as a "supplemental jouissance," supposes this passage through the Other, the Law of the Other in which the drive encounters not only its limit, but the radical impossibility of its quest for an object. . . . [It therefore raises] the question of the feminine subject's ethics with respect to the need to articulate the drive to the Law of the signifier, despite its inadequacy or deficiency. It is not obvious how a woman can get out of the logic of the drive and enter into the space of desire, if desire is always the desire of the Other's desire where jouissance, even if it always eludes the signifier, nonetheless finds balasts and modes of expression other than those involved in its inscription on the body. Access to the other jouissance supposes this articulation of the Letter to the signifier, in which the real works upon the signifier to evoke the unsayable, to make visible the invisible, to find a form for the impossible and what cannot be said: but in a mode and in a space that does not bypass the Other.
>
> (76)

In responding to the constraint imposed by her confessor, Teresa might be understood as submitting to the law of the symbolic in its most prevalent institutional form: the protocols of Church doctrine. Yet Cantin argues that her position is actually subversive with respect to the "official" symbolic of her day in that it insists on the hole or defect in the Other the Church represents. This is because Teresa confronts much more radically than the Church the absence of the Other called God, and apprehends Christ not as a savior or source of eternal life, but as the source of words of love that allow this absence to be borne but not denied: "The God of Teresa of Avila is not that of Jeanne des Anges. . . . Teresa's 'conversion' marks a moment of passage, the moment at which the loss or renunciation through which she accedes to the lack of any possible object for the drive is inscribed. God is the name given to this Absence, and Christ becomes the Other who offers the signifiers that allow her to bear this lack" (79).

Moreover, her "submission" is in tension with the fact that Teresa also radically *transforms* the symbolic by inventing new forms and structures through her written practice and approach to meditation. What she submits to is therefore not really Church doctrine, but the constraints internal to these practices. In writing, she finds a limit that the Church was unable to provide. The same is true of her approach to convent life and her eventual choice of a strictly cloistered existence that rejects the laxer institutional practices of her milieu. In Cantin's words, Teresa feels that the absence of a strict cloister in the convent where she took her vows does not allow her to "mark out the loss (of the world) that she must assume in order to attain the degree of perfection in her relation to the Other that she wants to be absolute" (78). Like the practice of writing, the constraints of the cloister establish a symbolic framework within which she can inscribe and contain her experience.

The experience of possession to which Jeanne des Anges attests does not actually challenge the existing order, but confirms its identity by defining its "outside" and therefore facilitates the repression of what remains consigned to the unspeakable. In contrast, Teresa submits to the constraints of the symbolic while nonetheless insisting on its remainder, the experience of a jouissance for which there are no words and in the face of which language fails. In other words, her practice consists not merely in inscribing everything within the order of the signifier, "symbolizing" it all, but in locating a hole in the symbolic, attempting to find words that are adequate to the experience of its deficiency or to find a form for what it cannot treat or limit. Their experiences thus elucidate two different functions of the signifier: repression (where feminine jouissance is relegated to the inadmissible) and evocation (what Cantin describes as a process of "giving visibility to the invisible," or metaphorizing the real).

In finding a way to metaphorize her experience, Teresa obliges Church authorities to recognize her mystical experiences as a legitimate contribution to the spiritual practices of the Catholic Church, rather than as something diabolical or pathological. The result is that instead of existing as a mere object of fascination or horror, a miraculous or diabolical body offered up to the gaze of others, she leaves her own stamp on the "official" symbolic of the time by enlarging and transforming the parameters of religious practice. Her writings are subsequently recognized by the Church as major contributions to its theology and practice, setting in motion a process that leads to her canonization as a saint and eventual designation as a Doctor of the Church, along with Catherine of Siena (the first two women to be so recognized).

In her meditational practices as in her choice of the cloister, Teresa seeks not so much to control or negate her experience as to give it a form or create a space in which it might unfold. Moreover, Teresa's experience never loses its corporeal dimension, even as it ceases to be expressed solely through what Cantin calls the "fascinating" or deadly jouissance of the symptom. Her "rapture" is sensual as well as spiritual, and continues to be defined by a kind of surrender to the Other that "annihilates" her, exceeding the control of her will or her faculty of reason.[24] "The experience of God," Cantin writes, should thus be understood as

a call to the Other: a place in which to lose herself, as Michel de Certeau puts it. For Teresa of Ávila it is above all an experience, that is, an encounter that relies upon the letter of the body but is measured by its truth effects for others: truth effects in which her being is ravished, but nonetheless participates in the transformation of jouissance through the signifiers of love proffered by the Other that fulfills her. Henceforth this jouissance is no longer deadly, because it is articulated and counterbalanced by the signifiers of the lover's discourse.

(80)

An "experience measured by its truth effects for others" captures perfectly what I want to express in invoking the notion of an "experimental symbolic": a symbolic that gives form to an experience, and so elaborates its public or interpersonal dimension.

Teresa's trajectory sheds light on the difference between desire and passion: desire differs from the passion at stake in the fantasy in requiring to be negotiated in public. It demonstrates that the corollary of the lack of any object for the drive is the need to create, and thus the attempt to find a form for a desire that is neither anchored nor exhausted by any object. This desire is what drives Teresa's activities as a reformer. She begins to write at the age of forty-seven, and in the same year founds the first of many convents of a reformed order—the Discalced (or "barefoot") Carmelites—that will be known for their rule of extreme poverty and strict enforcement of the cloistered life. Cantin remarks that the work of founding convents all over Spain "gives a social form to Teresa's desire, which henceforth will seek to inscribe itself in the symbolic space it also transforms" (83). This dual action of seeking inscription within the symbolic and *at the same time* transforming it is crucial. It is not a matter of "submitting to" the symbolic, but of re-creating or transforming it, expanding its possibilities while retaining its function as a limit or constraint. Teresa shows that the symbolic is not merely an institutional order or a system of beliefs, but a way of approaching or working on the real. The convents she founds might be understood as contributing something of particular value to other women, by creating a constrained space that enables a form of spiritual practice specific to the feminine experience of the Other's inconsistency (and so making convent life the scene of another possible articulation of the symbolic for women, and not a space of exile from it).

The act founded on desire provides a way for what is at work in the body to find a social expression by channeling the drive toward new aims, providing an outlet for what previously was expressed only through the fascinating jouissance of the body. Cantin concludes her reading by stressing that the work of the real can deconstruct the order of meaning and evoke the unsayable only if it is sufficiently articulated to the space of the believable and the possible recognition of the subject's truth—otherwise it is entirely absorbed in a logic of the drives. "The relation to the Other," she writes,

> establish[es] the boundaries that define . . . just how far the letter can go in evoking the unsayable without falling back into the space of the body proper and enclosing itself within the work of the drive. If the aim is to find a form for what is not contained, barred, and limited by the symbolic, there where neither the Law nor the order of Meaning can serve as references, then all that remains is the requirement of an aesthetic form "recognizable by the Other." It may well be that there can be no aesthetic of the other jouissance without an ethics of speech, in which the signifier comes to bound and contain the real with respect to the Other that delimits the space of the believable.

(85)

With this conclusion Cantin not only underscores the aesthetic dimension of the symbolic, but subtly extracts the former from the latter by suggesting that it is necessary to give an aesthetic form to what is not contained, barred, or limited by the symbolic. Her point is not to make the symbolic all-inclusive, but to identify a limit point where the symbolic gives way to aesthetics, or to a presentation of the unpresentable (a subject I will return to in the final chapter of this book).

SUBJECTIFICATION AS DISIDENTIFICATION: THE SYMBOLIC IN THE THOUGHT OF JACQUES RANCIÈRE

I turn next to the political philosophy of Jacques Rancière. While the symbolic is often understood as almost diametrically opposed to anything like the "political" in the stakes that contemporary political philosophy gives to the term, their rapprochement is central to Rancière's work. He understands the symbolic not as a normative "order," but as the interruption of the (imaginary) order of identification and meaning—what he calls the "police logic"—by the emergence of a political subject who exposes its "miscount" of the social by giving voice to a specific "wrong." The symbolic is not a "better" or "more complete" count however—a better-founded or more just order— but is completely *unfounded*: hence its importance for the political. The unfoundedness of the symbolic differs from the "miscount" that defines the police order in that the latter proposes an arithmetic division of the social that presumes to represent or give a place to all of its parts; the symbolic, in contrast, lays bare the "lack of foundation" that defines the political, the gap or breach that is also the necessary condition of political subjectification. "Any subjectification," Rancière writes, "is a disidentification, removal from the naturalness of a place, the opening up of a subject space where anyone can be counted since it is the space where those of no account are counted, where a connection is made between having a part and having no part."[25]

In the opening pages of his influential book *Disagreement* (*La mésentente*), Rancière suggests that the eruption of this symbolic dimension is what distinguishes the political as such from a mere revolt with no subjectivizing character:

> Politics exists when the natural order of domination is interrupted by the institution of a part of those who have no part. This institution is the whole of politics as a specific form of connection. It defines the common of the community as a political community, in other words, as divided, based on a wrong that escapes the arithmetic of exchange and reparation. Beyond this set-up there is no politics. There is only the order of domination or the disorder of revolt.
>
> (11–12)

He develops the difference between revolt and politics with two examples from classical antiquity: the unsuccessful revolt of the Scythian slaves, and the secession of the Roman plebeians of the Aventine. The first example is taken from the *Histories* of Herodotus. The Greek historian reports that the Scythians customarily put out the eyes of those they reduced to slavery, to better restrict them to their menial tasks as slaves. This normal order of things was disrupted when the Scythians left to undertake a great military campaign that kept them engaged in Asia for an entire generation. During this time, a generation of sons was born to the slaves and raised with their eyes open. Looking around, they saw they were born with the same attributes as their absent masters, and concluded there was no reason why they should be slaves. They therefore decided that they were the equal of the warriors, and prepared to hold their ground when the latter came back by arming themselves and digging a great trench around the territory. When the Scythian conquerors returned from their campaign and sought to quell the slaves' revolt with an armed assault, they failed. At this point, Herodotus writes, one of the shrewder warriors took stock of the situation and presented it thus to his comrades: "Take my advice—lay spear and bow aside, and let each man fetch his horsewhip, and go boldly up to them. So long as they see us with arms in our hands, they imagine themselves our equals in birth and bravery; but let them behold us with no other weapon but the whip, and they will feel that they are our slaves, and flee before us" (cited in 12). The spectacle succeeds: struck by this *display* of mastery, the slaves flee without a fight. What the tale illustrates, writes Rancière, is that "the paradigm of the slave war is one of a purely war-generated achievement of equality between the dominated and the dominator" (13). While the rebels' demonstration of their equality in arms manages at first to shake their former masters, they have no comeback when the latter once again "show the signs of their difference in nature." "What they cannot do," writes Rancière, "is transform equality in war into political freedom" (13).

Something very different is at stake in the plebeian secession. Here Rancière draws not from the classical source material, but from a dramatic restaging of the Aventine secession penned by the nineteenth-century French writer and philosopher Pierre Simon Ballanche, a campaigner for social justice who criticized the canonical account of the revolt by the Latin historian Livy and attempted to reimagine its fundamental stakes.

The secession in question was the first of five such actions involving the Aventine Hill, an area outside the city walls of Rome that was inhabited

primarily by the commoners who made up the vast majority of its popu-
lace. Although they produced most of its food and goods, the plebs enjoyed
none of the rights of the patrician upper class. A secession was an informal
exercise of power by the commoners, not unlike an extreme form of general
strike. During a *secessio plebis*, the plebs would abandon their posts, exit the
city, and leave the patrician order to themselves. A *secessio* thus meant that
all workshops would shut down and most commercial transactions cease.
In 494 BC, in response to the harsh rule of Appius Claudius, the plebeians seceded to the Mons Sacrum and threatened to found a new town.
This action resulted in the patricians agreeing to free some of the plebs
from their debts, as well as conceding some of their power by creating the
office of the Tribune of the Plebs (the first government position held by the
commoners).[26]

Livy's account recalls in certain respects Herodotus's tale of the foiled
slave revolt. What he stresses is not the collective power of the plebs, but
the success of the patricians in persuading the commoners to return to their
posts and assume once again their place within the community. He reports
that Menenius Agrippa, a consul of the Roman Republic, was chosen by the
patricians to persuade the plebeian soldiers to end the secession and reenter
the city. Menenius tells the soldiers a fable about the revolt of the body's
members, in which the organs and limbs are metaphors for the different
parts of the Roman Republic. The rest of the body, thinking the stomach
was contributing nothing, decided to stop providing it with food. Soon,
however, the other parts grew weary and unable to function. They realized
that the stomach did serve a purpose, and that they were nothing without
it. The stomach is therefore meant to represent the patrician class, and the
other body parts the plebs. With this fable, Menenius manages to convince
the plebs that they are a part of the social body, and to bring about a return
to order. Eventually, Livy reports, the patricians conceded to some of the
plebs' demands by guaranteeing certain legal protections and creating a Tribune of the Plebs; in return, the soldiers agreed to reenter the city. In this
narrative, the extension of certain rights and protections, and even the creation of political representation, is part of a strategy to maintain the existing
order by better inscribing the plebs within it.

Ballanche, in his reimagining of the conflict, reproaches the Latin historian for (in Rancière's words) "being unable to think of the event as anything other than a revolt, an uprising caused by poverty and anger and sparking a power play devoid of all meaning" (23). He shows that Livy "is incapable of supplying the meaning of the conflict because he is incapable of locating Menenius Agrippa's fable in its real context: that of a quarrel over the issue of speech itself" (23). Ballanche offers a restaging of the conflict that centers on the discussions between the senators and the speech acts of the plebs, in which, Rancière writes,

> The issue at stake involves finding out whether there exists a common stage where plebeians and patricians can debate anything. The position of the intransigent patricians is straightforward: there is no place for discussion with the plebs for the simple reason that plebs do not speak. They do not speak because they are beings without a name, deprived of logos—meaning, of symbolic enrollment in the city. Plebs live a purely individual life that passes on nothing to posterity except for life itself, reduced to its reproductive function. Whoever is nameless *cannot* speak. . . . Between the language of those who have a name and the lowing of nameless beings, no situation of linguistic exchange can possibly be set up, no rules or code of discussion.
>
> (23–24)

In Livy's account Menenius manages to convince the plebs they are a part of the social, albeit a marginal part. In the fable of the body's members, however, being a necessary part of the whole does not imply having speech: the "part" that the plebs constitute is the animal part of the community that has no logos. This is why Rancière's reading—by way of Ballanche—insists instead that they constitute a part that *has no part* in the current count of the community, which is counted as nothing because it is deprived of membership in the community of speaking beings.

Rancière writes that the plebs gathered on the Aventine, faced with this fundamental inequality, "do not set up a fortified camp in the manner of the Scythian slaves." Instead,

They do what would have been unthinkable for the latter: they establish another order, another partition of the perceptible, by constituting themselves not as warriors equal to other warriors but as speaking beings sharing the same properties as those who deny them these. They thereby execute a series of speech acts that mimic those of the patricians: they pronounce imprecations and apotheoses; they delegate one of their number to go and consult their oracles; they give themselves representatives by rebaptizing them. In a word, they conduct themselves like beings with names. . . . They write, Ballanche tells us, "a name in the sky": a place in the symbolic order of the community of speaking beings, in a community that does not yet have any effective power in the city of Rome.

(24–25)

Rather than asserting their equality in arms or accepting the merely *functional* equality of body parts that are all "equally" necessary to the body's smooth operation, the plebs *claim* an equality that does not yet "exist" in the current partition of the social, but inheres in their status as speaking beings. Their speech acts demonstrate that their equality is not arithmetically inscribed, but inheres in these acts themselves.

Ballanche's rewriting makes Menenius crystallize the stakes of speech in the event. Instead of being placated by his fable or even attempting to overturn the order on behalf of which he speaks, the plebeians cause Menenius to recognize their mere "noise" as speech. The result is not a Habermasian "dialogue," however, but a "dazzling" or confounding of Menenius that leaves him without words. Ballanche attributes a discourse to Appius Claudius in which he accuses the consul of making a fatal error in imagining that words are coming from the plebs' mouths, and not noise:

They have speech like us, they dared tell Menenius! Was it a god that shut Menenius's mouth, that dazzled his eyes, that made his ears ring? Did some holy daze take hold of him? . . . He was somehow unable to respond that they had only transitory speech, a speech that is a fugitive sound, a sort of lowing, a sign of want and not an expression of intelligence. They were deprived of the eternal word which was in the past and would be in the future.[27]

Rancière glosses the passage by concluding that "before becoming a class traitor, the consul Menenius, who imagines he has heard the plebs speak, is a victim of sensory illusion" (24), that is, he has admitted the possibility of another "partition of the sensible," one that contests the permanence and inevitability of the patrician order.[28] "Somehow unable to respond," he cannot simply brandish the signs and emblems of power, as the Scythians do. His lack of a response is an implicit acknowledgment of the effectiveness of the plebs' speech act, since this act is not receivable within the existing order. But neither can it any longer be dismissed as "meaningless," as a mere "noise" or sign of want. This is because the plebs have forced Menenius to recognize them as speaking beings, and therefore as capable of *disagreement*. Disagreement is more radical than being a necessary part of the social body; it involves a conflict between two discourses or claims that cannot be resolved, because there is no common language in which they can be arbitrated, no Other who can mediate or decide. At stake is a speech act, an act tout court, and not a discourse or "exchange." As speaking beings, the plebs must be answered in speech, a speech suddenly unavailable to Menenius because what is required is not mere words, a discourse or fable in which the speaker attempts to "make sense" of the conflict or impose a role upon his addressee, but a subjective speech that must proceed in the absence of any guarantee of its receivability. This is what makes the speech scene symbolic, and not reducible to the imaginary of a "meaning" that functions only through the repression of intersubjectivity.

This example is important for the question of norms. Previously the plebs were excluded from the symbolic, their speech dismissed as mere "noise," the lowing of beasts. This prejudicial exclusion from what is *recognized* as speech nevertheless does not prevent them from speaking, from giving themselves names and so claiming a place in the symbolic order of the community, a place whose occupation is not contingent upon being recognized, accepted, or valued—or for that matter even tolerated—but inheres in the speech act wherein the plebs forcibly inscribe their name within the symbolic, and so extract and distinguish it from the patrician "partition of the perceptible," the imaginary order that ascribes visibility only to those who "count" and that is therefore nothing more than a play of identities and representations.

Against the normative reading, Rancière emphasizes the "sheer contingency" of politics, which democracy exposes in a radical way: "The foundation of politics is not in fact more a matter of convention than of nature: it is the lack of foundation, the sheer contingency of any social order" (16). When he questions "whether there exists a common stage where plebeians and patricians can debate anything," "common stage" (*scène commune*) does not imply some hypothetical "public sphere" or notion of "consensus," but the dissensus in which a speech act's lack of foundation is also its condition of possibility. It is the scene of the "partition of what is common" (5), and thus of disagreement or debate.

This reading allows us to cast in a different light the adoption of published written laws, which is one of the lasting legacies of the plebeian secessions. Taken together, the effect of the five secessions is to expand political representation, to extend rights and legal protections to those who did not previously have them, and, in particular, to see those rights inscribed in a written constitution:

> In 449 BC the plebs seceded a second time to force the patricians to adopt the Twelve Tables [the first constitution of the Roman Republic]. Unlike the earlier secret laws which only the priests had access to, these new laws amounted to a written and published legal code. And unlike the earlier non-published laws, the Twelve Tables presented a basic set of laws and rights to the Roman public, as opposed to hidden and secret laws that gave no specific rights to the ordinary plebeian Roman. . . . In 287 BC the plebs seceded one last time to force patricians to adopt the Lex Hortensia, which gave plebiscites the force of law.[29]

Rancière's argument allows us to read the adoption of written laws not merely as the achievement of a marginalized group's quest for greater representation or fuller rights, however, but as the trace and inscription of the plebs' decision to "conduct themselves like beings with names," writing for themselves a place in the symbolic order of the community. The point is not that the plebs' secession leads to a new state or institutional order, but rather that the written law inscribes in the symbolic the principle of disagreement, and thus the constraint of a lack of foundation. It introduces the potential for dispute and dissensus that is integral to written law, which is neither occult and unverifiable nor reducible to a "spirit" presumed to be discernible to all but subject to contention and disagreement at the level of its letter.

While some might be tempted to assimilate the "symbolic order" in its common acceptation to what Rancière calls "the police logic" (the norms, procedures, or laws that enforce a given partition of the sensible by allowing some subjects to be counted and not others), this is not his own position. Instead, Rancière understands the symbolic as the scene of a disagreement that the police order attempts to neutralize by reducing the speech of one of its parties to a disruptive noise. It is thus integral to his understanding of the political as the encounter between the police logic and an egalitarian logic that contests its miscount. "Nothing," Rancière writes,

> is political in itself. But anything may become political if it gives rise to a meeting of these two logics. The same thing—an election, a strike, a demonstration—can give rise to politics or not give rise to politics. A strike is not political when it calls for reforms rather than a better deal or when it attacks the relationships of authority rather than the inequality of wages. It is political when it reconfigures the relationships that determine the workplace in its relation to the community. The domestic household has been turned into a political space not through the simple fact that power relationships are at work in it but because it was the subject of argument in a dispute over the capacity of women in the community. The same concept—opinion or law, for example—may define a structure of political action or a structure of the police order.
>
> (32–33)

Rancière, then, does not reject written laws and legal jurisprudence as inherently unpolitical or antipolitical, as many contemporary thinkers do.

As we see in the example of the Aventine secession, the according of legal rights or the adoption of written laws can lend itself either to a police order reading (the one offered by Livy, where the extension of rights and protections has as its aim the preservation of the existing order) or to the political staging proposed by Ballanche (where the adoption of written laws is an expression of the act in which the plebs "write a name for themselves" as a contestatory political community). The difference depends upon whether or not it gives rise to a meeting of the police logic and the egalitarian logic.

Rancière's argument not only allows us to distinguish the literality of law (its properly symbolic dimension) from its content or representational function, but stresses that "the modern political animal is first a literary animal, caught in the circuit of a literariness that undoes the relationship between the order of words and the order of bodies that determine the place of each" (37). The difference political disorder inscribes in the police order is "the difference between subjectification and identification," since it "inscribes a *subject name* as being different from any identified part of the community" (37, my emphasis). "Worker," "woman," or "proletarian," for example, is "the subject that measures the gap between the part of work as social function and the having no part of those who carry it out within the definition of the common of the community" (36). What makes politics fundamentally symbolic, then, is the capacity of political speech to interrupt the imaginary of identification, to "space" the social order and so open up a space for the subject. Political disorder introduces a gap into "what is," provoking a "disidentification" or "removal from the naturalness of a place" by "opening up a subject space where . . . a connection is made between having a part and having no part" (36).

Rancière illustrates the difference between subjectification and identification with a speech scene he describes as "one of the first political occurrences of the modern proletarian subject," a dialogue occasioned by the trial in 1832 of the French revolutionary August Blanqui:

Asked by the magistrate to give his profession, Blanqui simply replies: "proletarian." The magistrate immediately objects "That is not a profession," setting himself up for the accused's immediate response: "It is the profession of thirty million Frenchmen who live off their labor and who are deprived of political rights." The judge then agrees to have the court clerk list proletarian as a new "profession." Blanqui's two replies summarize the entire conflict between politics and the police: everything turns on the double acceptance of a single word, *profession*. For the prosecutor, embodying police logic, profession means job, trade: the activity that puts a body in its place and function. It is clear that proletarian does not designate any occupation whatever, at most the vaguely defined state of the poverty-stricken manual laborer, which, in any case, is not appropriate to the accused. But within revolutionary politics, Blanqui gives the same word a different meaning: a profession is a profession of faith, a declaration of membership in a collective. This collective is of a particular kind, however. The proletarian class in which Blanqui professes to include himself is in no way identifiable with a social group. The proletariat are neither manual workers nor the labor classes. They are the class of the uncounted that only exists in the very declaration in which they are counted as those of no account.

(37–38, translation modified)

In showing that the name "proletarian" corresponds neither to a set of properties shared by a multitude of individuals nor to a collective body of which those individuals are members, but is "part of a process of subjectification identical to the process of expounding a wrong" (38), Blanqui's speech act also illuminates the specifically political function of the slogan or popular rallying cry, which could be understood as a form of political speech uniquely charged with articulating this disidentification: May '68's "We are all German Jews," Occupy Wall Street's "We are the 99%."

Rancière's account of politics as a meeting up of two orders—and thus as the staging of a polemic—departs not only from an understanding of politics as "representation," but also from any brand of revolutionary politics that emphasizes violent struggle or armed conflict to the exclusion of the symbolic features of the political. The last example is especially interesting in this regard. Blanqui is known for his advocacy of a dictatorship by force that would bring about a new order, and for his willingness to enforce revolutionary change with violence. In emphasizing the force of his speech act instead, Rancière introduces a different take on what makes Blanqui's stance truly political. As in the distinction between the slave revolt and the plebeian secession, the difference is not merely between violent and nonviolent resolutions of conflict. Blanqui's claiming of a profession, like the plebs' action against the patrician order, is in fact still violent, but it is the violence of speech (a symbol that is always inadequate to the complexity of what it signifies) rather than (or at least in addition to) physical force.

This nuance modulates the problematic of revolutionary class struggle in suggestive ways. Like the strategy of the *secessio plebis*, Blanqui's revolutionary activity anticipates a recognizably Marxist paradigm of political action within the framework of class struggle. Rancière himself affirms class struggle not only as the ultimate political question, but as the very "institution of politics itself" (11). Yet he also stresses that class struggle cannot be limited to a power play; it cannot simply be a mode of revolt, but must have a symbolic dimension if it is to "establish another order" altogether, rather than merely expanding upon or revolting against the existing order. So, while we do not usually associate dialectical materialism with the symbolic—much less the affirmation of the symbolic—Rancière's work not only enables this connection but implies that neither can be thought effectively in isolation from the other. Just as he makes clear that the symbolic character of law does not necessarily relegate it to complicity with the police logic, Rancière invites us to consider whether there is a necessary symbolic dimension to revolutionary class struggle, and in what it might consist (a question I will return to in chapter 6, through a reading of Walter Benjamin's "Critique of Violence").

Another major (if less obvious) interest of Rancière's work, in my view, is that it allows us to appreciate that a woman's relation to the symbolic is deeply political. "In politics," he writes, "'woman' is the subject of experience—the denatured, defeminized subject—that measures the gap between an acknowledged part (that of sexual complementarity) and a having no part" (36). This is the case of Jeanne Deroin, a socialist feminist and early advocate of women's suffrage who, in 1849, "presents herself as a candidate for a legislative election in which she cannot run" (41). Her example demonstrates that "a mode of subjectification does not create subjects ex nihilo; it creates them by transforming identities defined in the natural order of the allocation of functions and places into instances of experience of a dispute" (36). While "'workers' or 'women' are identities that apparently hold no mystery," the process of political subjectification "forces them out of such obviousness by questioning the relationship between a *who* and a *what* in the apparent redundancy of the positing of an existence" (36). It therefore "bring[s] out the contradiction between two logics, by positing existences that are at the same time nonexistences—or nonexistences that are at the same time existences" (41).[30]

In placing the "wrong" of sexual inequality alongside wrongs of a more conventionally "political" nature, Rancière's work acknowledges something that is generally disregarded by accounts of the political as a scene of violence, power, and armed struggle: the "war of the sexes" could never be resolved through armed conflict or a simple friend-enemy distinction. As a wrong or inequality sited in speech, the inequality of the sexes must also be confronted and addressed in speech. It is thus an inherently symbolic wrong, the wrong that actually founds the symbolic, that is, the impossibility of speech being counted as *full* speech, inasmuch as the phallic signifier represents the desires of all subjects "equally" and thus inadequately.

Rancière's comments relate very well to the case of Teresa of Ávila, who aspires through her meditational practices and institutional reforms not merely to find a way for her experience to "be counted," but to evoke in speech what *fails* to be counted: her experience of a jouissance that eludes meaning, that has no "place" in society. Instead of allowing her mistrust of speech to become a refusal of speech or language—and thereby reverting to the "fascinating jouissance" of the body as the only site of truth—Teresa's experience attests to the importance of constructing in speech the "wrong" that language does to women specifically, and contesting the phallic signifier in its partition of what "counts" as meaningful, useful, or beneficial to society. The choice Teresa is compelled to make between the symptom and speech in turn illuminates Rancière's distinction between "revolt" and "politics." The symptom, like an armed revolt with no symbolic dimension, is unable to liberate its subject precisely because it takes place outside the register of speech, the "opening of a subject space" that for Rancière defines the political. Teresa's experience closely parallels analysis, while Rancière's work concerns the political. Both authors, however, develop an account of the symbolic as the arena of subjectification, the site of inscription of a desire that in finding a public or political expression ceases to be purely particular and assumes general (if not universal) consequences.

As these two cases make clear, there is nothing particularly flashy about the kinds of examples this book takes up, but neither can they be reduced to the normative or "bourgeois individualist" slant that is often ascribed to them in much contemporary scholarship. This charge is frequently leveled at psychoanalysis, and not without some justification; but it also extends to some of the approaches to social and political change that I intend to highlight. Peter Hallward, for example, regrets in an appraisal of Rancière's thought that the latter "is not interested, as a rule, . . . in the group dynamics of collective mobilization or empowerment," since "the model in each case is provided by the isolated process of intellectual *self*-emancipation," a choice in which Hallward sees a "certain degree of social resignation."[31] As I hope to have made clear in this introduction, I do not see self-emancipation as something qualitatively distinct from—much less at odds with—social change; I will tend to emphasize instead the ways in which the latter can result from, if not necessarily depend upon, the former.

MAKING ROOM FOR THE IMPERCEPTIBLE: SOPHIE CALLE AND THE "CITY TO COME"

Finally, and more briefly, let me turn to one last example: the work of the contemporary French artist Sophie Calle, whose site-specific works and collaborative projects with ordinary urban residents all share an emphasis on the refashioning of public space, and more broadly on the reinvention of the social tie. Calle's work foregrounds the enabling function of artistic constraints, and by extension the symbolic status of the artwork itself, which does not merely evoke or envision another reality, but anticipates or even precipitates alternative linkages and modes of relation. Most of Calle's projects are structured by formal constraints, a trait her work shares with the aesthetic endeavors of the Surrealists, Situationists, and Oulipians, among others. But the singularity of her work with respect to other constrained creative practices is that it uses constraints to refound the social link on another footing, to establish new ties and connections.

In two rich essays devoted to her work, Juliet Flower MacCannell suggests that Calle's photographic work "constitutes a demand that public space (our most common metaphor for the work of the Symbolic) confess how it is populated—and haunted—by all the desires it embraces yet fails to symbolize. She thus aims her camera at nothing less than a re-functioning of the Symbolic, ridding it of its outdated, overly 'phallic' style."[32] Calle's first work to pursue this project in detail is *Suite vénitienne* (*Venetian Pursuit*), a photo essay structured by the constraint she gives herself of following a man she meets at a gallery as he leaves on a trip to Venice, and then pursuing him incognito through its streets and canals with her camera. As MacCannell understands it, Calle's quest is devoid of the voyeuristic intentions most viewers have been content to read into it. Her aim is not to expose the intimate details of her quarry's life (she never follows him into private or interior spaces, and mainly photographs his back and his feet), but to explore a fundamental *social* question: Does a woman have a place in the streets? Can she enter the public arena only on the condition of "following" in a man's path, or can she also remap and remake public space? Under what conditions can society recognize a woman's right to the public sphere?

Why pursue this quest in Venice, then? Because "with its watery ways," writes MacCannell, "[it] becomes the one city of *all* cities that most fully voids standard patriarchal symbols for channeling desire" (63). Lacking conventional avenues, grand boulevards, or gridded streets, Venice challenges the phallicized model of urban design that dominates in most cities. As such, it also "deprives you of the illusion that you (and by analogy your civilization) have drive under control" (63). To follow Calle to Venice, MacCannell suggests, "is to follow Woman into the beyond of our civilization's pleasure principle, to where it meets up with death drive and answers for it, where civilization resymbolizes itself in a new narrative space, in a new city space" (58).

Disguised in a hyperfeminine blond wig and dark sunglasses, Calle spends long hours attempting to locate Henri B. or waiting for him to emerge from a building. In her journal she records her efforts, as well as the strangely excessive emotions (tragic ennui, rage, even the desire to see a little boy finally catch and kill one of the pigeons he's pursuing . . .) that seize hold of her in this uniquely feminine *désoeuvrement*. At numerous junctures, Calle is obliged to rely upon "the kindness of strangers" to locate and identify Henri B., telling them she needs to know the whereabouts of a man with whom she is in love. "Only love," Calle writes in her journal of the pursuit, "seems acceptable." How can a woman "walk the streets" legitimately, she seems to ask, if not in pursuit of a man? Does she really belong there?

Hence although Calle follows "her man" incognito, attempting to elude recognition, she ultimately also *aspires* to be recognized—differently. Finally Henri B. does recognize Calle beneath her disguise: "because of her eyes," he tells her. After a few awkward moments, he calls her out of the shadows and proposes that they walk through the streets together. He is unsettled, unsure, and does not quite know how to proceed. This is completely new terrain for both of them, but the point is that they now proceed to walk it *together*. MacCannell suggests that this may be what Calle was looking for all along: recognition as a *legitimate* streetwalker, who has as much claim to the streets as he does. In inviting this unknown man to experience differently or anew the streets and citified spaces that are now as foreign to him as they were to her, Calle's artwork "tilts the symbolic lightly on a feminine axis" (67) by asking it to apprehend public space from the perspective of the feminine, and so open itself to another possible understanding of the common.

Echoing Rancière, MacCannell concludes from Calle's work that the "woman who does not exist" must show us the way toward a new symbolic, one capable of encompassing the "imperceptibles." Importantly, however, she asserts that Calle's "in-your-face-femininity" is not only concerned with its own possible destiny, but directly related to her "sustained address to the great political hot spots of our time" (71), and to the insight they provide into a "symbolic in distress" that is woefully in need of remaking. In an essay titled "Making Room: Woman and the City to Come,"[33] MacCannell returns to Calle's work in the context of an argument devoted to the contemporary city and its future. Her focus is Calle's installation from 1996 at the Jewish Museum, "Public Spaces-Private Places," subsequently published as *L'EROUV de Jerusalem* (*Eruv of Jerusalem*).[34] Like *Suite*, it explores the state of the symbolic through a specific city: not an elusive alternative to the stale phallic model this time, but the distillation of its most intractable impasses.

MacCannell reads Calle's piece as an intervention into the conflict over how to divide Jerusalem. As the "cradle" of both the Jewish and the Islamic civilizations, Jerusalem presents a specific dilemma: is its division the object of a truly symbolic social contract, or a merely phallic one? Drawing on Fethi Benslama's psychoanalytic study of the Jerusalem conflict,[35] MacCannell observes that "each side is unconsciously invested in whatever once stood 'erect' or is still upright: essentially phallic in form and affective force. Each also speaks of the site as the *cradle* of their people. This thus makes it a primal scene haunted by 'maternal spectrality': the scene of the mother's bed or one's own birthing." The result is an "irresolvable *psychological* paradox," since "the phallic that would regulate its own 'natal bed' is also enfolded within it. To take the site as exemplary of the *birth* of our civilization(s) is thus to render it psychologically immune to alteration by reason, law or mere political sovereignty." The dilemma the conflict presents, therefore, is whether Jerusalem can be situated "within a truly symbolic rather than a merely phallic order."

The question becomes: would it be possible to reconceive symbolic order and thereby its civilization and cities (including this city of cities) from a post-Oedipal but not anti-Oedipal perspective? If an unconscious conflict over the mother's bed is the underside of phallic order, that order is no longer (if it ever really was) identical to *the symbolic*. To pretend that the phallic and the symbolic are the same is to doom us to the artificiality and the false reassurance of today's postmodern ironic city, gesturing toward an inert phallic order by repeating its lifeless forms in order to save us from

Jerusalem. Jerusalem's case is completely unique, psychologically speaking, yet this extreme case exposes how open to challenge the phallicized symbolic must now be.

Calle, she claims, courageously faces this challenge by giving us "*another* Jerusalem: a place that is in fact a *living* symbolic, though not organized along phallic lines of division, hierarchy, and force."

Calle's installation draws upon the Orthodox Jewish tradition of erecting an *eruv*, a physical and symbolic enclosure created by stringing wire from poles in and around a Jewish community. This practice is used as a way of stretching the Talmudic law that prohibits the transfer of objects outside of the home on the Sabbath by defining the space within the *eruv* as "home." Calle asked fourteen residents of the city, Palestinian as well as Israeli, to take her to public places they considered private and share their personal associations with the sites. In the completed installation, the stories of her subjects were documented anonymously through framed photos of these "private" sites and the texts describing their importance, which were placed on a map of Jerusalem in the center of the gallery. Twenty panels of black and white photographs of Jerusalem's *eruv* lined the walls of the gallery, symbolically re-creating the sacrosanct space.

In the text accompanying the exhibition, Calle suggests that a literal translation of *eruv* might be "mixture" (*mélange*): it represents the possible articulation of the public and the private. The wires defining the *eruv* pass high above the street level and do no actually interfere with the passage of pedestrians; although of paramount importance to Orthodox Jews, they are virtually invisible to everyone else. Unlike the Jerusalem "security wall" to which it is implicitly opposed, this "boundary" is permeable. It is also a mobile border, expanded every time a new community is added to the edge of the city. Because it is mobile and frequently crosses over lands that are under construction, residents are obliged to pay close attention to the changes in its boundaries over the weeks and years.

The *eruv* is thus a metaphor for the possible expansiveness and malleability of the symbolic, but at the same time for the risk it necessarily runs—which it also must somehow find a way to avoid—of simply being collapsed with the "Oedipal" logic of the "home." That is, even as the *eruv* renders public spaces intimate, there is an implied violence involved in turning into a Jewish home (and by extension an Israeli "homeland") what are in fact spaces that figure in the public and personal lives of every one of the city's residents. A true symbolic cannot simply be an expansion of the familial (the Oedipal model) or the home; it cannot be absorbed into identity and identification.

Calle's artwork responds to this challenge by proposing a different kind of *eruv*, which extends the reach not of the "home" (or of identity more broadly speaking), but of a symbolic simultaneously constituted and decompleted by the subjects it inscribes without actually representing them. MacCannell writes that "hidden beneath the Holy City—the traditional holy sites that officially divide its people from each other—Calle unearths a secret sharing that fundamentally recasts the argument over Jerusalem's sacred sites." Its "truly sacred sites," she finds, "are the *common spaces* where (and only where) *the dreams of the one do not interfere with and displace the desires of the other*. Calle discovers *who belongs* in the contested City—and *to whom this City belongs*: both Palestinians and Jews." Importantly, their experiences are concerned not primarily with being Israelis or Palestinians, Jews or Arabs, but with the desires that animate real lives. A Palestinian girl, for example, leads Calle to an enormous modern shopping center on the city's outskirts where she used to walk hand in hand with her boyfriend, hiding in plain view from the disapproving gazes of parents and community. In Calle's reimagining, the *Eruv of Jerusalem* is not the extension of a religious or group identity claim (the "common predicates" that the phallic signifier privileges); it is about real desires that are singular, inassimilable to group norms. In MacCannell's assessment,

> The piece is obviously about the flawed way we grasp Jerusalem, but it is also about a crucial defect in any symbol: no symbol *can in fact ever fully represent the human links that animate it*. Calle's work makes strikingly clear the multiplicity of unacknowledged desires in Jerusalem; it demonstrates that they can co-exist *only* where a truly *symbolic space exists*—in this case, the space of her *Eruv* artwork, where the paradox of the symbol is made salient rather than willfully ignored. Our spaces

must accommodate the indefinable, incompatible desire of the other (including the other sex)—without brutally overexposing it, stereotyping it, or enforcing borderlines around its hardened *identity*. Which means our spaces, in order to be truly symbolic, must allow for recognizing the *imperceptible* other, the subject beyond the visibly gendered, racialized, ethnically categorized person before our eyes, the subject of surveillance and control. Executed in charming, quirky, unexpected ways, Calle's work documents unflinchingly the blindness of the official phallic-symbolic order to the new subjects a true symbolic must include.

Calle's project recalls that of another great champion of truly public art, the British street artist Banksy (whose guerrilla graffiti on the West Bank security wall—one of more than twenty such works to date—is represented on the cover of this book). Both attempt to create in art a symbolic space that is missing in the public sphere, that fails to be represented in its "partition of the perceptible." Banksy's work proposes surreal reversals of the existing order (a physically imposing masked man lobbing a bouquet of flowers rather than the expected bomb, a little girl patting down a soldier to look for concealed weapons, an Israeli border guard scrutinizing a donkey's identity papers as it tries to pass a checkpoint) that expose the failings of the existing "symbolic" order and call for a new conception of public space.[36]

David Fieni, in his suggestively titled article "What a Wall Wants, or How Graffiti Thinks," reminds us that in the hands of a motivated graffiti artist a wall can be a space of desire as well as a tool of containment and oppression,[37] recapturing "security" walls for the representation of those they contain and control. He sees in the work of Banksy and others a project of "nomad grammatology," a term that both recalls and revises the "nomad thought" theorized by Gilles Deleuze and Félix Guattari in their *A Thousand Plateaus*.[38] While the latter is invariably aligned with "smooth" spaces unwritten or unmarked by the law or symbolic, Banksy and other politically engaged graffitists attempt to rewrite and reinscribe public space, to recapture it for the social link as distinct from the state order.[39] This is what makes their projects social and even symbolic and not anarchistic or nihilistic, despite their illegality. While a striated "partitioning" may fall away, grammatology does not. Along with Calle's *Eruv*, it offers a great example of what Ballanche describes as the need to write a new "name in the sky," a new place in the symbolic order.

These three examples correspond roughly to the three different sections of this book. The first takes up the constrained experience of the transference in psychoanalysis, and the perspective it offers on the conditions and possible consequences of an act founded on desire. The second and longest section deals with the function of speech and writing in politics and legal theory, and the symbolic function of the written law in particular. The final chapter concludes with an examination of aesthetic constraints, and their role in enabling a "presentation of the unpresentable." Let me turn, then, to a first (re)invention of the symbolic: Freud's discovery of the unconscious.

PART 1
REINVENTING THE SYMBOLIC

1

INVENTIONS OF THE SYMBOLIC

Lacan's Reading of Freud

"**T**O GO THROUGH a psychoanalysis marks a passage, on the condition that my analysis of the unconscious as founding the function of the symbolic be completely admissible."[1] With these words, Jacques Lacan sums up the two claims that this chapter will attempt to elucidate: that the analytic experience constitutes a "passage"—a transformation of the subject's position with respect to the fantasy—only on the condition that the subject traverse the field of the symbolic, and that it is the unconscious that founds the symbolic function, and not the norms, ideals, or prohibitions that regulate social coexistence. Psychoanalysis is an experience structured by a confrontation with symbolic constraints, and not a process of behavioral modification or adaptation.

In one of his last seminars, Lacan recalls that he was led to the triad of the real, the imaginary, and the symbolic "by the hysterics," since "it was in trying to say something coherent about hysterics that Freud constructed his technique."[2] Why, then, does Lacan feel compelled to invent a new set of terms, rather than simply employing the vocabulary and theoretical constructions Freud already proposed? Because he finds that psychoanalysis after Freud has appealed increasingly to behavioral and social norms to repress the unconscious, and therefore to buttress—rather than dismantle—the defenses the subject erects against the real that are at stake in the fantasy and her own unconscious desire. Although for Lacan it is ego psychology that bears the brunt of the blame (for disseminating an understanding of psychoanalytic technique that completely distorts—when it does not efface altogether—Freud's invention), Freud's own formulations are part of the problem as well. The conceptualization of the symbolic should be understood as an attempt on Lacan's part to reduce the analytic experience to its fundamentals, and to make possible the analysis of those subjects that the clinical practices of his day failed to address in a satisfying way.

While "the symbolic" is not a concept in Freud's writing, his work can be read as elaborating a nascent account of its structure and function. Where do we look for it? In a series of essays on infantile sexuality from the 1910s and 1920s, Freud offers what is often taken to be the basis of Lacan's account of the symbolic when he advances that the traversal of the Oedipus complex is the condition of successful entry into social life, and equates ethical comportment with the internalization of the paternal superego.[3]

To the extent that Freud does found intersubjectivity—and the possibility of an ethical relation to desire—on the Oedipus complex, this approach is problematic. It predicates successful coexistence on the phallic function that structures the Oedipal complex in the little boy, for whom narcissistic investment in the organ facilitates internalization of the father's law. The flip side of this masculine emphasis is a failure to conceptualize femininity in other than phallic terms and the charge that the "passing" of the Oedipus complex in the girl's case is at best incomplete, at worst a failure. (Hence the notorious claim in his lecture "Femininity" from 1933 that a woman's superego is less firmly installed than a man's, rendering her less capable of developing a sense of justice or morality or of participating in collective undertakings.)

A related problem is the tendency (both in Freud's own practice and in psychoanalysis more generally) to privilege the experience of the obsessional neurotic. Lacan is from the outset concerned with those structures and subjective positions that fall outside the neurotic structure and the challenges they present to analytic treatment: first the psychoses, then perversion and hysteria, and finally femininity. If it is all about the passing of the Oedipus complex and the internalization of the paternal superego, then there is no way to treat most clinical structures, and psychoanalysis becomes nothing more than a clinic of obsessional neurosis: a clinic for neurotics, but also a clinic that sustains and perpetuates the social norms and prohibitions to which the neurotic appeals to repress the subject of the unconscious and its inadmissible desire.[4] Lacan's theorization of the transference and the analytic maneuver takes aim at both.

A symbolic that only describes the experience of the (masculine) neurotic is not a symbolic at all, but a normative codification of values and ideals. Lacan seeks not only to distinguish and further theorize these clinical structures, however, but to consider the stakes of the symbolic from the perspective of those who are marginal to its most familiar iterations. His early career is devoted to the possible psychoanalytic treatment of the psychoses. More than any other psychic structure, psychosis makes clear that the function of the symbolic cannot be conflated with social prohibitions and conventions, and underscores the decompletion or unfounded character of the symbolic as its essential trait. This is Lacan's core argument, and across his work he explores it, first in relation to psychosis, then in relation to perversion and hysteria, and finally in relation to femininity. Each of these positions reveals in a different way the *unfounded* character of the symbolic and its tension with the societal norms and ideals that supplement or obscure it.

A normative account of the symbolic as the internalization of patriarchal law derives from an understanding of the symbolic as a by-product of the Oedipus complex and its passing. I maintain that this understanding is not Lacan's, however, and ultimately not Freud's either. In introducing the three orders of the real, the symbolic, and the imaginary, Lacan radically disjoins the symbolic from the sphere of ideals and morality. In so doing, he allows us to pinpoint a latent theory of the symbolic in Freud's work that cannot be assimilated to the Oedipus complex and its passing. When we read his first major works (*Studies in Hysteria*, *The Interpretation of Dreams*, *Dora*) alongside his last (*Moses and Monotheism*, "Constructions in Analysis"), we see that Freud's investigations both begin and end with a set of preoccupations that are central to what Lacan elaborates as the symbolic. I contend that these works allow us to identify two distinct "inventions of the symbolic," both of which foreground its experimental character: the inauguration of the analytic transference in the Freudian clinic, and the founding of the Mosaic law. While the choice of the second is probably not surprising, I suggest that its true stakes emerge only in comparison with the first. My thesis is that Lacan's account of the symbolic is best understood as an attempt to take stock of the broader implications of the transference as the constraint that allows the subject to construct and sustain an unconscious desire.

This chapter will not attempt to offer a comprehensive clinical or critical genealogy of the concept of the symbolic, since such a project has already been tackled by a wide range of critical studies and far exceeds the scope of this book.[5] In limiting myself to a discussion of the transference and the Mosaic law, I aim instead to foreground the dynamic or experimental dimension of the symbolic that these mechanisms and practices sustain in allowing the subject to "mark a passage" or undertake a transformative experience.

The first section briefly situates the importance of the Oedipus complex in Freud's work, which can be understood as a representation—but also as a repression—of the problematic of castration. The second will turn to the first of the two "inventions of the symbolic" I see as latent in Freud's work: the elaboration of the signifying chain under transference that allows for the construction of the discourse of the unconscious. In Lacan's reading, the transference interrupts the narcissistic or paranoid character of the interpersonal relation by substituting for it a "minimal social link" defined by the intersubjective relation between the subject and the Other, or the locus of speech as such. The third section develops these implications by offering a reading of Freud's *Moses and Monotheism* in light of the clinic, advancing that Freud makes an important contribution to legal theory by allowing us to distinguish the properly symbolic dimension of law from its real and imaginary manifestations, an interpretation that would not have been possible without his earlier experience of the transference.

BEYOND THE OEDIPUS COMPLEX

Fundamentally, Freud's account of the Oedipus complex is concerned with the staging of castration. It describes the way in which the little boy (and the obsessional boy in particular) confronts castration, finds a representation for it, and attempts to manage its effects. For a man, Oedipus articulates the body to the law of the Other by inscribing in the body the reality of castration. It involves a loss of a part of his own body, and an assumption of lack (the impossibility of full enjoyment) as the condition of entering the social link. To put it another way, it marks the phallus as belonging to the race or group, and not solely to the individual (which explains why the incest prohibition is invariably addressed to men and not to women). By symbolizing this loss, the phallus serves as the guarantor of the cultural articulation of meaning for a man by linking his jouissance to his role in the procreation of the speaking being. The Oedipus complex articulates castration (which is not a matter of society or of inscription in the social order) to the norms and ideals of society, as well as to meaning. It sifts out what counts as meaningful jouissance and what remains unanchored, unspoken, outside of meaning.

Lacan's work can be understood as attempting to extract the concept of the symbolic from the institutions, norms, and prohibitions that represent it for the neurotic in order to reveal its structural dimension. We are all obliged to confront the locus of the Other and the constraints it imposes on desire. It does not follow, however, that we all confront it within the social order, if the latter is understood as a sphere defined by the embrace of certain ideals and norms. This is certainly not true of the psychotic and the pervert, but I would maintain that it is ultimately not true of anyone, even if the specifically neurotic way of avoiding castration often involves an appeal to ideals and values to repress unconscious desire.

While Lacan retains and affirms Freud's emphasis on castration as a core concept of psychoanalysis, he also seeks to expand it beyond the strictly phallic understanding of castration that tends to dominate in Freud so as to address the experience of women and of nonneurotic psychic structures. He argues that castration is not merely a matter of submission to a paternal or social order that imposes a renunciation of some share of sexual satisfaction or of a given sexual object, but, more structurally, a matter of the traversal of the field of the Other (of language as such) that causes every human being to lose the object that would satisfy the instinct and means that every interpersonal exchange is overdetermined by demand.

Although this structural fact and the consequences that result from it have been represented in certain fundamental and largely stable forms throughout human history (notably in the incest prohibition that Claude Lévi-Strauss posits as universal in human culture),[6] these are still only representations, and representations that are addressed to, and pertinent for, half of humanity at most. The *representation* of the structure has to be distinguished from the structure itself. In exposing the structure of castration, Lacan also opens up the possibility of—and the need for—other representations, other stagings. Whether or not we adhere to the ideals and prohibitions of the group, we are all castrated: the symbolic is concerned with how we encounter castration, how we attempt to repress it or manage its effects, and how we go about developing an ethics in response to it.

Castration could be defined most simply as the loss of full being to language, or the fact that for the human being it is not possible to return to a purely instinctual existence (defined by the successful fulfillment of specific instinctual aims or by the infallible ability to locate and obtain certain objects within a given natural environment). Lacan's understanding of castration is therefore indebted less to Freud's theorization of Oedipus and the castration complex than to his *Three Essays on the Theory of Sexuality*, published in 1905, which theorizes the emergence of the drive in relation to the loss of instinctual sexuality. For the human being, the sexual drive has neither an instinctual aim (the reproduction of the species) nor an instinctual object (the genitals of the other sex). In Freud's early formulation, the drive is "the psychical representative of an endosomatic, continuously flowing source of stimulation," which can only be partially bound—and therefore never exhausted or fulfilled—by any given object or aim.[7]

More specifically, castration denotes the fact that the quest for satisfaction, in the human being, must necessarily pass through the locus of the Other (the field of the address, or language as such), which results in the transmutation of need into a demand that cannot be fulfilled directly. Once a man has to address a woman, for example, he necessarily loses her as a sexual object; it is no longer enough to have a penis or be guided by the reproductive instinct to be able to obtain the object. The structure of the address imposes a detour with respect to the object, which can only be approached metaphorically or approximately. Fundamentally, then, the symbolic describes the constraint of the Other, this third term or locus that supplements and undermines every would-be dyadic relation. What Lacan calls the "delusional normalism of the genital relation" (*Écrits* 234) is calculated to hide this castration, by attempting to reintegrate sexuality into a pseudonatural order.

Lacan questions the Oedipal slant Freud gives to the symbolic in three different ways. First, he questions the priority of the phallic function that structures a man's relation to castration by defining masculinity and femininity as two different attitudes taken up with respect to castration. Second, he draws on the experience of the hysteric, the pervert, and the psychotic to extract the symbolic function from the mechanisms of law, and in particular the "imaginary" dialectic of frustration and identification that defines the father's Oedipal role as an agent of prohibition. Third, more broadly, he explores across his entire corpus the implications of both for the study of culture, which Freud generally approaches from an obsessional perspective (especially in his studies of religion).

THE SYMBOLIC AND SEXUAL DIFFERENCE

While Lacan retains Freud's emphasis on castration as a fundamental experience for men and women alike, he also questions his tendency to frame it solely in phallic terms (and specifically in terms of having or not having the penis). While a woman may potentially experience her lack of a penis as a "narcissistic wound" or as a threat to her unified body image, the anatomical absence of the organ cannot found the ethical experience of castration for a woman because it does not serve to inscribe in her body the effects of submitting to the law of the Other (the loss of the organ of sexuality to the social order, for example). This is why Freud views women as less moral than men: they appear not to be inscribed in the order of ethics, understood as an order of renunciation or lack.

Lacan does not refute Freud's observation about the marginality of women to the mores of the phallocratic order, but interprets it differently. He challenges the purported universality of the Oedipus complex by advancing that the feminine subject is "not wholly inscribed within the phallic function" and the particular modality of castration it imposes. This is because she is confronted not with the lack in drive—the impossibility of obtaining its object that the prohibition metaphorizes—but with an excess that is not anchored by any object, and that the law (and more broadly the signifier itself) is therefore unable to limit. Because Freud defines castration in phallic terms, he can imagine no other way for a woman to assume the ethical consequences of castration than through maternity, which subjects a "piece of her body" to loss (in the form of the child she must eventually relinquish), thereby articulating castration to the demands of society. Yet maternity is only one possible role or function among others for a woman; it cannot be the only way for a woman to encounter and assume castration. Moreover, while maternity may metaphorize loss, it does not address the specificity of a woman's relation to the drive (which Freud himself characterized as "especially constant").[8] Because she bears the brunt of embodying not the lack in drive, but its excess, a woman is confronted with the lack of any adequate limit to the drive (the lack of lack, as it were).

If Freud sometimes leaves us with the impression that woman is an extra-symbolic being, Lacan's elaboration of the symbolic can be understood as an attempt to rectify the prejudices of this argument. For Lacan it is not that men participate in the symbolic and women do not, but that women relate to the symbolic in its inconsistency or lack of foundation. In the feminine contestation of the signifier or law, he sees not a repudiation of morality or justice, but a unique knowledge concerning what Apollon has termed the *Infondé*, the "unfoundedness" of the symbolic.[9] This is because femininity is qualified by what Danielle Bergeron describes as "its failure in relation to the rules defined by the phallus as the representative of lack: to be a woman is not only to be situated within the phallic as a subject of language, but also to be one who cannot trust language or bring herself to make phallic laws the sole foundation of the meaning of her life."[10] Without renouncing the phallic signifier altogether, the ethics of the feminine subject must therefore be founded upon something other than the particular kind of limit it represents. It follows that a woman is not incapable of moral behavior, but driven by her experience to question the foundations of the moral order and the law of the signifier it supposes. Her quest for a limit supposes an interrogation of the signifier's defect—its failure to regulate jouissance—that leads her to seek a solution outside the sphere of societal norms and prohibitions.

A SYMBOLIC BEYOND THE LAW

While Freud devotes considerable attention to the function of the law, both at the level of the individual psyche and at the level of the social, Lacan is just as interested in thinking about the limitations of law, what lies beyond it. Freud's interest in questions of law is closely tied to his focus on the structure of obsessional neurosis (notably in his studies of religion and culture); Lacan's exploration of the "beyond" of law, on the other hand, is motivated in large part by his attention to the experience of the hysteric, the psychotic, and the pervert, as well as to the question of femininity. Because they are all confronted with an excess that the law is unable to limit, each of these positions attests in different ways to the limitations of patriarchal forms of social organization and to the inadequacy of traditional paternal laws (the laws of lack) in the face of the disorganizing effects of the drive and the fantasy it structures.

What they reveal is not the irrelevance or parochialism of the paternal function, however, but the urgent need to theorize a paternal function beyond the law, and so distinguish its psychic function from the patriarchal norms and ideals that structure a social or moral order defined by the renunciation of enjoyment or the embrace of certain values. In contesting its efficacy, these structures help to clarify the structural function and psychic importance of the paternal metaphor, which need not imply the imaginary investment of the paternal figure that is a feature of the Oedipal fantasy (and of the group psychological mechanisms that Freud sees as essential to the identity and cohesion of such "artificial" groups as the Church and the army).[11] While they appeal to the paternal imago as an imaginary authority (and even as an agent of severe privation) in order to not confront the unfounded character of the symbolic, each of these structures reveals in a different way that the paternal metaphor is necessarily nothing more than a "fiction," a fiction that can alternately sustain and support the subject in its confrontation with the real of the drives or that (in its imaginary guise) can be enlisted in its attempts to repress them.

These structures are thus uniquely poised to teach us something about symbolic life "after" the patriarchy, when traditional authorities no longer appear as credible guarantors of the social order. From a feminine, perverse, or psychotic perspective this appears not as a "loss" of ground, but as the exposure of a groundlessness that is a structural condition of the symbolic. They help us appreciate that the "unfoundedness" of the symbolic is key to its true function and to why, ultimately, it matters.

In his seminars of the 1960s, Lacan returns to the origins of psychoanalysis to propose that the function of the symbolic must be sought not in the Oedipal prohibition and the social order to which it gives rise, but in a reexamination of the "discourse of the hysteric" that founds psychoanalysis by revealing the transformative potential of the signifier (or the symbolic function of speech) as distinct from the "imaginary" of the social bond (the norms, values, and ideals with which the ego identifies in order to repress the fragmented body of the drives). Commenting upon Freud's strategy in the Dora case, Lacan marvels that after years of listening to hysterics Freud can come up with nothing better than the Oedipus complex to make sense of their experience: "Why did Freud mislead himself to this extent? . . . Why does he substitute for the knowledge he gathers from all these mouths of gold—Anna, Emma, Dora—this myth, the Oedipus complex?"[12] In Lacan's rehabilitative reading, the hysteric is the one who reveals the significance of the signifier as such in its relation to the field of the Other. The upshot of this critique is to show that the symbolic function of the signifier is not reducible to the law or prohibition, but is instead intimately linked to the clinical experience of psychoanalysis and the mechanism of the transference.

As women who were not addressed by the patriarchal prohibitions that metaphorize a man's relation to the lack in drive (the incest prohibition), Freud's first hysterical patients were confronted with a jouissance not limited by the law. The fact that they were able to benefit from analysis, however, demonstrates that they encountered through the transference another modality of the symbolic, the elaboration of the signifying chain that functions to limit and constrain the jouissance at stake in the symptom. The logic of the transference reveals that the assumption of castration is a matter not solely of internalizing the phallic laws of lack (as Freud sometimes suggests), but more fundamentally of encountering and assuming the lack in the Other, its structural decompletion. That there is no signifier for jouissance means there is a lack in the Other (in language as such), a defect in the signifier inasmuch as it cannot name—and so cannot repress—jouissance. The elaboration of the signifying chain under transference does not furnish this missing signifier, however, but allows the analysand to elaborate a knowledge about her encounter with the real of jouissance, to construct that lack in the Other (as well as the fantasy staging that sought to repress it) and to thereby free herself from the repetition-automatism it unleashes by ceaselessly inscribing—in the form of symptoms—the real that fails to be inscribed in the order of the signifier (in Lacan's formulation, "*ce qui ne cesse pas de (ne pas) s'inscrire*": what never ceases (not) to be inscribed).[13] At stake is thus the possibility of constructing, through the clinic of the symptom, the real that writes itself upon the body in failing to be inscribed in the order of language. The hysteric reveals that the analytic experience—and specifically the constraint of the transference—can function as a limit to the drive where the law was unable to.

THE INVENTION OF THE TRANSFERENCE

We can understand Lacan's theorization of the symbolic as a return to Freud—and in particular to the fundamentals of the Freudian clinic—in an effort to peel away the highly codified practices characteristic of the psychoanalysis of his day and so to rediscover the conditions that allow the analysand to encounter the unconscious, to elaborate a knowledge about her fundamental desire, and to construct an ethics capable of sustaining it. Lacan's understanding of the mechanism of the transference is central to this endeavor, and establishes a clinical basis for the concept of the symbolic that is all too often overlooked in its broader theoretical dissemination.

My claim is that the unconscious elaborated under transference is an exemplary articulation of the symbolic. The transference and the symbolic are not interchangeable terms, of course; but it is only with an understanding of symbolic (as opposed to imaginary or "affective") transference that psychoanalysis as a constrained experience (as opposed to a scene of diagnosis, therapy, or rehabilitation) becomes possible, and it is only with the elaboration of the transference that it becomes possible to separate the logical or structural dimension of the symbolic from the norms and practices that define its most traditional iterations. Lacan's theorization of the transference breaks with a widespread understanding of psychoanalysis as directed toward social adaptation by returning to Freud's emphasis on unconscious desire. It shows that the transference in its symbolic dimension not only is not reducible to norms and rules, but actively counters them.

Lacan's understanding of the transference as a symbolic constraint not only departs from the dominant clinical views of his day, but responds to an equivocation in Freud's own conception of the transference that is never fully settled. In Freud's lexicon, transference refers primarily to the patient's relationship to the analyst as it develops over the course of the treatment. Yet as Dylan Evans notes, Freud's understanding of the transference undergoes significant elaboration and modification over the course of his work. Initially Freud viewed the transference as a form of resistance that interferes with the recall of repressed memories, and thus as an obstacle to the treatment that the analyst must "combat" if he is to effect a cure. Over time, however, he modified this view, and came to see the transference as a factor that is not only inevitable in analysis, but even beneficial to its progress. This is because the analysand, in the way he relates to the analyst, inevitably repeats or restages earlier relationships with other figures in his life (and his parents in particular). The transference therefore enables important elements of the patient's past to enter the treatment in a form other than the imperfectly remembered experiences narrated by the patient. As such, it is not merely opposed to the elaboration of the unconscious, but internal to its operation. This paradoxical dual nature of the transference continues to define all of Freud's subsequent writings on the topic.[14]

In one of his most extended early meditations on the transference (from the final chapter of *Dora: An Analysis of a Case of Hysteria*), Freud writes:

It may safely be said that during psychoanalytic treatment the formation of new symptoms is invariably stopped. But the productive powers of the neurosis are by no means extinguished; they are occupied in the creation of a special class of mental structures, for the most part unconscious, to which the name of "transferences" may be given.

What are transferences? They are new editions or facsimiles of the tendencies and phantasies which are aroused and made conscious during the progress of the analysis; but they have this peculiarity, which is characteristic for their species, that they replace some earlier person by the person of the physician. To put it another way: a whole series of psychological experiences are revived, not as belonging to the past, but as applying to the person of the physician at the present moment. Some of these transferences have a content which differs from that of their model in no respect whatever except for the substitution. These, then—to keep to the same metaphor—are merely new impressions or reprints. Others are more ingeniously constructed; their content has been subjected to a moderating influence—to sublimation, as I call it—and they may even become conscious, by cleverly taking advantage of some real peculiarity in the physician's person or circumstances and attaching themselves to that. These, then, will no longer be new impressions, but revised editions.

If the theory of analytic technique is gone into, it becomes evident that transference is an inevitable necessity. Practical experience, at all events, shows conclusively that there is no means of avoiding it, and that this latest creation of the disease must be combated like all the earlier ones.[15]

When Freud characterizes transference as the "latest creation of the disease," he implies that it is merely a further manifestation of the illness to be "combated" by the physician. But as manifestations of the "productive powers" of the neurosis, the transferences are also creative formations, even "sublimations," whose status as "a special class of *mental* structures" might justify classing them alongside such formations of the unconscious as dreams, slips of the tongue, parapraxes, and jokes. The same ambiguity characterizes the textual metaphor. As "facsimiles" or "reprints" of earlier tendencies or fantasies, the transferences appear to follow the script laid down by past lived experiences, which is then reread or restaged in relation to the person of the analyst. As "revised editions" or as "sublimations," however, they seem not merely to follow a script or reenact a pattern of behavior, but to represent the elaboration of a text that is constantly undergoing revision and expansion. What, then, is the status of the transferences as "unconscious structures"? Are they primarily the restaging of tendencies and fantasies that remain unconscious, in the sense of being unavailable to consciousness? Or are they themselves formations of the unconscious, instances of unconscious speech or interpretation?

As the passage continues, Freud maintains this ambiguity without clearly resolving it:

> It is easy to learn how to interpret dreams, to extract from the patient's associations his unconscious thoughts and memories, and to practise similar explanatory arts: for these the patient himself will always provide the text. *Transference is the one thing the presence of which has to be detected almost without assistance and with only the slightest clues to go upon*, while at the same time the risk of making arbitrary inferences has to be avoided. Nevertheless, *transference cannot be evaded, since use is made of it in setting up all the obstacles that make the material accessible to treatment, and since it is only after the transference has been resolved that a patient arrives at a sense of conviction of the validity of the connections which have been constructed during the analysis.*
>
> (*Dora* 107, my emphases)

Transference brings into play something that the patient's discourse is unable to elucidate, that is not of the order of memories, events, or conscious complaints. As a repetitive staging that is outside of speech and not represented in the patient's discourse, the transference is strongly identified with the fantasy, and therefore with the repetition of something that has failed to be inscribed or represented. It stages the tension between what can be inscribed in language and what repeats in silence, as behaviors or gestures, which explains why transference sometimes appears as an obstacle to free association, or as a silence in the middle of speech. The question is: how does the analyst respond to this phenomenon?

If the patient does not provide the "text" of the transference, whose presence must therefore be "detected" by the analyst without any assistance, it might seem that the role of the analyst is to infer or intuit what is being played out in the patient's behavior and to interpret it for her benefit. Yet Freud specifies that it is not the analyst who convinces the patient of the validity of the constructions elaborated over the course of the analysis, but the transference itself; it alone "sets up all the obstacles that make the material accessible to treatment," and confirms or refutes the accuracy of the constructions put forward by the analyst. The passage concludes with Freud affirming that "transference, which seems ordained to be the greatest obstacle to psychoanalysis, becomes its most powerful ally, if its presence can be detected each time and explained to the patient" (*Dora* 108).

What then does it mean to "detect" and "explain" the transference? Lacan's whole approach to the theory and clinic of psychoanalysis can be understood as an intervention on this question. At the time of his first presentations on the topic in the early 1950s, the dominant receptions of Freud emphasized the pathological dimension of transference, understood as a distorted perception of reality. In the "ego psychology" that held sway at the time (and to a large extent still does), the analyst's interpretation of the transference was supposed to allow the analysand to gain insight into—and thereby resolve—his distorted perceptions and irrational behavior. Dylan Evans explains,

> Quite early on in the history of psychoanalysis it became common to distinguish between those aspects of the patient's relationship to the analyst that were "adapted to reality" and those that were not. In the latter category fell all the patient's reactions which were caused by "perceiving the analyst in a distorted way." . . . [The assumption] was that the analyst could tell when the patient was reacting to him not on the basis of who he was but rather on the basis of previous relationships with other people.

The analyst was credited with this ability because he was supposed to be better "adapted to reality" than the patient. Informed by his own correct perception of reality, the analyst could offer "transference interpretations"; that is, he could point out the discrepancy between the real situation and the irrational way that the patient was reacting to it, [helping] the analysand to gain "insight" into his own neurotic transference and thereby resolve it.[16]

Lacan argues that the "adaptation" paradigm is entirely circumscribed within the "specific conditions of obsessive neurosis" (*Écrits* 509), in which the ego appeals to social norms and behavioral ideals to repress the scene of the unconscious. Because it defines the end of analysis as "the subject's identification with the analyst" (513), it turns psychoanalytic treatment into a form of "emotional reeducation" (517) that serves merely to uphold the normative criteria upon which the ego relies for its sense of integrity. When the analyst assumes that he is better adapted to reality than his patient, Lacan writes, he has no choice but to "fall back on his own ego" since this is the only "reality about which he knows a thing or two" (494). The analytic encounter is therefore reduced to a "dyadic relation" (508) between the patient and the analyst, an imaginary staging whose only effect is to repress the unconscious and deepen the subject's alienation.

Lacan takes aim at this conception of the treatment and the "reality" it promotes in advancing that "the transference is not the enactment [*mise en acte*] of the illusion that seems to drive us to this alienating identification that any conformity constitutes, even when it is with an ideal model"; instead, "the *transference is the enactment of the reality of the unconscious*."[17]

Several important consequences ensue. First, Lacan breaks with the dominant clinical approaches of his day in maintaining that transference is an *intersubjective structure*, and not an interpersonal relationship. "Like any other situation involving speech," he reasons, the analytic situation "can only be crushed if one tries to inscribe it in a dyadic relation" (508). Lacan therefore consistently locates the essence of transference in the symbolic and not the imaginary. While he acknowledges that transference often "reveals itself in an emotional guise" (for example, as feelings of love or aggressivity directed toward the person of the analyst), Lacan states that transference does not consist in any "mysterious property of affectivity" but instead "has a meaning only as a function of the dialectical moment at which it occurs" (184). He identifies the symbolic nature of transference with the solicitation of unconscious speech, in the form of the signifiers, acts, and symptoms through which the subject's unconscious transmits a knowledge about her encounter with an unassimilable real, that is, how she attempted to explain its causality or manage its effects.

Because the subject of the unconscious cannot be observed, and is witnessed only in speech, the reduction of the patient to an object of observation can only represent a silencing of the subject. In Lacan's words,

> Doesn't the fact that a dialectical conception of psychoanalysis has to be presented as an orientation peculiar to my way of thinking indicate misrecognition of an immediate given, and even of the commonsensical fact that psychoanalysis relies solely upon words? Must we not recognize, in the privileged attention paid to the function of the nonverbal aspects of behavior in the psychological maneuver, a preference on the part of the analyst for a vantage point from which the subject is no longer anything but an object? . . . Whereas Freud assumed responsibility for showing us that there are illnesses that speak (unlike Hesiod, for whom the illnesses sent by Zeus come over men in silence) and for making us hear the truth of what they say, it seems that this truth inspires more fear in the practitioners who perpetuate this technique.

(177)

In speech (which Lacan identifies with the formations of the unconscious rather than with the heavily sutured character of everyday discourse) the subject is not describing a verifiable or shared reality, but speaking about a psychic reality: the reality of the unconscious. As a result, speech is necessarily fragmentary, approximate, and evocative rather than descriptive, figural rather than literal (as in the metaphoric and metonymic processes that Freud identifies in the dreamwork). Speech concerns the evocation of a mental object, a mental representation that has no empirical equivalent or counterpart in the world, and that is therefore not perceptible or comprehensible to anyone else.

Ego psychology perceives the subject through the lens of a pseudoscientific behavioralism; it assumes that the human being is the inhabitant of an environment, and is successful or unsuccessful to the extent that it understands and reacts appropriately to the constraints of that environment. The subject of the unconscious must be distinguished from the biological organism or living being, however, since it results from the subjection of the living being to the structures of language that compromise its organic functioning by introducing the structure of the address into the human universe, thereby causing it to turn around an absent center. In Lacan's words, "one should see in the unconscious the effects of speech on the subject—in so far as these effects are so radically primary that they are properly what determine the status of the subject as subject" (*Seminar XI* 126). If "the unconscious is structured as a language" (149), it is because it responds to and attempts to construct the effects of speech on the living being. Speech is therefore not merely the medium in which the analytic situation unfolds (the alternately transparent, dissembling, or distorting medium in which the subject's history and complaints are communicated), but the *true object* of analysis inasmuch as it attests to a different reality altogether: the intersubjective relation of the subject to the locus of the Other.

Unlike the object of biological science—the living being whose survival depends upon its ability to perceive and respond to the cues of its environment—the subject of the unconscious is a subject addressed to the Other, an Other that cannot be located in an environment because it is merely the empty locus supposed by every act of speech. In his development of Lacan's metapsychology, Willy Apollon proposes that the advent of language, in introducing this empty center into the human universe, disrupts the logic of communication that defines the language of animals (the hormonal signals and visual cues of the mating ritual, for example), understood as the integral transmission of a piece of information from an emitter to a receiver.[18] Unlike the dyadic model of communication or identification, speech always supposes a third locus, the Other. It follows that the human being who speaks is not transmitting information to another member of the species, but rather addressing the locus of the Other in and beyond any given interlocutor. Hence the paradox that the hallmark of true (that is, unconscious) speech is the *failure* of communication, in the form of the slips of the tongue, parapraxes, and symptomatic acts that interrupt what the speaker "meant" to say and attest to the insistence of another scene. "Intersubjective" therefore means "between the subject and the Other," and not between one person and another.

Transference supposes not only a repetition of past behaviors in relation to the person of the analyst, therefore, but the way in which every interpersonal relationship—and every instance of speech—is at once a restaging and a repression of a more fundamental intersubjective relation, between the subject and the Other. It follows that for Lacan the concept of transference is not narrowly applicable to the patient-analyst relationship, but refers more broadly to the dialectical nature of the treatment that this intersubjective structure brings into play, and therefore to every aspect of the analysis. Analysis re-creates this intersubjective structure, in which the Other of the patient's address is not "someone" (a *semblable*, or "little other"), but the absent Other at stake in the empty locus of speech. (I will return to this point in more detail.) It therefore has the effect of provoking symptoms, hallucinations, and *passages à l'acte*, and not diminishing their appearance through recourse to stabilizing identifications.

Lacan's conception of the transference and the analytic act is thus closely tied to his elaboration of the stakes of language within the Freudian metapsychology. Because the human subject is always getting its bearings in relation to this absent Other, and not in relation to its environment, the perception-consciousness apparatus that orients the animal to external cues tends to give way to a hallucinatory perception of reality. What Lacan calls the imaginary is really the response of the subject to this hole in the perceived environment, which compels him to hear or to see something in the place of this absence. If for human beings there are "illnesses that speak," it is because illness—"mental" illness in particular—bears witness to the hallucinatory reality that surges forth to account for this absent Other, causing the subject to lose its environmental and social reference points. Hence the importance of the psychoses for Lacan. Persecuted by voices that no one else hears, that undermine his ability to communicate with other people or even to accomplish the most basic tasks of everyday life, the psychotic is acutely and viscerally aware that human beings are controlled by an Other who takes possession of their bodies and minds, speaks through them, and dictates their behavior. When Dr. Schreber complains of the malicious and uncomprehending God who forcibly rapes him, alters his physiognomy, and forces him to blurt out nonsensical or humiliating phrases against his will, he gives vivid expression to a fundamental human experience that is in no way unique to psychosis.[19]

In *Beyond the Pleasure Principle*, Freud stresses that there is no real perception of reality in the human being, since the perception-consciousness apparatus understands even "internal" or psychical threats as threats coming from the environment.[20] This is what accounts for the phenomenon of projection, in which the mental apparatus posits an external source for what it experiences or perceives. While the psychotic delusion may offer an especially vivid illustration of this phenomenon, it is an avoidable fact of human life, one that Lacan will ascribe to the effects of language upon the human subject. To the extent that the analysand evinces a "failure of adaptation," this failure characterizes all human beings and not just the pathologized patient. The imaginary is the strategy of the subject who does not and cannot adapt to reality, because it is responding to something that is not perceptible or verifiable within its natural *or* social environment. It would be a mistake to conflate these imaginary constructions with the behavioralist notion of attitudes and emotions "unadapted to reality" though, since "reality" is necessarily an imaginary construct for the human being whose conflation of its inner world or psychic reality (*Innenwelt*) with its environment (*Umwelt*) is a structural feature of the speaking being (*Écrits* 97).

The theory of the drives is Freud's attempt to account for this phenomenon. Unlike the instincts, which allow the living being to survive in its environment, the drives (which Freud defines as lacking any proper aim or object) respond to this absent Other. Freud even characterizes the drives as a kind of "mythology," advancing that the drives are "mythical entities, magnificent in their indefiniteness."[21] Apollon adds that this is because "they respond to an Other of whom we have no idea."[22] From the beginning of recorded history, human beings have testified to an obscure Other that haunts human life, but whose presence cannot be verified; it is known only by the effects it leaves on us. Myths tell of an Other at the origin of the human world, an Other who gave us life, who controls our actions, who shapes our destinies, who persecutes us or who loves us, who causes our lives to be a living hell or who promises a paradise of eternal life. But while myths provide a shared or collective representation of the Other, the drive is the response of the individual psyche; it constructs a mental representation to account for an Other that no one else sees, hears, or experiences in quite the same way. The fantasy that structures the drive surges forth to "stage" what cannot be tested or verified, articulating the subject's relation to one of the four "objects a"—voice, gaze, breast, and feces—that give partial expression to this primordial Other. When Lacan adds the voice and the gaze to the breast and feces that Freud already emphasized as fundamental objects of fantasy, he underscores the relationship between the object-cause of desire at stake in the fantasy and the locus of the Other, the Other whose absent presence is attested to by aural and visual hallucinations, but also by the locus of speech as such inasmuch as it gives rise to a purely mental object that cannot be located in the world.

The subject and the ego are both addressed to this Other, but in different ways. The ego discourse gives a face to this absent Other by confusing the locus of the Other with some specific other (a parent, a malevolent God, a person in the patient's life who played a decisive role in her current suffering, and the like) who is made to answer for the effects of the drive or who is called upon to repair their debilitating effects (a demand that invariably applies to the person of the analyst as well). The ego's relation to the others of the social scene is therefore overdetermined by the imaginary and by the strategy of seduction, which posits an imaginary Other (or what might be described as a hallucinatory Other) in the place of that absent Other. The aim of the analytic maneuver is to occasion the "fall" of the imaginary

Other by dismantling the seduction fantasy that allows the subject to refuse responsibility for the drives, and so to confront him with the castration implied in the passage through the symbolic locus of the Other that alone will allow him to construct his unconscious desire.

If the subject of the unconscious is fundamentally addressed to the Other, then it must be constrained to manifest itself in speech. This is what Lacan means by the "dialectical nature" of the transference. The analyst constrains the analysand to evoke in speech what is at stake in the drive, as well as in the symptom that encodes the subject's relation to the excess jouissance that language unleashes even as it renders impossible the natural satisfaction of the instincts.

In foregrounding the symbolic dimension of transference, Lacan radicalizes Freud's emphasis on the transferences as "obstacles that make the material accessible to treatment." We saw already that Freud described the transference as at once an "obstacle" and the analyst's "most powerful ally." The obstacle is that words are all we have and yet we are dealing with something that is unspoken or that exceeds the patient's discourse. As Freud puts it, the patient does not provide the "text"; something insists that is not spoken. For ego psychology, this means that the analyst must complete what is missing by interpreting the patient's behavior. But Lacan reads Freud differently: this "obstacle" is not an impediment to the treatment, but the *constraint* that is its condition of possibility (and thus the analyst's *only* real ally). This is because the exhaustion or "frustration" of the patient's discourse obliges the unconscious and the drive to answer where the analysand is unable to. The transference is an "ally" inasmuch as it locates the limits of the sayable, and thus forces a repetition or restaging of the subject's confrontation with a real. Where the patient cannot speak, the illness speaks in his place, and thereby identifies the site from which the subject (as opposed to the ego) speaks. The constraint consists in getting it to speak or in creating the conditions in which its speech can be heard, and not in attempting to overcome this obstacle by filling in the blanks or devising extraverbal means of interpretation. Interpretation is the affair of the unconscious alone; the transference merely calls it forth.

THE "SUBJECT SUPPOSED TO KNOW," OR THE CONSTRAINT OF THE ADDRESS

The concept of the "subject supposed to know," which Lacan elaborates most fully in his seminar *The Four Fundamental Concepts of Psychoanalysis* from 1964, develops this core insight by framing the transference as the attribution of a knowledge to the Other, in the form of the supposition that the Other is a subject who knows: "As soon as the subject who is supposed to know exists somewhere . . . there is transference."[23] Transference therefore does not merely substitute the analyst for someone in the patient's history, but constitutes an "address to the Other" inasmuch as this address subtends all interpersonal relations. It shows that the interpersonal must be understood in relation to this intersubjective dimension that it both derives from and attempts to repress.

The patient appeals to the analyst as an expert who will know how to cure his symptoms or lead him out of his impasse and thereby take control of the jouissance that is disorganizing his life. But the analyst can respond to that demand only at the cost of sustaining the seduction fantasy, by positioning himself in the place of the imaginary Other of the subject's fantasy, who is either held responsible for castration or called upon to solve it, and who therefore functions to repress the Other's absence or inconsistency.[24] In "The Mirror Stage," Lacan shows how the child attempts to build an ideal ego by identifying with the image it takes to be the object of the mother's love, seeking in her gaze a unified body image that might allow it to repress the fragmented body of the drives (*Écrits* 75–81). His analysis implies that such a mechanism potentially subtends every interpersonal relationship, from the familial to the social to the religious or political.

If the analysand must be *constrained* to encounter the reality of the unconscious that the transference enacts, it is because the intersubjective dimension of this "address to the Other" can only be overdetermined by the imaginary when it occurs on the social stage. Although the patient appeals to the analyst as a "subject supposed to know," the analysis can advance only on the condition that the analyst refuses to occupy this position, and instead maintains the lack in the Other: the fact that there is no other who knows, that the Other is not "someone." At the level of the analytic maneuver, this lack manifests itself in the analyst's way of listening to the patient. She offers no guidance, advice, or assistance, and generally responds to the patient's questions or appeals with silence. Lacan specifies that the analyst's role is one of "positive nonaction,"[25] which he relates to the function of the dummy hand in bridge: a structural locus whose inactivity obliges the player opposite to play the hand by himself, drawing on the dummy only as a repository of his own cards (the signifiers at play in his own subjective history).

The silence that responds to the subject's appeal is more generative than any answer or reply, because instead of implicating two interlocutors in an imaginary "conversation" or discourse it interrupts that conversation and allows something else to emerge: the speech of the unconscious (*Écrits* 206). Symbolic transference takes place not between the patient's ego and the person of the analyst, but between the analysand and the unconscious.[26] The signifiers of the dream, and later the symptom, contest the ego narrative and the social values, norms, and ideals that sustain the ego by facilitating its repression of the unconscious. If for Lacan "the presence of the analyst . . . must be included in the concept of the unconscious" (*Seminar XI* 127), it is because the analytic maneuver sustains and supports the discourse of the unconscious as the "discourse of the Other" (131). As Freud emphasizes in *The Interpretation of Dreams*, the analyst is not the dream's interpreter; rather, *the dream is itself an interpretation* of the subject's unconscious position, which the analyst merely upholds against the patient's attempts to repress it. Or, as Lacan puts it, "the analyst's interpretation merely reflects the fact that the unconscious, if it is what I say it is, namely, a play of the signifier, has already in its formulations—dreams, slips of tongue or pen, witticisms or symptoms—proceeded by interpretation. The Other, the capital Other, is already there in every opening, however fleeting it may be, of the unconscious" (130). If the subject's answer comes to it "from the Other,"[27] it is important that this means "from the unconscious" (inasmuch as it supposes a lacking or absent Other) and not "from the other person" (as expert, as diagnostician, and so forth).

If the analyst's action is really a nonaction, a matter of letting the unconscious speak, then what justifies speaking of the transference as Freud's "invention"?

Lacan asserts that "the transference is an essential phenomenon, bound up with desire as the nodal phenomenon of the human being" (*Seminar XI* 231). In not responding to or affirming the ego narrative, and especially in wanting to know about something that is not spoken there, the analyst does not merely expose the vacuity of the ego's discourse with his silence, but literally calls forth the unconscious with his desire to know. The transference is not merely a set of behaviors, affects, or associations that emerge spontaneously, but a logic of call and response, question and answer, in which the subject's unconscious responds to a question (stated or unstated) on the part of the analyst. This is why Lacan emphasizes repeatedly that Freud did not "discover" the unconscious, but literally *invented* it by calling upon the dream to respond to his desire to know with the production of a knowledge, in the form of the signifiers that interpret the subject's encounter with a real. The cornerstone of Lacan's "return to Freud" is thus the call for "an ethics . . . that would place at the foreground the question of the analyst's desire" (*Écrits* 514).[28] Because nothing qualifies the analyst to interpret the patient's symptoms or evaluate his grip on "reality," what he brings to the analytic experience is nothing more or less than a *desire to know*, which necessarily implies a lack of knowledge that only the unconscious can begin to fill. Desire is thus the active dimension of lack: it "enacts" the unconscious by calling it forth.

THE UNSPEAKABLE AND THE SYMPTOM

The unconscious formations that respond to the analyst's desire elaborate a knowledge about the analysand's unconscious fantasy. But they also show the knowledge of the unconscious to be a knowledge that is always wanting, because there is no signifier for the jouissance at stake in the fantasy. The lack in the Other is not only descriptive of the analyst's way of functioning, therefore, but is the object of his desire to know. In the clinic of the dream, for example, the dream furnishes signifiers that elaborate a new knowledge. But it also contains a "navel," something the analysand is unable to explain or associate upon. The role of the analyst is to uphold the navel of the dream, the lacking center around which the signifiers of the dreamwork turn. The analyst's act aims to expose the failure inherent in repetition, "what never ceases (not) to be inscribed" (*ce qui ne cesse pas de [ne pas] s'inscrire*).[29] At these moments the patient stops free-associating, is unable to say anything more, and retreats into silence or pointless conversation. This is not a failure of the symbolic transference or a transferential obstacle to the treatment, however, but the moment the transference has been driving toward, its true beginning.

When in the course of an analysis the subject's dreams and associations either fail to furnish further signifiers or cease altogether, the unconscious produces a symptom in response to the analyst's desire to know. Willy Apollon designates this moment as the true inauguration of the transference, in which the analyst "constrains the analysand to an ethics of speech with respect to the jouissance of the fantasy, which the symptom hides and protects."[30] Freud, in his early account of the transference, emphasizes that something insists that is not articulated by the analysand's discourse, that repeats in the form of behavior; yet as the metaphor of the "revised edition" suggests, it also takes the form of a "text." Importantly, however, this text is not put into words by the patient herself. Instead, the drive inscribes in the erogenous zones (or what Lacan calls the "letters of the body") what cannot be inscribed in the signifier. Under the transference sustained by the analyst's desire, what is written in and by the symptom must therefore be constrained to speak itself.

The aim of the analytic act is thus to *provoke* the formation of symptoms—even potentially deadly symptoms—and not to resolve them or to restore the patient to "health." The analyst is the ally of the symptom itself, and not of the patient who complaints of its effects and seeks to be relieved of it. The wager implied in the analytic act is that the patient can be relieved of the threat the symptom presents only if he "traverses" the fantasy it encodes (which means not merely understanding that fantasy, but assuming it as the basis of his ethics as a subject).

Freud's "Wolf Man" case offers one of the best examples of this transferential procedure. When the case reaches an impasse where the patient's dreams and memories are no longer moving the analysis forward, Freud turns his attention to the symptom of constipation, which has recently become so severe that the patient is unable to produce a bowel movement at all without the application of an enema.[31] In an effort to overcome his resistance, Freud promises to cure his constipation within a prescribed period of time. The aim of the analytic maneuver is to show that the symptom is a form of speech that responds to the analyst's desire to know about the subject's unconscious desire, and that it answers to a logic that can be constructed on the basis of the work undertaken so far. When Freud manages to treat the symptom psychoanalytically, much to his patient's astonishment, he writes with satisfaction that the Wolf Man's bowels "began, like a hysterically affected organ, to 'join in the conversation,'" furnishing a response to the analyst's questions where the patient's own associations were unable to.[32] At this point a new phase of the transference begins, in which the response of the bowels—as the erogenous zone implicated in the fantasy of the primal scene—functions to confirm or refute the accuracy of the fantasy's construction. The body "converses" or "responds" through the evacuation of the bowels, which elucidates the series of equivalences (feces = father's penis = baby) that relate the different components of the fantasy staging. More importantly, it allows the position of the Wolf Man himself within the fantasy to be located with precision.

In appealing to the symptom itself to elucidate the subject's position in the fantasy, Freud isolates the clinic of the symptom as a distinct phase of the analysis that cannot be assimilated to the construction of the signifying chain. The act of inviting the bowels to "join in on the conversation" supposes the exhaustion of the signifying chain, the lack internal to the chain inasmuch as it abuts—but cannot inscribe—the real. Lacan speaks of an "inherence of a (-1) in the set of signifiers,"[33] which is due to the fact that there is no signifier for the jouissance that marks the place of the subject.[34] This (-1) means that the signifying chain is necessarily incomplete. At stake is thus "a lack inherent in the Other's very function as the treasure trove of signifiers," precisely "insofar as the Other is called upon (*chè vuoi*) to answer for the value of this treasure . . . in terms of the drive" (*Écrits* 693).

This example makes clear that the elaboration of the subject's symbolic determinants through the transference does not serve merely to "symbolize," or to represent in language, a real that was only provisionally resistant to being spoken (because forgotten, because too traumatic to name, and so forth). Instead, the elaboration of the signifying chain has no other purpose than to drive toward what Lacan calls the "-1 inherent in the field of signifiers," the structural decompletion of the signifying order that the real of jouissance exposes. It leads to an impasse where only the drive can respond, in the form of a symptom or act. In its symbolic dimension, therefore, the transference does not merely impose a signification upon what was previously outside of sense, but allows the real to be approached and worked on in its resistance to signification. In other words, it provides the constrained conditions that allow the analysand to confront a real that insists and repeats in the form of something unsayable, which until now has been inscribed or "written" only in the "letter of the body," the erogenous zone where the jouissance of the fantasy is inscribed in the organism.

Implied in the transference are thus two fundamental constraints. The first is the address to the analyst as a "subject supposed to know" inasmuch as it is fundamentally an address to the locus of the Other; the second is the ethical constraint that the subject attempt to find words for what insists wordlessly (and so elaborate the knowledge that was initially attributed to the other, a knowledge that can only be lacking). The analytic act that "makes present the Other's absence" is the essence of both. The postulation of the analyst as a "subject supposed to know" turns the repetition or restaging of the seduction fantasy (or, in the case of psychosis, the delusion) into a constraint that obliges the patient to encounter the unconscious, rather than repressing it. In upholding the ab-sense of the Other, the analyst evacuates the site posited as a "subject supposed to know," and in the process redirects the interpersonal dynamic implied in seduction onto the intersubjective structure of the address, the dialectical nature of the transference. The transference is thus a symbolic mechanism that allows the subject to experience and work upon the lack in the Other so as to elaborate a knowledge, and more importantly to formulate an ethics capable of sustaining desire.

THE INSTITUTION OF THE MOSAIC LAW

The insights we glean from clinical practice about the "unfoundedness" of the symbolic are key to understanding how the symbolic works and why, ultimately, it is important. Freud's *Moses and Monotheism* brings full circle the investigation of the symbolic as constraint that begins with *Studies in Hysteria* and *The Interpretation of Dreams*, emphasizing the continuum between the clinical function of the signifying chain and the written commandments of the Mosaic Decalogue. Each elucidates in a different way the stakes of the symbolic as the "laws of speech."

In the critical reception of Freud's work, the major cultural writings that attempt to elaborate the social consequences of the Oedipus complex often tend to marginalize or even displace the importance of his early clinical papers and case studies, in which a latent account of the symbolic is being developed that counters in important respects the argument of these other works. Yet I maintain that *Moses* ultimately has more in common with the early work than with the later. *Totem and Taboo* and *Group Psychology* delineate the Oedipal and totemic logic in which the father, conceived as an agent of prohibition, both forbids access to the object that would fulfill desire and at the same time functions as an ideal ego for each of the sons by holding out possibility that there is "one who enjoys" and that jouissance is therefore possible. The clinical works lay the foundation for a different reading of *Moses*, allowing us to understand the stakes of the Mosaic law and to see it as something other than a set of prohibitions, ideals, or norms. To consider law alongside the transference is to stress that law has multiple dimensions that cannot be reduced to the representation of authority, and to elaborate a properly symbolic understanding of law as an intersubjective field distinct from the narcissistic logic of identification that binds the group or collective.

If the Freudian clinic introduces the experimental dimension of the symbolic, *Moses* represents Freud's fullest elaboration of its role in enabling subjective freedom and desire. At face value, of course, there is nothing particularly "experimental" about the Mosaic law; indeed, it may be the ultimate example of the normative symbolic. For Freud, however, it actually represents the emergence of this experimental dimension as a break with a normative order of rules and prohibitions that is not at all symbolic, namely, the logic of totemism and the group psychology that results from it.

In a reading I will expand upon in subsequent chapters, I propose that *Moses* locates the origin of the symbolic in the foundation of a fundamentally new kind of law that attempts to interrupt the function of the imaginary. It revises in important ways the earlier argument of *Totem and Taboo*, which advanced that all forms of social and religious life could be understood as responses to the primeval murder of the father and the totemic belief structures that result from it. The totemic logic Freud elaborates there can be defined most simply as the postulation of a source or ground of authority, in the form of an exceptional figure who incarnates the law: the father of the primal horde, the animal substitutes that are worshiped and feared in his place, and finally the omnipotent father-God of monotheism. It gives rise to an imaginary understanding of law that dominates all subsequent iterations of the social order. After the sons' murder of the father, the laws of the fraternal pact impose equality and mutual privation in an attempt to exclude the exceptional authority and unlimited enjoyment that defined his position with respect to his sons. Yet Freud finds that far from being excluded, this exceptional figure actually persists as a powerful psychic imago in and through the very laws that purport to displace his exceptional authority. The first "laws" of the fraternal pact are really just the internalization and codification of what the sons take to be the father's will: notably the ban on any other male taking possession of the women of the horde, in which Freud sees the origin of the incest prohibition. Structurally, therefore, they function at once to postulate the existence of an exceptional authority "outside" the law and to sustain the fantasy that one might oneself accede to this exceptional site of enjoyment through identification with the father. This ambivalent attitude is given ritual expression in the "totemic feast" that persists as a displaced commemoration of the repressed patricide, as well as in such religious rituals as the Catholic Eucharist. Freud understands it as a reenactment of the collective cannibalism that followed the father's murder, in which the father was at once decisively destroyed and preserved as an ideal ego through the act of incorporation:

> The brothers who had been driven out and lived together in a community clubbed together, overcame the father, and—according to the custom of those times—all partook of his body. This cannibalism need not shock us, it survived into far later times. The essential point is, however, that we attribute to those primeval people the same feelings and emotions that we have elucidated in the primitives of our own times, our children, by psychoanalytic research. That is to say, they not merely hated and feared their father, but also honoured him as an example to follow; in fact, each son wanted to place himself in his father's position. The cannibalistic act thus becomes comprehensible as an attempt to assure one's identification with the father by incorporating a part of him.[35]

Almost thirty years later, Freud returns to the totemic thesis in *Moses and Monotheism*, but this time attempts to isolate the specificity of the Mosaic moment within this larger development. Previously the monotheist religions were considered only through the lens of Christianity, and specifically such Catholic traditions and rituals as the Eucharistic feast. But Freud now considers Mosaic monotheism, and in particular the Ten Commandments of the Hebrew Decalogue, not merely as a continuation of the totemic trajectory but as the first true break with its logic. In essence, his thesis is that the Mosaic religion introduces a fundamental absence or lack where the totemic structure places the all-powerful father that functions as the ideal ego for each member of the fraternal pact. The ascendance of the Mosaic law does not represent the replacement of one normative order by another, therefore, but the institution of an *experimental symbolic* that requires each subject to pass through the lacking locus of the Other rather than relying upon identification with—and submission to—an imaginary authority. Among its innovations with respect to earlier forms of law and religious observance, Freud stresses the repudiation of sacrifice and the ban on incarnate manifestations of the deity. Both have the effect of evacuating the place of the all-powerful father and the superegoic character of his "law," which is really nothing more than the rule of his exclusive right to enjoyment. The first marks a shift away from ritual practices intended to satisfy the deity's demands, while the second can be read as a break with the totemic foundations of sovereignty, or the belief in a law spiritually incarnated in a living body.

Moses is a leader who evacuates the place of the leader, who undercuts the logic of identification binding the group and refounds the collective undertaking on a nonimaginary basis. In Lacan's terms, one could say that the key innovation of the Mosaic tradition is the invention of the symbolic as distinct from either the real (the exceptional jouissance of the primal father and the superegoic imperatives that sustain it) or the imaginary (the father imago that persists as an ideal ego even after his murder, as well as the norms and prohibitions that take the father's place in the logic of the fraternal pact). This is the upshot of Freud's careful attempt to distinguish between the two gods of Israel that subsequent traditions have collapsed into a contradictory composite: the bloodthirsty Yahweh of the original Hebrew tribes (a rapacious god of sacrificial demand) and the sublimely distant Aton/Adonai of the Egyptian Moses whose absence confronts the Israelites with the ethics of desire.[36] In emphasizing the singularity of the second, *Moses* is really an attempt to extract this symbolic dimension from what would otherwise be a dialectic of real and imaginary: real father and father imago, real murder and ritualized Eucharistic feast, and so forth.

The second and third commandments of the Hebrew Decalogue, which forbid representations of the deity or the speaking of his name, underscore the decompletion of the symbolic, the emptying out of the logical place of the Other that manifests itself as a rupture or breach in the field of representation and as a hole in language. In early Jewish ritual practice this negative space is given form in the Holy of Holies, the innermost sanctum of the Israelite tabernacle. It is associated with the deity not as the site of his manifestation or presence, but as a space that must not be entered on pain of death, a "holy hole." In identifying God with a space that cannot be breached or transgressed, the Mosaic law does not simply establish the parameters of religious observance. It articulates something fundamental about the symbolic function of the law, which in institutionalizing this distance also *opens up a space* in which the subject of desire can come into being. This is why Lacan says of the Ten Commandments that "whether or not we obey them, we still cannot help hearing them—in their indestructible character they prove to be the *very laws of speech*."[37] The condition of speech is the signifier's limitation or negation of the real, which opens up a space in which subjectivity becomes possible. This logic is nowhere better expressed than in the fourth commandment, to honor the Sabbath day. According to Lacan, "that suspension, that emptiness, clearly introduces into human life the sign of a gap, a beyond relative to every law of utility" (81). It memorializes or sanctifies God's creation of the world, which paradoxically concludes with the insertion of a gap.

In a gloss of Lacan's reading, Julia Lupton and Ken Reinhard observe that "God completes the world by subtracting something from it, namely his own activity."[38] He withdraws to create a place where "something is missing," namely, his own full presence. In this way, the commandment links the emergence of the human subject to the negation of the fullness of the real, the unmediated presence of *das Ding*: "the subject of religion," they write, "only emerges in the decompletion of the symbolic universe, through the positive addition to the cosmos of an instance of negation, of suspended activity. In this moment of ar-rest, the subject comes forward as the bearer of the lack that has engendered him" (83). In privileging the structural function of speech, the Mosaic tradition allows us to distinguish between two fundamentally different registers of law: *imaginary authority* and *symbolic constraint*. As the "laws of speech," the commandments mark a break not only with every prior understanding of law, but also with the "law of the spirit" that comes to displace the Mosaic law in Paul's gospel of salvation. They function not as placeholders for a force or authority figured as "beyond" the law, but as the articulation of a symbolic structure whose spacing or negation of the real undercuts the fantasy of a possible incarnation of the law implied in Pauline Christianity.

In the second part of this book, I will argue that this symbolic dimension of law is fundamentally linked to the formal and structural innovation implied in the advent of written law. Admittedly, this problematic is not taken up in any detail by Freud. But while his argument places no particular stress on the question of writing, he does pause to consider the hypothesis of one scholar that the "early Israelites, the scribes of Moses, had a hand in the invention of the first alphabet" (51). While Freud initially presents their mastery of a written alphabet as further evidence that Moses and his immediate cohort were Egyptians, he also muses that "if they were bound by the prohibition against making images they even had a motive for forsaking the hieroglyphic picture writing when they adapted their written signs for the expression of a new language" (51n). For Freud the ban on images is therefore not merely the object of a written law; it is linked to a fundamental shift in the Israelite's attitude toward writing, away from the imaginary function of representation and toward the symbolic function of spacing or negation.

The broader stakes of writing for the Mosaic law are implicit, however, in Freud's discussion of the ethical code of Moses and above all the subsequent rejection and overturning of this innovation in Pauline Christianity. With respect to the Mosaic law, Freud suggests that Pauline Christianity represents a return to the totemic logic in all its ambivalence: in Paul's gospel the father takes second place to the son, who stands in his stead just as the sons of the primal horde had longed to do. While the *apparent* result of this destruction is the liberation of the sons from the old totemic logic that held them captive, Freud argues that the reverse is actually true: it is the old logic that triumphs once and for all. Even as Pauline Christianity dispenses with the law that took the father's place in the Jewish religion, it cannot dispense with the supposition of an all-powerful and all-knowing Other. The proof is that the Christian innovation culminates in the "return of the one and only father deity whose power is unlimited" (105).

Ultimately the sons' victory is not a victory *over* the logic of totemism, but a victory *of* that logic in its fundamental ambivalence. Freud concludes that the deity's unlimited power is his most crucial feature, and argues that the success of Christianity is due to the enduring memory of the all-powerful primal father: it is "the religion of the primeval father, and the hope of reward, distinction and finally world sovereignty is bound up with it." In other words, it is here that the omnipotent God of unlimited power emerges for the first time.

Freud's conclusion is that "Paul, by developing the Jewish religion further, became its destroyer." What is destroyed, however, is not only the compulsive character of the law that is the explicit object of Paul's polemic (the imaginary function of the law that designates and so "brings to life" objects of covetousness), but the *symbolic function* of the Mosaic law that empties out the locus of the Other. If the function of the Mosaic law was to negate or exclude the exception, the effect of Paul's innovation will be to negate that negation, to *exclude the exclusion*, such that the fantasy of the exception reasserts itself once again in a particularly powerful form: the gospel of salvation and the imaginary relation to the Other that it sustains. This resurrected exceptionalism expresses itself as the reign of "spirit," whose authority is directly opposed to the function of writing. In Paul's words, "we no longer serve under the old written law, but under the new law of the spirit" (Romans 7:5–6). At stake is thus an exclusion of the symbolic itself, and more importantly of the structural lack in the Other that it metaphorizes.

2

DEMANDING THE IMPOSSIBLE

Desire and Social Change

T HE TRADITIONAL PESSIMISM of psychoanalysis with respect to social change is well known. Even from its greatest innovators, we are used to a kind of jaded critique of social reform or political engagement as enthusiasm, wish fulfillment, or worse: Freud's dismissal of Marxism as a delusional worldview,[1] or Lacan's telling the student militants of May '68 that "what you aspire to as revolutionaries is a master: you will get one."[2] Both judgments point to the imaginary character of most social and political projects, or their tendency to aid and abet the idealization and wish-fulfillment that are the hallmarks of the ego's repression of the subject of the unconscious: a subject that appears only as a rupture in the world, and that has no social dimension. While such a critique is undeniably justified from many points of view, an unfortunate side effect is a refusal among psychoanalysts and psychoanalytically informed critics to consider the social and political spheres as sites where the subject (and not merely the ego) intervenes, sites that may be transformed by subjective desire.

At the same time, psychoanalysis does not always live up to its own standards where respect of the subject is concerned. Lacan complains of the displacement or erasure of Freud's invention of psychoanalysis—a psychoanalysis centered on the experience of the subject and the transformative potential of desire—by a supportive psychotherapy centered on the ego and its accommodation to the world. He accuses the practitioners of ego psychology not only of limiting themselves to the concerns of the obsessional neurotic, but of themselves behaving neurotically in repressing the subject of the unconscious and the radical challenge it presents to the ego.[3] One form this repression takes is the imposition of structures like the Oedipus complex as generic theoretical paradigms, or the tendency to "diagnose" the subject rather than listen to his speech. The result is that the analytic maneuver tends to become mired in the same impasses as the group psychology: an investment in the ego to the exclusion of the subject, and an appeal to interpersonal relationships to facilitate repression. For Lacan, analysis has to be about something other than accommodation to the world, successful adaptation, or integration. His "return to Freud" is a return not merely to the conceptual or methodological foundations of psychoanalysis, but to its cause: the desire of Freud, the desire that founded the practice of psychoanalysis and without which it could not have been born.

The question I would like to consider here is: what is the relationship between desire and social change?

My approach is inspired in part by the recent work of Peter Hallward, whose subject is the role of will or determination in changing the world. Hallward calls for a "dialectical voluntarism" that would affirm the "practical primacy of will," condensed in the adage "where there's a will there's a way."[4] He frames his project with a reference to the charge famously leveled at philosophy by Karl Marx: "philosophers have hitherto only *interpreted* the world in various ways; the point is to *change* it." But while broadly Marxist in inspiration, his work departs from most materialist approaches to social change in foregrounding the experience of the willing subject, rather than broad social and historical dynamics. In this context, he discusses a number of historical figures whose examples have galvanized popular movements, and the slogans that condense their exemplarity: "What would Jesus do?" in the context of the liberation theologies so influential in Latin America, but also "What would Mao do?" "What would Robespierre do?" and so forth.[5] In these examples, I am intrigued by the relationship between the individual act and the people who bear witness to it, or the notion that the ethical stance or subjective position of an individual might incite a change of position in other people.

Of course, these examples instantly raise all kinds of questions and objections relative to what Freud called the group psychology, in which the leader, through identification, is called upon to function as an ideal ego for each member of the group. Freud emphasizes that identification can never be a foundation for real willing, because it works to repress castration by making some Other responsible for guaranteeing the ego. The same is true of ideals and values, no matter how lofty.

Yet I wouldn't want to dismiss the interest of these examples on that basis, or deny their significance as forces for change. In underscoring the function of the leader, founder, or model, Hallward is interested not in the role of the ideal in soliciting identification, but in the force of will and the voluntarist dimension of change. His examples are all the more provocative in that they include not only the great leaders who have given their names to religious and political movements, but individuals working in relative obscurity whose apparently very modest acts have unexpectedly brought about important social transformations: a man whose decision to clear room for a soccer field in a poor slum in Port-au-Prince led to a mass mobilization of young people who reclaimed their neighborhood from the multinational corporations that had set up business there, or a doctor working in the poor highlands of Haiti (the Harvard immunologist Paul Farmer) who decided to give his patients the most expensive and complex treatment for drug-resistant tuberculosis, despite its unfeasibility, on the grounds that a human life is worth as much in Haiti as it is in the developed world (and whose decision has had the unforeseen consequence of making such treatment much more widely available, by spurring production and bringing down its cost). The larger question these examples raise is whether the subjective stance of one person can initiate broad change or inspire collective action by means other than the group psychology: in other words, not by appealing to a particular set of values or ideals, or by cementing the group through identification or libidinal cathexes, or by offering some kind of external or even transcendental foundation for the ego, but by foregrounding the experience of the willing subject.

This chapter takes inspiration from this project. But I propose to take a more psychoanalytic approach to the problem by considering the individual act not principally as an instance of will or determination, but for the way it lays bare the stakes of desire. What distinguishes desire from determination or will? Fundamentally, desire raises the question of where this determination or resolve originates, of what within us is determined or willing. One can be determined to live a good or a moral or a selfless life, and yet this determination often fails inasmuch as it is fundamentally in conflict with an unconscious position that it attempts to repress or control. Desire, on the other hand, supposes the subject of the unconscious: it is not sustained by identification with something "outside" the subject that allows it to repress the drives or facilitate its refusal to know anything about the unconscious. When Lacan offers as a formulation of the ethics of psychoanalysis the imperative not to give up on one's desire—*ne pas céder sur son désir*[6]—he suggests that desire is what admits of no compromise or concession, and that it therefore always bears some relation to death.

Desire is thus immediately in tension with any notion of a collectivity or group; there may be collective ideals, but there is nothing like a collective desire. Nonetheless, desire differs from a private passion or enthusiasm in being negotiated in public. Hence the fundamental link between desire and sublimation: desire gives rise to a new object, an object that didn't exist before, that intervenes in the world so as to transform it. But this also means that desire is structurally without object, and thus invariably concerned with an impossible object: it is not a striving toward some object that is in the world, even a principle or ideal. When Hallward links the question of will or determination to the imperative to change the world—to change the *whole world* and to change it *absolutely*, and not simply to modify or improve the world[7]—he makes clear that this determination can never be reduced merely to the resolute pursuit of a specific goal, but must instead be understood as the quest for an impossible. Whenever the impossible as such is at stake (and not simply as an impossibility that would be veiled or repressed by a sense of hope or possibility), it's a question of desire. (I am reminded of the slogan of May '68: "Be objective: demand the impossible.") Desire is uncompromising because it takes no account of what is practical, capable of gaining acceptance, or likely to please; it is fidelity to an impossible cause of desire, not fidelity to a constituency.

Willy Apollon writes that "psychoanalysis is a scandalous discipline, insofar as it is founded on the desire of a subject, Freud."[8] In an interview given shortly before his death, Freud spoke of the "desire to know" that guided him for his entire life, a desire to know about what causes the human subject that led him away from the empirical sphere of science and toward an object that could not be verified empirically, but only witnessed in speech. The subject is itself an "impossible object" in this sense, a pure hypothesis that cannot be observed scientifically or explained as a product of culture. In what way is this desire affecting? It is not only inspiring, although that may be part of it. If it produces effects in other people, it is because an act founded on desire supposes the subject, and is therefore fundamentally at odds with any ideal or value.

The interest of the question "What would Jesus do?" (for example) is that it makes an implicit distinction between Jesus as a support for identification and Jesus as a subject of desire. The question supposes a kind of immovability in the desire of Jesus, something nonnegotiable: it implies that Jesus would not make concessions, that he would not waver. If the answer to the question is somehow obvious, it is not because it concerns some specific content or principle, but because desire is an orientation or a stance with respect to the impossible object that causes it, and not a *response* to a particular case or circumstance. The question is of a very different order than "What would Jesus say?" or "What would Jesus teach?" because it is not a matter of ideals, agendas, or programs. It is also different from "What would Jesus want?" or "What would Jesus tell you to do?" because it is not a matter of demands or of satisfying a leader or an idealized role model by doing what we think he wants.[9]

In his best-selling biography of Dr. Paul Farmer, *Mountains Beyond Mountains*, Tracy Kidder offers an extraordinary portrait not only of the man and his unwavering commitment to serve the poor, but of the effects that this desire produces in Kidder himself as he accompanies Farmer on his daily rounds over a period of several years.[10] He conveys with remarkable honesty and insight the irritation, resentment, and even hostility that Farmer sometimes provokes in those whose admiration and support for his work are beyond question: this includes Kidder himself, as well as the dedicated coworkers and volunteers who collaborate with Farmer on his many projects. The freshness of Kidder's approach consists not merely in exposing, in the usual biographic mode, the irritating imperfections of the great man (although Farmer, like everyone else, certainly has them), but in revealing how the unwavering or uncompromising quality of his desire itself is irritating: this irritation is not a distraction or detraction from the force of will that drives his accomplishments, but absolutely of a piece with them. Kidder finds himself becoming exasperated with Farmer at precisely those moments when he gives expression to an uncomfortable truth, takes on a monumental new project widely deemed to be "impossible," or refuses to turn a blind eye to what almost everyone else manages to accept as inevitable: the gross disparity between the rich and the poor. Desire presents a challenge because it concerns the status of the act, and not the affirmation of ideals or beliefs. Indeed, it makes us aware of how the ideals we espouse make it possible *not* to act. In this case, it provokes an uncomfortable self-examination: Why is it that most of us refuse to see the situation of the poor as the scandal that it is? Why don't we do anything about it? This question never comes from Farmer himself, however, who neither proselytizes nor judges the people around him. The challenge has to do with his act itself, and its refusal of compromise or concessions. This example suggests that it is easy to embrace the ideals the founder embodies, but much more difficult to rise to the challenge of his act or to accept without contestation or resistance the desire that drives him.

Unlike the love at stake in the group psychology, desire invariably appears as something violent, scandalous, or unbearable, whose first effect is often to solicit resistance and even aggressivity. Perhaps this explains why betrayal is a leitmotif of all social movements that emerge around the desire of an individual subject, and why assassination is so often the fate of the public figures who have marked history with the force of their desire. It may also shed light on the basic problem that groups rarely survive their founders. Once the desire of the founder is no longer at the center, groups tend to dissolve or lose their momentum, or even to become reactionary or repressive. This is the dynamic Freud identifies in *Moses and Monotheism*, where the desire of Moses gives rise to new forms of religious practice and social organization that are rapidly stripped of their force and even brutally repressed by his followers. This is a problem that affects almost all groups. But psychoanalytic groups bear witness to it in a particularly dramatic (or even melodramatic) way. Freud and Lacan were both "betrayed" by large numbers of their followers, and both had difficulty finding heirs to continue the work and even found themselves denounced or excommunicated by their disciples. Where desire is most central, it seems that the prospects of a collective undertaking are most uncertain.

In insisting on the way in which collective movements tend to fail or falter, my aim is not to render one more pessimistic judgment on the possibility of bringing about social change (a pessimism that is all too common in psychoanalytic circles), but rather to think about how desire differs from the idealizing love at stake in identification, and therefore about its transformative potential.

ANXIETY AS A RESPONSE TO THE DESIRE OF THE OTHER

Lacan offers a unique approach to the question of desire when he proposes that anxiety is the affect that responds to the desire of the Other. If love is about the strategies of seduction that sustain the imaginary coherence of the ego, desire is linked to the anxiety induced by the loss of the ego ideals and the encounter with castration. The corollary is that the practice of psychoanalysis is founded on the confrontation with the anxiety provoked by the desire of the Other, and the assumption that only this can result in real change.

What then is at stake in the "desire of the Other," and how does it relate to the question of the leader or founder? What does desire mean, if not passion, will, or determination? What exactly provokes anxiety, and what light does it shed on the problem of social change?

In *Group Psychology and the Analysis of the Ego*, Freud already underscores the relationship between anxiety and the loss of the leader as ideal ego. He argues that panic erupts when the emotional ties binding the members of the group break down, or when the group experiences the loss of the leader:

> The typical occasion of the outbreak of a panic is very much as it is represented in Nestroy's parody of Hebbel's play about Judith and Holofernes. A soldier cries out: "The general has lost his head!" and thereupon all the Assyrians take to flight. The loss of the leader in some sense or other, the birth of misgivings about him, brings on the outbreak of panic, though the danger remains the same; the mutual ties between the members of the group disappear, as a rule, at the same time as the tie with their leader.[11]

He further specifies that the panic associated with the loss of the leader is the group equivalent of anxiety in the individual. Unlike fear, which is provoked by an increase in danger, panic and anxiety are both provoked by the "cessation of emotional ties," the loosening of the libidinal cathexes that support the ego through identification (37).

Lacan approaches the same problem from a different angle, advancing the thesis that in anxiety, the subject is affected by the desire of the Other.[12] The analysis of children reveals that anxiety emerges when the child becomes aware of the lack in the Other, which first takes shape in the mother's desire. When the child perceives that the mother is wanting something, anxiety responds with the question: what can I do to satisfy her? The logic of perversion in particular reveals that the child imputes demand to the mother in an attempt to disavow her desire, and so avoid confronting the lack in the Other. The pervert offers himself up as an object for the mother (or undertakes to restore the missing phallus) so as to avoid confronting her "castration," which really means the lack of any object that would satisfy her desire, including the child himself. The point is that the mother's desire, like all desire, cannot be satisfied. It therefore points to the structural lack of the object that for Lacan is the essence of castration. His reading of Freud emphasizes the interdependence of two faces of castration: the lack in the subject, and the lack in the Other. The child first encounters the possibility of his own castration in the castration (or lack) of the mother,[13] just as the soldier of Freud's example is struck with castration anxiety at the news that the general has lost his head.[14] This is why the child imputes demand to the mother and the soldier surrenders to the will of his superior officer: the question "what does s/he want (from me)?" leaves open the possibility that there is an object that could satisfy desire, or that the relation with another person might represent a solution to the impasse of castration.

These are two possible avatars of the fantasy of seduction, where the ego comes into being as an object for an Other who is either held responsible for castration or called upon to solve it. In "The Mirrror Stage," Lacan suggests that the child attempts to build an ideal ego by identifying with the image it takes to be the object of the Other's love or desire, seeking in its gaze a unified body image that would allow it to repress the fragmented body of the drives.[15] His analysis implies that such a mechanism potentially subtends every interpersonal relationship, from the familial to the social to the religious or political. If the function of the interpersonal relation or group psychology is to support the ego by sustaining the strategies of seduction, psychoanalysis takes aim at seduction and the ego it sustains in order to gain access to the subject of the unconscious, the subject of desire.

Psychoanalysis is not simply antagonistic to social mechanisms, however; it is itself a form of social tie: one that opposes the symbolic articulation of desire and castration to the imaginary mechanisms of love and seduction. Apollon describes the transference that inaugurates the analytic experience as a "minimal social link"[16] in which analysand and analyst are bound not by love or by identification, but by the desire of the analyst that solicits a response from the subject's unconscious in the form of a dream. The signifiers of the dream contest the ego narrative and the social values, norms, and ideals that sustain the ego by aiding and abetting its repression of the unconscious. But the logic of the transference reveals that only the desire of the Other can solicit the unconscious, and so provoke a shift in the subject's position. This is why analysis requires two people. Where the analysand is concerned, repression stands in the way of change; his position is determined by a *je n'en veux rien savoir*, a "not wanting to know anything about it" that precludes any examination of the fantasy structuring his symptoms and his relations with others. The desire of a second subject, a desire to know about what causes the subject, is necessary to solicit the response of the unconscious in the form of signifiers attesting to another knowledge (or savoir) about the subject's encounter with the real of the drives.

Like Hallward's "What would X do?" (which underscores the role of one subject's act in transforming the position of a second subject), the logic of the transference reveals that under certain conditions, the desire of one subject can have the effect of liberating another subject's desire and allowing it to find expression in an act. From a psychoanalytic perspective, only a subject can act: there is nothing like a shared or collective act. But the singular act of a subject may *respond* to the act of another person without taking it as a model or ideal. The mechanism of the transference reveals that the difference inheres in the operation of anxiety, which makes the act of the other a motor of change, and not the source of stability or support implied in identification. This is because anxiety exposes the *lack* implied in the desire of the Other.

The analyst does not know anything about what is happening to the subject; she has no generalizable knowledge or expertise born of experience that might be applied indifferently to each new case. But she *desires* to know, and this desire is what drives the transference by soliciting a response from the subject's unconscious.[17] What, then, provokes anxiety? The analyst's desire points to a *lack in knowledge*, a lack the ego narrative attempts to repress through recourse to the seduction fantasy that rationalizes or compensates for castration.[18] It therefore sets in motion the process that will lead to the falling away of the seduction fantasy and the displacement of the ego by the subject of the unconscious.

In *The Interpretation of Dreams*, Freud points to the indispensable role of affects in confirming the operation of the transference. While dream thoughts are subject to distortion through condensation and displacement, affect leads infallibly to the latent dream thoughts because it does not undergo alteration.[19] Anxiety is *the* affect of psychoanalysis, because it responds to the analyst's desire to know by overcoming the censorship applied to unconscious thoughts.[20] Only by traversing this anxiety can the subject come to have another knowledge about what is happening to him, and thus liberate himself from the repetition-compulsion of the fantasy.

While psychoanalysis may be unique among forms of the social tie in explicitly placing anxiety at the center, it also draws out something that is implicit in some of the most significant examples of social transformation, if not always noticed or emphasized. The remainder of this chapter will be concerned with three examples of the social tie that are structured around the desire of the founder and the anxiety it induces: the interdiction of sacrifice and the worship of an absent God in the religion of Moses, the role of the transference in Freud's invention of psychoanalysis, and the "love of the enemy" in the discourse of Jesus.

What might be gained by considering the desire of the founder that prompts social or political change alongside the desire of the analyst? The role of the analyst's desire in installing the transference suggests that at the level of the subject, real change necessarily involves the falling away of imaginary supports, and thus the loss of ideals and values as motives for action. Moses and Jesus, in the respective challenges they present to the Jewish people, might in this sense be understood as early avatars or anticipations of the analyst's function. Both figures have the effect of completely transforming—indeed dismantling—an existing conception of God. They could therefore be understood as opposing desire (an intervention in the world that makes no concessions, even to the point of death) to the appeal to an all-powerful Other who is charged with the subject's fate. In this sense they anticipate the evacuation or dismantling of the imaginary Other of the seduction fantasy that is the first aim of the analytic experience, without which it is impossible for the subject to engage his own desire.

The clinical context sheds light on the violent resistance and repression that erupted in response to the founding acts of Moses and Jesus, and offers some insight into the structural antagonism between the founder's desire and the possibility of a collective movement. At the same time, the examples of Moses and Jesus develop or draw out a dimension of the analytic experience that is not always given sufficient weight or attention, even within the clinical context: that desire must find expression in an *act*, or in the production of a new object that intervenes in the world so as to transform it.

This is the essence of sublimation, in which the absolutely singular and subjective nature of desire manages to find expression in the production of an object that is collectively valorized. In *Three Essays*, Freud maintains that the sublimated form of the drive cannot be characterized without reference to the object. Sublimation differs from the fantasy in providing a direct satisfaction of the drive through "objects that are socially valorized, objects of which the group approves, insofar as they are objects of public utility."[21] This is the possibility Freud explores in his analysis of the paintings of Leonardo da Vinci. If Leonardo's *Madonna and Child with Saint Anne* originates in a childhood fantasy, then what makes his painting a great masterpiece and not merely a neurotic symptom? The answer is that in transforming the pictorial space in order to give visibility to his own psychic object, Leonardo makes the artwork into an object of sublimation by expanding the boundaries of what can be seen.[22] The collective dimension of sublimation is what accounts for the motif of the "great man" that appears in so many of Freud's cultural analyses: the "great man" is someone whose object constitutes a sublimation not only for himself, but for his age.

THE MURDER OF MOSES, THE LEADER WHO WOULD NOT LEAD

Sublimation for Freud is practically synonymous with the name of Moses, the ultimate example of the "great man." In Freud's reconstruction of the Exodus story, Moses the Egyptian introduces the uncultured Hebrew tribes to the rigorous monotheism he learned in the court of the Pharaoh Ahkenaton, which teaches that "the Deity spurns sacrifice and ceremonial; he demands only belief and a life of truth and justice."[23] Moses is a leader who evacuates the place of the leader, who undercuts the logic of identification binding the group and refounds the collective undertaking on a nonimaginary basis. This function is most evident in the first tablet of the Mosaic Decalogue, which prohibits worshiping idols, making images of God, or invoking the divine name. In consigning God to the place of the unrepresentable, the law is the sublimation that allows the collectivity to explore the absence or loss of the leader in a way that promotes and sustains the desire of the Other, rather than repressing it.

Why, then, is Moses murdered? Freud argues that the Mosaic religion does not simply allow the subject to "expand his soul" in the absence of barriers or supports, but introduces a fundamental absence or lack where the totemic structure puts the all-powerful father that functions as the ideal ego for each member of the fraternal pact.

Freud hypothesizes that the people's lingering guilt over the repressed primal murder is the source of their initial enthusiasm for the new religion, which exalted the primeval father as the source of all life and so satisfied their craving for a powerful ideal ego. The great Moses was not satisfied with a mere father cult, however, but set forth a rigorous ethical doctrine that attempted to "form their character for good" by encouraging them to abandon their magical practices and "progress in spirituality and sublimations" (*Moses* 108). This Mosaic innovation failed to catch on with the broad mass of the Hebraic people, who never completely overcame the superstitions and hostilities of the totemic mind. Freud suggests that the episode of the golden calf encodes the people's falling away from the new religion and demand for new father substitutes, which eventually lead them to repeat the original murder on Moses himself. Although an elite minority of the Jewish people (the priestly class) manages to keep the Mosaic message alive and preserve his vision for later generations, the purity of this rational monotheism could at best be said to exist alongside—rather than in place of—all the rest: the broad mass of the people are still subject to the totemic logic and the group psychology that is its social and political expression.

In his own reading of the Mosaic legacy, Lacan explores the psychic function of sacrifice in a way that casts new light on the repression of the Other's desire and the lack it exposes. When Moses teaches that the Deity "spurns sacrifice," he does not simply relieve the Israelites of the oppressive demands of a bloodthirsty deity, but also takes away the sacrificial object whose function is to repress the Other's desire by giving form to the *object a*: the purely mental object of the fantasy that has no correlate in reality. In the process he not only dismantles the all-powerful God of the original Hebraic religion, but obliges the Israelites to confront the lack in the Other and the anxiety it provokes.

Lacan suggests that the Mosaic religion marks a radical break from its antecedents in being organized not around the demand or jouissance of an all-powerful being, but around "the desire of a God who is the God of Moses" (*Television* 90). He elaborates his reading through a commentary of the Sacrifice of Isaac (Genesis 22:1–14).[24] On God's orders, Abraham binds his son on the altar and prepares to sacrifice him as a burnt offering. But as he lifts his knife over the boy and prepares to slit his throat, the angel of the Lord appears beside him and stays his hand.

Lacan declares that "a God is something one encounters in the real, inaccessible. It is indicated by what doesn't deceive—anxiety."[25] But what exactly provokes anxiety? Until this moment, Abraham sees God as a God of demand or jouissance; the proof is that he is prepared to sacrifice everything to him. God's bloodthirsty demands are not what give rise to his anxiety, however:

Prior to that restraining gesture, Abraham has . . . bound [Isaac's] hand to his feet like a ram for the sacrifice. Before waxing emotional, as is customary on such occasions, we might remember that sacrificing one's little boy to the local *Elohim* was quite common at the time—and not only at the time, for it continued so late that it was constantly necessary for the Angel of the Name . . . to stop the Israelites, who were about to start it up again. . . . Don't reproach me for having made too short shrift . . . of Abraham's feelings, for, upon opening a little book that dates from the end of the eleventh century by one Rashi, . . . you would be quite astonished to hear him give voice to a latent dialogue sung between Abraham and God, who is what is at stake in the angel. When Abraham learns from the angel that he is not there in order to immolate Isaac, Rashi has him say: *What then? If that is what is going on, have I thus come here for nothing? I am at least going to give him a slight wound to make him shed a little blood. Would you like that?*

(Television 93, emphases in original)

In Lacan's reading, sacrifice is not a gesture of propitiation or submission, but a preemptive act whose aim is to avoid any confrontation with the Other's desire or lack. Rather than staging the demands of a ruthless and capricious God, the episode really instantiates the *interdiction of sacrifice* that obliges the subject of the covenant to confront his own anxiety by acknowledging the lack of any object that might satisfy the Other's desire. Charles Shepherdson suggests that the importance of this transformation is that it reveals a God who is lacking, who wants something, but who does not want Abraham to take responsibility for his lack or to try to figure out what would satisfy him; instead, Abraham has to be able to tolerate the anxiety of not knowing what the Other wants, as opposed to the security of merely doing God's bidding.[26] In the words of Psalm 51: "For thou desirest not sacrifice; else would I give it: thou delightest not in burnt offering."

In his seminar on anxiety, Lacan develops this argument by explaining that sacrifice has nothing to do with offerings or gifts. Its true function is to entangle the Other in the network of desire, and so be relieved of one's own anxiety. He notes that the practice of sacrifice assumed its importance at a time when the gods were part of the fabric of everyday life; its true objective was to figure out "whether these gods desired something":

> Sacrifice consisted in acting as if they desired just like us, because if they desire just like us, then *a* has the same structure. This doesn't necessarily mean that they're going to eat whatever we sacrifice to them, or even that it is of any use to them at all; the important thing is that they desire it, and, more importantly, *that it doesn't cause them any anxiety.* There is a trait that I don't believe anyone, until now, has ever explained in a satisfying way—it was always specified that the victims must not have any flaws or blemishes [*devaient être sans tache*]. Now, you will recall what I've said to you about the flaw or stain at the level of the visual field. With the flaw

we see emerge the possibility of the resurgence, in the field of desire, of what is there behind it, hidden; for example, that eye whose relation to this field must necessarily be elided if desire is going to remain . . . and that allows it to keep anxiety at bay. When one ensnares the gods in the trap of desire, it is essential not to awaken their anxiety.[27]

The underlying logic of sacrifice is that the Other has to be able to handle the objects that cause us anxiety (or, even better, be willing to take them off our hands, whether or not they are of any use to him). The demand that the victim be unblemished or "pure" really works to repress the fact that the object offered up is not a "good" object, but an object of anxiety. Lacan links it to what psychoanalysis identifies as the first gift, the anal object. His own feces is the first part of himself that the child relinquishes, though it is, importantly, an object that he does not know what to do with, that must be disposed of somehow and that has no real value, no utility: as such, it becomes the gift par excellence, what is "generously" offered up precisely because one must get rid of it at all costs. Anxiety erupts when God is no longer willing to take these "gifts," no longer able to dispose of them for us.

In foregrounding the question of God's desire, the Mosaic religion substitutes for the jouissance of an all-powerful Other a law-based observance predicated on lack. In Lacan's words,

Here may be marked the knife blade separating God's jouissance from what in that tradition is presented as his desire. . . . That is the key to the mystery, in which may be read the aversion of the Jewish tradition concerning what exists everywhere else. The Hebrew hates the metaphysico-sexual rites which unite in celebration the community to God's jouissance. He accords special value to the gap separating desire and fulfillment. The symbol of that gap we find in the same context of *El Shadday's* relation to Abraham, in which, primordially, is born the law of circumcision, which gives as a sign of the covenant between the people and the desire of he who has chosen them what?—that little piece of flesh sliced off.[28]

(*Television* 94)

When he describes the "little piece of flesh cut off" as the symbol of the gap separating desire from jouissance, Lacan suggests that the severed foreskin is not an object of "sacrifice," but an inscription of lack: a lack that the logic of sacrifice is designed to circumvent by disposing of anxiety. In its affirmation of the gap separating desire and fulfillment, the Mosaic tradition underscores not only the impossibility of fulfilling the Other, but the necessity of renouncing such an undertaking. Importantly, though, it signals the castration not only of the human subject, but of God himself: if God cannot be satisfied, neither is he all-powerful.

Lacan hypothesizes that the fantasy of God's omnipotence (which implies that he is not only *all-powerful*, but *powerful everywhere*, without exception) marks the emergence of a specifically obsessional response to the problem of anxiety:

> The correlation of omnipotence with omnivoyance reveals to us what is at stake in this fantasy: the projection of the subject into the field of the ideal, split between, *on one side, the specular alter ego, the ideal ego, and on the other, what lies beyond it, the Ego Ideal.* At the level that is concerned with covering over anxiety, the Ego Ideal assumes the form of the All-Powerful, the Almighty. It is there that the obsessional seeks and finds the complement of what he needs to constitute himself in desire.
>
> (356–57)

This is why, no matter what he might say to the contrary, "the obsessional always believes in God: the same God that everyone believes in without believing it—namely, this universal eye that surveys all of our actions" (357). The true atheist, says Lacan, is the one who manages to eliminate the fantasy of the all-powerful Other altogether.

Lacan's analysis seems to offer a reexamination of Freud's account of the group psychology by suggesting that the overestimation of the leader and the belief in his omnipotence are concerned not merely with love (or the narcissistic ties of identification that bind group members to the leader as ideal ego), but with the refusal of the lack in the Other that is veiled by the imaginary object of identification. When he states that "the object *petit a* is what falls from the subject in anxiety" (*Television* 82), Lacan seems in part to be alluding to Freud's thesis concerning the leader as ideal ego. If what falls away from the subject in the experience of anxiety is the leader as object a or ideal ego, does this not suggest that to confront desire is to relinquish this object?

While Freud's analysis suggests that panic-anxiety is structurally incompatible with group coexistence, at least in the case of such "artificial" groups as army and Church (*Group Psychology* 34–38), Lacan's reading of the Sacrifice of Isaac finds in the Mosaic religion an example of a group that is not organized according to this logic, and that even accords special value to the falling away of the object and the anxiety that accompanies it. Historically we know that the sublimely unrepresentable God of Moses evolved from a "leader god" or "god of way," who even in the Book of Exodus takes his place at the front of his people in the form of a column of fire.[29] But over the course of the narrative, we witness his transformation first into a God with whom one can no longer identify (exemplified by the ban on graven images), and finally into an entirely absent God who obliges his people to wander the world indefinitely, with no leader to guide them. What this trajectory really attests to is the loss of the leader as the one who cements the identity of the group.

With respect to the question of the group psychology, Lacan's implicit suggestion seems to be that the Mosaic community is founded not on the repression of panic or anxiety through the emotional bond of love uniting each of the members to its leader, but on the confrontation with the desire or lack of the Other and the anxiety it induces in each member of the covenant. Yet Freud and Lacan both stress that while the Mosaic tradition may be exemplary in the value it accords to the falling away of the object and the anxiety it provokes, the broad mass of the Jews are unable to tolerate this situation. Freud reads the Israelites' forging of the golden calf as an attempt to reconstruct a leader around whom they can rally: one that immediately follows the handing down of the prohibition on making images (or having "imaginary" ties of identification with the leader) by the God who cannot be seen (*Moses* 57–58). But the ultimate example of the Jews' refusal of the Other's desire is their eventual murder of Moses himself, who is sacrificed precisely for having sustained the lack in the Other.

The paradox is that the Jews must kill Moses—the man who truly led them out of Egypt and secured their freedom—in order to keep alive the fantasy of the leader as ideal ego. After his death, Moses is deified as a stern and demanding God, his traits and actions attributed to a fearsome volcano deity who better satisfies the popular imaginary and its craving for an all-powerful Other. The result is that the deeds of the man Moses and the desire that engendered them are effaced by the very legend that immortalizes them as supernatural acts:

> Since the Moses people attached such great importance to their experience of the Exodus from Egypt, the deed of freeing them had to be ascribed to Jahve; it had to be adorned with features that proved the terrific grandeur of this volcano-god, such as, for example, the pillar of smoke which changed to one of fire by night, or the storm that parted the waters so that the pursuers were drowned by the returning floods of water. . . . The bestowal of the Ten Commandments too was said to have taken place, not at Qades, but at the foot of the holy mountain amid the signs of a volcanic eruption. This description, however, did a serious wrong to the memory of the man Moses; it was he, and not the volcano-god, who had freed his people from Egypt.
>
> (48)

Freud follows Ernst Sellin in supposing that the murder of Moses "was the basis of all later expectations of the Messiah," giving rise to the hope that the man the Jews had murdered would "return from the realm of the dead and lead his contrite people—and perhaps not only his people—into the land of eternal bliss" (42). This impulse finds its ultimate expression in Pauline Christianity, in which Freud sees the triumphant return of the omnipotent father-God who secures the identity of the ego and supports the fantasy of resurrection (108). The gradual displacement and repression of the Mosaic innovation could therefore be understood as a refusal to go any longer without a leader or ideal ego, a refusal to live with anxiety, and thus the birth of the group psychology.

In *The Ethics of Psychoanalysis*, Lacan suggests that the process of sublimation is concerned not merely with the construction of a new object, but with the fall of the imaginary object or ideal ego and the emptiness it exposes: "in every form of sublimation, emptiness is determinative." Religious forms of social organization are therefore inherently at odds with sublimation, since "religion in all its forms consists of avoiding this emptiness. We can illustrate that in forcing the note of Freudian analysis, for the good reason that Freud emphasized the obsessional traits of religious behavior" (130). Nonetheless, the Mosaic religion reveals that in some instances, religious practice can actually establish the conditions under which sublimation becomes possible. In its case, says Lacan, "a phrase like 'respecting this emptiness' perhaps goes further. . . . The emptiness remains in the center, and that is precisely why sublimation is involved" (130). In terms of the preceding analysis, the obsessional posture of "avoiding this emptiness" can be witnessed not only in the illusion of an all-powerful, all-seeing Other, but in the logics of demand and sacrifice that sustain it. Conversely, the "respect" of emptiness appears in what Lacan calls the "special value the Hebrew accords to the gap separating desire and fulfillment," which finds expression in the Ten Commandments of the Mosaic law.

Moses founds an institution (the Jewish law), and this institution is the legacy of his desire. It provides a structure or a space in which the subject can encounter and explore the lack in the Other in a creative manner, without being so consumed by his anxiety that he violently rejects and represses it. This is what we see in the practice of the oral law or Talmud, where the collectivity engages in the exploration of God's absence as the creative foundation of the rabbinic community. The law is a structure that allows for a work on the absent Other, and in this respect functions as a sublimation for the age (and indeed for subsequent ages, since the sublimation functions not only for members of the Mosaic religion, but potentially for anyone who takes up this object). In its negative character, the Decalogue underscores the emptiness at the center of the real, the lack that gives rise to a desire without object that only the signifier can sustain.

THE CONSTRAINT OF THE TRANSFERENCE

Freud introduced a radical new conception of the social link when he made this desire and the anxiety it induces the foundation of the new social movement he called psychoanalysis. The desire of the analyst is a desire to know about what causes the human being, a desire that necessarily leads to the originary castration that Freud identifies with the uniquely human experience of the drives that detach instinctual energies from their natural aims and objects, structuring human life as a quest for an impossible. This desire is what drives the transference, leading the subject toward the incompleteness of the Other and the castration it implies as the only possible support for desire.

In stripping away the imaginary accoutrements of the Hebraic religion and instituting the absent God of the Decalogue, Moses anticipates the function of the analyst by obliging the Israelites to confront the desire or lack of the Other. But while the institution of law provides a space in which the subject can explore the lack in the Other in a creative way, nothing guarantees that a given subject will actually do so. Although Moses induces anxiety in the Israelites, he is not able to make them abandon their earlier practices simply by imposing the imageless worship of God and banning sacrifice. The result is that for the vast majority, the confrontation with the Other's desire simply provokes repression and violence, and a reversion to the very practices Moses allowed them to evolve away from. His example raises the question of how desire can provoke change, and not simply resistance, hostility, and repression.

This is the question Freud confronts at the beginning of his practice. The failures of his first attempts at analytic therapy reveal the limitations of what Freud will subsequently call "wild psychoanalysis," or the attempt to effect a cure by delivering an interpretation of the patient's symptoms and then calling on her to avow the unconscious thoughts at their origin. Even when the interpretation is correct, it fails to produce enduring results: new symptoms emerge to replace those that have been treated, and even the patient's embrace of Freud's interpretation fails to bring relief.[30] How, then, can the analyst effect a shift in the subject's position? The transference is the innovation that responds to this problem. Its structuration of the social link establishes the conditions under which one subject's desire can affect another subject in such a way as to provoke a transformation. By calling upon the subject's unconscious to contest the ego narrative and to construct another savoir about what is happening to her, the analyst can *constrain* the subject to change her position (and generally avoid being murdered for his efforts).

While the Mosaic tradition emphasizes the necessity of confronting the desire of the *Other*, it has less to say about the process of becoming a *subject* of desire. The analytic experience is concerned with the transition from the first to the second. First the analysand must confront the desire of the Other and the anxiety it provokes, next he must assume this desire himself as a subject.

The analysand has to "traverse" the fantasy, to confront himself the fall of the Other of seduction such that this fantasy is no longer able to function. But this passage can occur only in response to the constraints imposed by the analyst's desire. In demanding an analysis, the analysand at the beginning is not looking for anxiety and castration; he is looking for a solution, in the form of a life free of suffering. Like the Israelites, he is looking to be led into the Promised Land, as it were. He appeals to the analyst as a "subject supposed to know" (*sujet supposé savoir*), as an expert who will know how to cure his symptoms or lead him out of his impasse. But the analysis can only advance if the analyst refuses to occupy this position, and instead maintains the lack in the Other.

At the level of the analytic maneuver, this lack manifests itself in the analyst's way of listening to the patient. In the way she "conducts" the session, the analyst exemplifies the position of the leader who does not lead. This is true on many levels, not least of which is the fact that the analyst generally sits *behind* the patient, where she cannot be seen. More importantly, she offers no guidance, advice, or assistance, and generally responds to the patient's questions or appeals with silence. These are the very elements of Freudian technique that often provoke indignant criticism from those expecting a supportive therapy, who complain that the analyst does not "do anything" or has "nothing to offer." But Lacan argues that the silence that responds to the subject's appeal is more generative than any answer or reply, because instead of implicating two interlocutors in an imaginary "conversation" or discourse, it interrupts that conversation and allows something else to emerge: the speech of the unconscious (*Écrits* 206). The analyst can enter into an interpersonal "relationship" or conversation with the patient only at the cost of sustaining the seduction fantasy, by positioning herself in the place of the imaginary Other who is the object of the patient's appeal or complaint.[31] The insistence on the analyst's lack or absence is really what distinguishes Freudian and Lacanian psychoanalysis from every other major school of analysis, and forms the basis of Lacan's critique of ego psychology and of therapy more generally. His reading of Freud stresses that the transference is not the staging of an interpersonal relation (as in the concept of "affective transference"), but a solicitation of the unconscious through a question or a silence, which results in the production of a dream that responds to that question by providing new signifiers.

Maintaining the lack in the Other involves more than silence, however. The lack in the Other is not merely descriptive of the analyst's position; it is the object of his desire to know. Willy Apollon, Danielle Bergeron, and Lucie Cantin suggest that the analyst's role is to maintain the "ab-sense of the Other," or what Apollon calls the "unfoundedness" (*l'Infondé*) of the symbolic ("Treatment" 219). They offer a detailed clinical account of how the constraint of the analyst's desire functions in the treatment of psychosis, which illustrates especially well the movement from seduction to castration.[32]

Like the seduction fantasy of the neurotic, the psychotic delusion ascribes to the Other a sense, a meaning. In *Memoirs of My Mental Illness*, for example, the psychotic Dr. Schreber speaks of a "flaw in the order of things," which the delusion ascribes to the machinations of an ignorant God: a capricious, infantile, and vindictive deity who persecutes men because he does not understand them.[33] The aim of the analytic act that sustains the transference is to distinguish the structural lack implied in the "flaw in the order of things" from the delusion that seeks to explain it, which posits an Other who is responsible for the defect and casts the subject in the role of a savior charged with the mission of repairing it. To the Imaginary Other of demand or jouissance, the analyst opposes the symbolic Other of lack. The "ab-sense of the Other" is the structural defect in the symbolic Other that the subject must confront if he is to be liberated from the fantasy and its particular structuration of the social link.

But he can confront it only on the condition that "the analyst, in the position of the missing Other, upholds and insists upon the flaw in the symbolic" (218). Rather than "helping" the psychotic or treating him as an object of care, as the doctor or psychiatrist does, the psychoanalyst does not presume to have any knowledge concerning the subject. With respect to the psychotic, he is in the position of a lacking Other, who listens to his speech with a "learned ignorance" (211). In the analyst, the subject therefore encounters a "listening ear that creates a kind of rupture in the place of the Other" (212), because it desires to know about something the delusion is unable to account for: "to say that the analyst is in the position of a lacking Other is thus to emphasize that his role is above all to *question the savoir* of the psychotic" (222). The object of his desire to know is not the solution proposed by the delusion, but the traumatic event that prompted its elaboration: an "encounter with a real unassimilable by the signifier, what we have called the defect in the Other" (219).

The analyst's desire precipitates the fall of the delusional Other by soliciting the elaboration of the signifying chain that allows for the construction of a subjective history. The supposition underlying the analyst's act is that only the unconscious can provide knowledge about what is happening to the subject: it is not a matter of applying a theoretical paradigm or bringing to bear an expertise based on clinical experience. Instead, "the logic of the signifier must come to cast doubt upon the psychotic certainty and object to the delusional interpretation" (224), in the form of dreams that contest the delusion by identifying details in the subject's personal history that run counter to the work of restoring the Other in which he is engaged, and that begin to allow for the elaboration of another knowledge concerning his encounter with a real that the signifier was unable to contain or assimilate.

Undergoing analysis involves confronting the lack in the Other. But it also involves a fidelity to the unconscious as the "discourse of the Other," the signifiers produced under transference that allow the patient to construct a savoir about his encounter with the Other's defect:

> Since what is at stake is the production of a savoir that will allow the psychotic to bear the defect in the Other, the constraint applied by the analyst's desire must accomplish two things at once. It must keep open the question of the hole in the symbolic—its "unfoundedness"—through the representation of a structural defect, linked to language. But at the same time, it must not give up on the requirement that the subject produce a savoir in the field of the signifier. . . . When it happens that one of the analyst's questions in the course of a session is left unanswered, and a dream then responds to it by furnishing the elements that allow a forgotten memory to resurface, the psychotic discovers a logic other than that controlled by the imaginary of the delusional solution, or what the imaginary constructs to account for the voices, injunctions, and nonsensical acts produced by the crisis. It is a moment of real vacillation, at which the psychotic can assume the position of an analysand by dedicating himself to the analytic work, to the production of his dreams and the *savoir* they allow him to construct, rather than to the delusion.

(223, 225)

The difference between the delusional knowledge and the savoir elaborated under transference is that the latter "sustains him in his relation to the hole in the symbolic" (221), *supposing* the lack in the Other rather than masking it over.

Lacan defines the transference as a "love" for the savoir produced by the unconscious, which differs from the love at stake in seduction in supposing castration, rather than refusing it: "The love of truth is the love of this weakness whose veil we have raised; it is the love of what the truth hides, which is called castration."[34] The traversal of the fantasy of seduction involves the encounter with castration, or the truth that there is no object that would satisfy desire and no Other who could answer for the effect of the drives. It involves an assumption that the psychic object is an impossible or inexistent object that no one else sees, that no one else wants, that no one else can provide. It therefore implies a kind of radical solitude, the assumption of which allows for a new relation to the social link, not as the scene of the ego and its complaints and demands or as the delusional certainty of the paranoid, but as the scene of ethics.

This is why every analyst has to undergo analysis. The desire of the analyst is the desire of the analysand, the desire of the subject who traversed the fantasy of seduction and discovered through his encounter with castration the transformative potential of the signifier that alone sustains desire.[35]

THE LOVE OF THE ENEMY
IN THE DISCOURSE OF JESUS

I will attempt to illustrate this passage with the same example discussed by Hallward: the desire of Jesus. I propose to read Jesus on the model of Freud's attempt to extract the subjectivity of Moses from the idealized figure of legend, by distinguishing the Jesus of ideals from the Jesus whose subjective position echoes in singular instances of speech.[36] My emphasis is on the desire of the mortal man Jesus rather than on the role of the risen Christ as a support for identification.[37] This is therefore a different Jesus than one finds in Freud's *Group Psychology*, which is concerned less with Jesus himself than with his function and meaning for Paul, for whom Jesus is the redeemer who absolves the sins of men by taking guilt upon himself, thereby vanquishing death once and for all.

If the Mosaic tradition exposes the lack or absence implicit in the unknowable desire of God, Jesus shows what it means not simply to encounter and accept the lack in the Other, but to find in the lack of the Other the support for his own desire. His story stages the tension between two modalities of love: the love for the ideal ego and the unified body image it sustains, and the "love for savoir" that implies a confrontation with castration and death, which Jesus calls "love of the enemy." With respect to the argument of the previous section, my claim is that Jesus models the position of the subject who undergoes analysis, whose acceptance of the "bitter cup" he must drink before acceding to the "new kingdom" provides an analogy for the embrace of castration implied in the "love of truth." His story exemplifies the solitude of one who traverses castration, who can never be part of a movement or group.

The early chapters of the Gospels tell how Jesus overcame seduction by assuming the lack in the Other as the condition of his desire. This ethical attitude is given mythical form in the legend that describes how Jesus overcame his temptation by Satan. The diabolical adversary might be read as a figure of the logic of seduction, in which someone else is appealed to as a support for the ego. In the trials imposed by Satan, Jesus is asked to call upon his father to perform miracles, or to secure his own enjoyment by assuming worldly power. In refusing to make these appeals, Jesus vanquishes temptation by assuming and sustaining the lack or absence of the Other as the condition of his desire as a mortal man.

The subsequent chapters of the Gospels could be read as the account of Jesus' passage from an analysand to an analyst, or of his transformation into someone who assumes the desire of the analyst by apprenticing himself to the discourse of the Other, which he calls "my father's word." In appealing to the father as a word, and not as an almighty being, Jesus recasts the father not as the support for an imaginary reality, but as the signifier of the lack in the Other: a signifier that is the *product* of the subject's desire, and not a substitute for or effacement of it.

In the words of the Gospel of John, "No man has ever seen God. It is his only Son, who is close to the Father's heart, who has declared him" (John 1:18). Jesus is not concerned with the imaginary father, in the form either of the protective parental figure imagined by the child or of the guarantor of rights and justice that Freud identifies with the fantasy of a loving God. Instead, his words point to the function of the symbolic father, whose word supports the subject's desire. Jesus tells us that his father's word creates a world in which the subject can live, a world that has nothing to do with the world of existence. Or as he puts it, "One does not live by bread alone, but by every word that comes from the mouth of God" (Matthew 4:4). When Jesus refers to God as his father, I do not think this should be interpreted as a claim about his own divinity. Rather, my point is that in the way Jesus speaks of his father, he introduces a completely new understanding of what the father is. The father is neither a man of flesh and blood nor an omnipotent being, but a word that gives eternal life: "Call no man your father on earth; for you have one Father, who is in heaven" (Matthew 23:9). In testifying to this "heavenly father," Jesus is not so much bearing witness to the existence of an immortal and all-powerful God as revealing the essence of the paternal function, in which the father is first and foremost a symbolic function that sustains the desire of a subject.

In deflecting attention away from the all-powerful God and onto the lacking Other of speech, Jesus also offers a new understanding of love: not the narcissistic love at stake in identification, but a "love for truth" that supposes a confrontation with castration and death. In Lacan's words, what he reveals is that "the love of truth is the love of this weakness whose veil we have raised; it is the love of what the truth hides, which is called castration."

This is how I interpret the words Jesus is supposed to have spoken at the moment of his death on the cross—"My Father, why have you forsaken me?" (Matthew 27:46). In my view, this is the episode that best reveals the true stakes of the father's love in the discourse of Jesus. On the eve of the crucifixion, Jesus prays to his father to release him from his destiny: "if it be possible, let this cup pass from me" (Matthew 26:39). But he realizes himself that it is not possible, and that his father cannot preserve him from what he must undergo. When one of the disciples tries to prevent the police from arresting Jesus, he says: "Put your sword back into its sheath. Am I not to drink the cup that the father has given me?" (John 18:11). But while the Father gives this bitter cup, his love also makes it possible for Jesus to face death. As Jesus explains to the disciples: "For this reason the Father loves me, because I lay down my life in order to take it up again. No one takes it from me, but I lay it down of my own accord. I have power to lay it down, and I have power to take it up again. I have received this from my Father" (John 10:17–18). With these words, Jesus makes clear that the father's love is not a means of avoiding castration; it is what condenses and distills the creative potential of the symbolic as the support for a desire whose stakes are inseparable from castration.

This understanding of love is what Jesus attempts to transmit to his disciples, and not the narcissistic love or eros at stake in identification. In emphasizing that only those who accept the loss and destruction of everything they hold dear will find life, he makes clear that this love is not a binding force that undoes alienation and death, but a love that involves the loss of the world itself:

> Do not think that I have come to bring peace to the earth; I have not come to bring peace, but a sword. For I have come to set a man against his father, and a daughter against her mother, and a daughter-in-law against her mother-in-law; and one's foes will be members of one's own household. Whoever loves father or mother more than me is not worthy of me; and whoever loves son or daughter more than me is not worthy of me; and whoever does not take up the cross and follow me is not worthy of me. Those who find their life will lose it, and those who lose their life for my sake will find it.
>
> (Matthew 10:34–39)

The reference to the sword cannot be interpreted as a militant battle cry or revolutionary call to arms. To call for the severing of worldly ties, and in particular the love at stake in the familial relation, is something quite different from waging war on tyranny or injustice in the name of a principle or ideal. What Jesus makes clear is that every worldly attachment must be called into question, must be scrutinized as an obstacle to finding life.

In psychoanalytic terms, his words could be understood as staging the tension between two modalities of love: the love for the ideal ego and the unified body image it sustains, and the "love for savoir" that implies a confrontation with castration and death. Indeed, it is possible to read the entire passage as if the unconscious itself is talking. Lacan defines the transference as a "love for the savoir" coming from the unconscious, a savoir that is necessarily a foe where the ego is concerned. To love Jesus, we are told, is to love the truth: "I am the way, and the truth, and the life: and no one comes to the Father except through me" (John 3:15). But like Lacan, Jesus makes clear that the love of truth is meaningless if it does not also become "the love of what the truth hides, which is called castration."

This is how I understand the injunction to "love the enemy" that is the centerpiece of Jesus' Sermon on the Mount: "You have heard that it was said, 'You shall love your neighbor and hate your enemy.' But I say to you, Love your enemies and pray for those who persecute you. . . . For if you love those who love you, what reward do you have? Do not even the tax collectors do the same? And if you greet only your brothers and sisters, what more are you doing than others?" (Matthew 5:43–48). Together with the last passage, these words suggest that to love Jesus is to love an enemy. In marked contrast with the way the words are usually glossed, the enemy is not someone whose enmity I might annul by inscribing him in the community of the faithful or showering him with my love; rather, the enemy is the enemy that Jesus—like the analyst—*is*, insofar as he sustains the field of the Other and the castration to which it leads, and not the discourse and ideals of the ego.

The desire of Jesus, like that of Moses, presents a challenge to his listeners: one that provokes anxiety. But Jesus differs from Moses in that his speech has a properly analytic function, which goes beyond simple iconoclasm to underscore the role of the signifier in effecting a confrontation with the lack in the Other and in sustaining desire. It appears in his predilection for the parable form, which in articulating a truth that can only be half spoken identifies speech as the locus where truth stumbles. But it is especially obvious in his frequent silences and his characteristic way of refusing to enter into a dialogue or conversation. Whenever he is asked "are you the Messiah?" or "are you the Son of God?" Jesus routinely responds with the distinctive formula that is one of the hallmarks of his speech: "you have said so."[38] Typically this formula is explained as an idiosyncratic form of assent. But for the purposes of my argument, it is interesting that Jesus does not articulate anything himself, but returns the questioner's speech to him in an inverted form, as if to force him to take responsibility for his own constructions. This strategy is most apparent in the way Jesus speaks with the apostles during the last supper, on the eve of the crucifixion. When Jesus tells the disciples that one will betray him, Judas says, "Surely not I, Rabbi?" To which Jesus replies, "You have said so" (Matthew 26).

The disciples have an interesting narrative function in the story, that of modeling the extreme anxiety and even paralysis that take hold of those who are affected by Jesus' words. The betrayal of Judas may offer the best illustration of the radical challenge that desire represents to the ego and the violent repression it provokes. But the betrayal of Peter, Jesus' staunchest supporter, is even more revealing (Matthew 26:69–75). It exposes the limitations of any engagement predicated merely on determination or will by demonstrating that neither resolve nor commitment to ideals is sufficient to confront the castration implicit in desire or the anxiety it provokes. Consider the extraordinary account from the Gospel of Matthew of the night preceding the crucifixion, when Jesus gathers the disciples together to await his certain arrest and execution:

> Jesus said to them, "You will all become deserters because of me this night; for it is written, 'I will strike the shepherd, and the sheep of the flock will be scattered.' But after I am raised up, I will go ahead of you to Galilee." Peter said to him, "Though all become deserters because of you, I will never desert you." Jesus said to him, "Truly I tell you, this very night, before the cock crows, you will deny me three times." Peter said to him, "Even though I must die with you, I will not deny you." And so said all the disciples. Then Jesus went with them to a place called Gethsemane; and he said to his disciples, "Sit here while I go over there and pray." He took with him Peter and the two sons of Zebedee, and began to be grieved and agitated. Then he said to them, "I am deeply grieved, even to death; remain here, and stay awake with me." And going a little farther, he threw himself down on the ground and prayed. "My Father, if it is possible, let this cup pass from me; yet not what I want but what you want." Then he came to the disciples and found them sleeping; and he said to Peter, "So, could you not stay awake with me one hour? Stay awake and pray that you may not come into the time of trial; the spirit indeed is willing, but the flesh is weak." Again he went away for the second time and prayed, "My Father, if this cannot pass unless I drink it, your will be

done." Again he came and found them sleeping, for their eyes were heavy. So leaving them again, he went away and prayed for the third time, saying the same words. Then he came to the disciples and said to them, "Are you still sleeping and taking your rest? See, the hour is at hand, and the Son of Man is betrayed into the hands of sinners."

(Matthew 26:31–46)

This is surely the most poignant passage in the Gospels, because we see that it is not easy for Jesus to confront his own death; what makes him Jesus is not some innate divinity, but rather his willingness to lose the world despite the intense agony it causes him. But even more striking than the solitude of Jesus in the face of death is the effect it produces in those around him. Judas betrays Jesus the old-fashioned way, to make a buck. But Peter betrays him first by falling asleep, and then later by claiming not to know Jesus after his arrest.

In the slumber of the disciples we see one kind of act in response to desire, an act that annuls its interpellating force. The call to "stay awake" is a call to live with the anxiety that desire provokes. In the famous words of Pascal, "Jesus will be in agony until the end of the world; there must be no sleeping during that time."[39] But to stay awake to desire is perhaps the most difficult thing of all, and the challenge that inevitably causes groups founded on nothing more than an ideal to founder. Just as Jesus anticipates, the sheep scatter the moment the shepherd is struck down. Strikingly, none of the disciples will go on to do much of anything, as if completely paralyzed by this confrontation with Jesus' desire. Their slumber recalls the forgetting that takes hold of the Jews in Freud's analysis of Moses, the forgetting both of the desire of Moses and of the murder that cut it short. But it also anticipates the slumber and forgetting that will follow after the death of Jesus himself, and of course the forgetting at stake in every act of repression.

Where Jesus is concerned, I would argue that the ultimate example of this forgetting is the founding of Christianity in the letters of Paul. We see it in the tension between the desire of Jesus (a desire that provokes anxiety) and the love that for Paul founds the community and the militant brotherhood, the love whose cornerstone is the possibility of resurrection.[40] Many authors have pointed to the fact that Paul differs from the writers of the Gospels in paying almost no attention to the words of Jesus, who he rarely cites and whose life and actions are of very little consequence for his conception of Christian ethics. Alain Badiou even celebrates this effacement as one of Paul's most original innovations—and if the goal is to conceive the possibility of a "militant brotherhood," as it is for Badiou, this effacement is in fact essential.[41] This dimension of Christianity is really born with Paul, who calls upon Jesus to function as its mascot and ideal; it is not there in Jesus himself.[42] But while Paul never mentions the words of Jesus, the resurrection of Christ is a constant motif. Even as he abandons Jesus as a subject, he cannot do without the ideal ego he represents. As he tells his young flock, "you are all one person in Christ Jesus" (Galatians 3:28).

Paul's immediate silencing of what is at stake in the words of Jesus and his replacement of it with the love of "resurrection" are similar in many respects to Lacan's argument about the effacement of Freud's innovation in ego psychology, which accuses analysts of immediately busying themselves with building up the ego again, as if to forget as quickly as possible the entire field opened up by Freud's desire. But just as the speech of the unconscious refuses to be silenced by the discourse of the ego, the speech of Jesus continues to resonate with an undeniable force in and beyond the religious discourses that attempt to contain and make sense of it.

As a counterexample of this silencing of the subject, we have the extraordinary phenomenon of *Moses and Monotheism*, where Freud becomes the "enemy" of his own people by dismantling the myth of Moses and revealing the founder of the religion to have been an Egyptian. Writing in 1939 during a period of institutionalized anti-Semitism, having himself fled Nazi persecution in Vienna, Freud opens the volume by writing: "To deny a people the man whom it praises as the greatest of its sons is not a deed to be undertaken lightheartedly—especially by one belonging to that people. No consideration, however, will move me to set aside truth in favor of supposed national interests" (*Moses* 3). While the Jews allow the wish for an omnipotent father figure and the myth of national "chosenness" to displace the memory of the man Moses, Freud combats the forces of repression by dredging up the subject whose desire caused anxiety. His exposure of the man behind the myth is a matter not of mere ideological unmasking, however, but of the extraction of the force of subjective desire from a legendary narrative whose function is to silence it by reinscribing it within a set of values and ideals. Freud supposes a subject of desire as the origin of a savoir, which the resulting text or legend attempts to repress or efface. In dismantling Moses as an ideal ego, Freud also allows the subject himself to speak.

Each of the examples I have discussed bears witness to the tension between the anxiety induced by desire and the effects it produces and the restorative tendency to silence or efface that desire and to shore up the ego. They also qualify the possible optimism about social change by reinforcing the extent to which this change occurs at an individual level, through a painstaking process of self-overcoming that is by no means certain and that only occurs in a small minority of cases. Religious history in particular suggests that it is much easier to hide behind the ideal ego or to take comfort in the illusion of the all-powerful father than to confront the Other's desire or absence. This is why psychoanalysis is ultimately pessimistic about the possibility of social change, and hesitates to affirm the social beyond the "minimal social link" inaugurated by the transference. If the members of the group do not also traverse castration, the anxiety that results from the confrontation with the Other's desire will simply provoke repression and violence, and not a change of position.

But while the desire of the founder may not be sufficient in and of itself to incite change, these examples also make clear that the anxiety it induces can have a transformative effect. This is because it exposes the profound freedom of an act founded on desire, in and beyond the castration or lack it implies. Translated into a more existential idiom, my argument is really that anxiety is the affect of freedom. Desire is what is most free in the subject, because it involves a liberation from the fantasy of seduction and its particular colonization of the psychic object. Freud sees in Moses a free man, one who threw off the shackles of superstition and nature worship to create a space for the subject as something other than a product of nature or the object of a capricious deity. While Jewish legend promotes the idea that Moses is the chosen instrument of God, the much more interesting truth is that the man Moses invents something new for civilization: something we can all draw upon, and that no God can take away. The difference between ideals and desire is the difference between ascribing freedom to an omnipotent God and assuming responsibility for that freedom oneself. In the same way, Freud himself will attempt to free the subject of the unconscious from the shackles of morality, and to prevent its reduction to an object of scientific observation. But he makes clear that this freedom can only come through traversing anxiety and not avoiding it. It is a difficult freedom, whose stakes are nowhere better expressed than in the words imputed to Jesus: "I lay down my life in order to take it up again." While these words have been interpreted by many as a promise of eternal life, I believe that the anxiety and solitude with which Jesus approaches his own death point to a more difficult interpretation. His act emphasizes that there is something more than "mere life," and that desire opens onto a life that can only be accessed by traversing death. In a similar vein, the practice of psychoanalysis is founded on the supposition that true freedom comes only from traversing the death drive and not repressing or avoiding it.

* * *

In the introduction to his seminar on the transference, Lacan writes that the fundamental question of psychoanalysis is "how to operate honestly with desire . . . how to preserve desire in the act. Ordinarily, the act is the extinction rather than the realization of desire, or at best nothing more than its exploit or heroic gesture. How then can we preserve a simple relation between desire and this act?"[43] The murder of Moses and the betrayal of Jesus are examples of acts that extinguish desire. But so, arguably, is any act that finds its value merely in the affirmation of an ideal.

If Freud's relation to Moses is so provocative where the question of desire is concerned, it is because it takes the form not merely of an interpretation, but of a response to the desire of Moses that finds expression in an act. It could be argued that Freud responds to the desire of Moses precisely by inventing psychoanalysis, as a structuration of the social link that puts lack at the center by underscoring the Other's absence. It is an invention that responds to *his* age, the age of the foreclosure of the subject from the empirical sphere of science.

Freud invents a mechanism that allows the analysand to free himself by confronting castration. But the end of analysis could be construed not merely as a liberation, but as a call to change the world by demanding that it make way for a new object. It involves the assumption of the truth that there is no object for desire, but more importantly the necessity of constructing a new object: if there is no object or aim that would satisfy desire, this also means that desire is not bound by any existing object, and is therefore innately transcendent. The logical conclusion of an analysis supposes that desire finds expression in an act, or in the production of a new object that intervenes in the world so as to transform it.

Where the question of social change is concerned, the three examples I have discussed are linked by the fact that this object takes the form of a new structuration of the social tie that creates a space for the subject, rather than silencing or repressing it. In Lacan's reading of the Hebrew Decalogue, his implicit thesis is that Moses invents the symbolic as a creative structuration of the absent Other that allows for the possibility of desire by introducing a gap in the world of natural existence. Moses' innovation is having carved out a space for the subject, negating "what is" in order to open up a space where sublimation is possible, where the subject can exercise reason in the pursuit of justice and truth. His legacy takes the form of a structure or an institution, the Jewish law and the practices of interpretation and debate that encourage spirituality and sublimation. The legacy of Jesus, on the other hand, is a legacy of revolutionary social transformation. If Jesus functions, as I suggest, like an analyst, one could argue that the constraint he imposes produces effects that spread out across history, inspiring the great revolutionary movements of the nineteenth and twentieth centuries in particular. His invocation of a "new kingdom" implies that the world is not a given, but something that must be created or transformed through love. In Freud's case, the invention of the transference could be understood as an attempt to give visibility to an impossible object, the subject that is neither a living organism nor a social construction, but a pure hypothesis sustained and given form by the desire of Freud.[44] But as Hallward reveals through the simple example of a man who clears space for a new soccer field, this new object need not be something so lofty. What is important is that it creates a space for the subject, a space that was not there before. The creation of this new object gives rise to social change without even aspiring to do so, because it is not guided by ideals or goals but by the desire of a subject.

PART 2

POLITICAL THEOLOGY AND THE QUESTION OF THE WRITTEN

3

WRESTLING WITH THE ANGEL

THE LEGAL THEORIST Pierre Legendre has argued that the Romano-Canonical legal traditions that form the foundations of Western jurisprudence "are founded in a discourse which denies the essential quality of the relation of the body to writing."[1] It emerges historically as a repudiation of Jewish legalism and Talmud law, where the rite of circumcision encodes the subject's entry into law as an "allegiance to the absolute Writing," or the "relationship between the human subject and the logical place of the Other" (110–11). In this shift, one understanding of writing is displaced by another: the material inscription of the letter, as an incommunicable limit or cut that defines the human being's relation to the Other of language, is supplanted by the fantasy of what Legendre calls a "living writing," a writing "in the heart" that promotes an ideal of perfect communication in which nothing is lost, in which meaning is lodged in an absolute Other who guarantees all knowledge.[2] In his words, "we belong to a culture in which a mystically alienated human body stands in the place of the absolute book. The state has emerged from this structure. . . . Its basic characteristics can be set out by means of a fundamental Romano-pontifical maxim: the Emperor carries all the archives in his breast (*omnia scrinia habet in pectore suo*)" (109).

The ultimate theological source of this Roman maxim is Paul's polemic against the Jewish law in the Epistle to the Romans. Paul's polemic is structured by a distinction between two orders of law: the "law of God" and the "law of sin." The first is associated with the intelligible "spirit" of the law, which is "written in the heart," and the second with the prescriptive "letter" of the Jewish law, which compromises or corrupts the first by binding it to a particular representation and consigning it to written form. Paul's solution is to bypass the law not merely in its imaginary or representative character, but as it is elaborated in language. The prescriptive "letter" of the Jewish law must be sublated by the law of the spirit, such that "we serve not under the old written code but in the new life of the Spirit" (Romans 7:6). Christ, as the living embodiment of the law of God, upholds the spirit of the law by "fulfilling"—and so rendering obsolete—its written form. Legendre sums up the logic implicit in the politico-theological conception of the act when he argues that Pauline Christianity, like the juridicism that emerges out of its melding with the Roman Empire, "is founded on an equivocation according to which the real and the symbolic would be one and the same category."[3]

The doctrine of Christ as the "living law" sustains what Legendre describes as a "banalization of writing" ("Masters" 111), a disregard for its material inscription that holds the letter to be nothing more than a place-holder, a flawed or incomplete representation of a meaning or truth that is itself beyond words. At the same time, it makes possible the legal and political fantasy of a living writing, located in a single body that is understood as the site of interpretive authority. The extraction of a meaning or truth from the intractable letter becomes the ultimate aim of the legal order and the loftiest task of its sovereign interpreter, who is uniquely charged with animating the dead letter. This notion permeates what Peter Goodrich describes as "the most standard protocols of legal reading," according to which "it is not the letter but the spirit that determines the meaning of the law":

> The text is composed of dead letters (*litera mortua*); the rule is no more than a "mute judge," a sleeping form, requiring the interposition, *anima*

legis, of jurist or judge. . . . The meaning of the law is internal to its living body, *viva vox iuris or lex loquens*, its image, interpreter, or legislator. In classical terms it is spelled out by reference to something beyond words: "to know the law is not to know the words of the law, but its force and power." In a renaissance formulation we are similarly told that "no words, forms, niceties, or propriety of language is of any regard in the Civil Law, in comparison to truth, faithfulness and integrity. For *verba menti, non verbis servire debet*; words are made as instruments to serve and express the mind, and not to command it."[4]

The forgoing of written laws and constraints in favor of an authority presented as antinomial to writing is an increasingly common phenomenon today, whose clearest expression is the resurgent political theology of decision that is a pervasive feature not only of modern politics, but of contemporary political theory and philosophy. In the modern era, this trajectory arguably achieves its fullest expression in the work of the conservative German jurist Carl Schmitt (considered in the next chapter), whose critique of normative law suggests that there is a "gap" in the law, which renders it incapable of addressing such threats to the legal order as revolution and the general strike. His *Political Theology* offers an account of the sovereign as the one who must on occasion suspend the written law so as to preserve the legal order (or the existence of the state as such), acting as the living embodiment of the state to decide on the exception in the absence of legal constraints. In this respect, the ultimate proof text for the strategy of exception is Paul's account of Christ as the "fulfillment of the law," the living logos who consigns the "old" written law to obsolescence, actualizing in his person the transcendent kingdom of God.

Paul's polemic is sustained not merely by the proponents of centralized power and consolidated interpretive authority, however. At the opposite end of the political spectrum, Alain Badiou, whose philosophy owes much to Marxist thought and to revolutionary and even anarchistic political practices (in other words, the very modes of political action Schmitt most fears as threats to state power), affirms Paul's polemic not as a proof text for sovereign authority, but as a message of subjective liberation from law.[5] He reads Paul's conversion experience as attesting to the liberatory potential of the "event," a decisive rupture with the normative worlds defined by Greek cosmology and Jewish ritual observance; it culminates in the production of a "New Man" who declares his emancipation from law and fidelity to a real that is beyond language and illegible to reason. Badiou's rigorously nonreligious reading of Paul's letters is in no way invested in promoting the resurrected Christ as a model of sovereign authority, or in reading the Gospels as a revealed truth. Nevertheless, its polemical confrontation between an exceptional event and a law understood as nothing more than a form of "enslavement" not only repeats the same familiar privileging of the "spirit" over the "letter," but gives new fuel to an already widespread disregard for the role of language in matters of law and politics.

Modern political and legal theory has arguably not surpassed the terms of Paul's polemic against the Mosaic law, with the result that the stakes of these terms and the specific understandings of the law to which they attest are rarely interrogated. Too often, we are left with a pejorative account of law as nothing more than a secondary representation or corrupting mediation of a force or authority, a simplistic and reductive view that is unable to acknowledge—much less account for—those functions of law that are not reducible to the communication of a message or meaning. What understandings of language and of writing—and of their relationship to the human subject—are promoted or repressed by the opposition of letter to spirit, norm to exception? When the function of law is reduced to normativity, what alternative approaches to law are lost or distorted in the process?

In the introduction I argued that the symbolic was irreducible to law, and claimed that to collapse the symbolic with law (and especially with norms) not only is highly misleading, but actually misses the very critique of law—in its normative *and* its superegoic or "real" dimensions—that the concept of the symbolic makes possible. In this section, I turn to the context of law in an attempt to elucidate its properly symbolic dimension.

In the juridical and political spheres, my claim is that the "experimental" dimension of the symbolic is exemplified by the structural role of the written law, as distinct from its principle or "spirit." I will begin by approaching it negatively, through a consideration of the displacement of the written law in the political-theological discourse of the "act" or "decision," as well as in contemporary theories of the "event" that could be understood as extensions of the same critical genealogy. From Paul to Schmitt to Badiou, the discourse of the decisive act is invariably structured as a polemic against writing, promoting a reductive understanding of the written law as nothing more than a "dead letter" or "rote norm" with respect to which the unscripted act, dictatorial decision, or explosive "event" represents the only possibility for a dynamic transformation of the situation. Through readings of a number of important legal and political theorists of the twentieth century, the next four chapters will question the lack of any serious meditation on the specificity of the *written* law in the pervasive critique of law as norm, and will attempt to elucidate a dimension of written law that is often overlooked: its function as constraint, which is irreducible—and in some cases even antinomial—to its function as a rule, or as the representation of an authority.

The Mosaic law (and Mosaic legal traditions more broadly) will continue to be important points of reference in this section, since they show this symbolic dimension of law to be inseparable from the formal and structural innovation implied in the advent of written law. In these chapters, however, my focus will shift away from the historical legacy of Moses in order to consider what I call the "practices of the letter" implied in Jewish legalism and the protocols and procedures that alternately develop or displace it in modern legal and political theory. In Talmudic legal traditions, law is viewed not as a description of an existing order or a representation of a lawgiving authority, but as a text whose meaning is uncertain.[6] Writing is understood not as a more or less transparent medium of communication, the bearer of a message that originates elsewhere, but as a form of inscription that implicates the subject in a process of interpretation determined from the outset as structurally incomplete. Fidelity to what Legendre terms the "absolute Writing" is thus a fidelity to the letter in its undecidable character, a writing that cannot be completed "spiritually." This fidelity to the letter of the text—and above all to a certain understanding of writing—is an important minor trend in legal theory, whose implications extend beyond the relatively narrow confines of Jewish and Islamic law. It is this precise conception of writing, I maintain, that is displaced by Paul's distinction between the "old written law" and the "new law of the spirit."

Let me begin, then, with a political-theological fable about the new law and what it consigns to obsolescence: Paul's interpellation by the voice of Christ on the road to Damascus. Why has this apocryphal story been of such decisive importance not only for the early appropriation of Paul within Romano-Canonical legal traditions, but also in modern political theory? My hypothesis is that it has to do with the spiritual authority assigned to the voice as the principle "behind" the law that at once fulfills it and renders it obsolete, both in Paul's letters and in his political and juridical reception. Significantly, however, this story is disseminated not by Paul himself (whose extant letters allude only indirectly to his conversion story), but by disciples of a later generation. As such, it arguably tells us more about the legendary importance of Paul for subsequent legal thought than it does about Paul himself. As many recent works on the subject have helped us to appreciate, there are other sides to the apostle:[7] the Paul who chides the Corinthians for succumbing to the "spiritualist" excesses of the *pneumatikoi* and for "speaking in tongues," who constantly emphasizes the importance of the literality of Jewish textual tradition, and who might even himself be understood as a proponent of a "constrained" relation to divine law, to which Immanuel Kant, among others, would be directly indebted.[8] While acknowledging that this other Paul exists, I want to focus here on the Paul that Western legalism canonizes, over and perhaps even against the intentions of the apostle himself.

THE ROAD TO DAMASCUS:
A POLITICAL-THEOLOGICAL FABLE

Of Paul's famous conversion on the road to Damascus, we have only the following apocryphal account from the Acts of the Apostles:

Now as he was going along and approaching Damascus, suddenly a light from heaven flashed around him. He fell to the ground and heard a voice saying to him, "Saul, Saul, why do you persecute me?" He asked, "Who are you, Lord?" The reply came, "I am Jesus, whom you are persecuting. But get up and enter the city, and you will be told what you are to do." The men who were traveling with him stood speechless because they had heard the voice but saw no one. Saul got up from the ground, and though his eyes were open, he could see nothing; so they led him by the hand and brought him into Damascus. For three days he was without sight, and neither ate nor drank.

(Acts 9:3–9)

Alain Badiou notes that after the event of Damascus, Paul turns away from "all authority other than that of the Voice that personally summoned him to his becoming-subject."[9] But what exactly does that Voice say? Although it does speak to him, it never transmits any specific directives or particular interpretation of the Gospel; it initiates a "conversion experience" that then follows its own course, unscripted: a difference both from the Hebrew prophets and from Moses, all of whom are conceived as mouthpieces for the speech of God.

What is the significance of this celebration of the fidelity to the Voice in the writings of Paul? The Voice that interpellates Paul on the road to Damascus, but also the inner voice of the Christian liberated from the law, the voice of freedom? In Paul's own discourse, it is opposed to Greek wisdom and to Jewish signs, and aligned with the mysterious "demonstration" of the spirit: "For Jews demand signs and Greeks desire wisdom, but we proclaim Christ crucified, a stumbling block [*skandalon*] to Jews and foolishness to Gentiles, but to those who are called, both Jews and Greeks, Christ the power of God and the wisdom of God" (1 Corinthians 1:22–24).

The authority of the Voice not only supercedes the articulations of prophecy or reason, however, but is itself strangely inarticulate. Consider this curious passage from the second letter to the Corinthians, where Paul speaks in the third person of his interpellation by the Voice: "I know a man in Christ who fourteen years ago was caught up to the third heaven—whether in the body or out of the body I do not know, God knows. And I know that this man was caught up into Paradise, . . . and he heard things that cannot be told, which man may not utter" (2 Corinthians 12:2–4). Paul does not hear—or at least cannot convey—*what* the Voice says to him, but only the *fact* that it calls upon him. What I want to consider here is the status of this authority of the Voice in Paul's discourse, and its relation to the problem of faith. Or, to put the question another way, what is at stake in Paul's insistence that the Jews open their ears to a Voice beyond the law? And why is the Jewish tradition unable, or unwilling, to hear this voice?

Emmanuel Lévinas, in an essay titled "The Pact," comments on a passage from the Babylonian Talmud that concerns the handing down of the law to the people of Israel. In this passage, the rabbis note that in the scene of law-giving reported in Deuteronomy 27, the Israelites are commanded not only to obey each individual interdiction of the Law, but to "uphold all the words of this Law" (Deuteronomy 27:26): that is, the Law taken in its entirety, or its general spirit.[10] Each law, therefore, has both a particular form and a general form. But why, Lévinas asks, does the law demand these two separate forms of adherence?

Can the adherence to the law as a whole, to its general tenor, be distinguished from the "yes" which is said to the particular laws it spells out? Naturally, there has to be a general commitment. The spirit in which a piece of legislation is made has to be understood. . . . For there to be true inner adherence, this process of generalization is indispensable. But why is it necessary to distinguish between this knowledge of the general spirit, and the knowledge of its particular forms of expression? Because we cannot understand the spirit of any legislation without acknowledging the laws it contains. There are two distinct procedures, and the distinction is justified from several particular points of view. Everyone responds to the temptation to encapsulate Judaism in a few "spiritual" principles. Everyone is seduced by what might be called the *angelic essence of the Torah*, to which many verses and commandments can be reduced. This "internalization" of the Law enchants our liberal souls and we are inclined to reject anything which seems to resist the "rationality" or the "morality" of the Torah.

(219)

Although the name of Paul never appears in it, this passage seems to engage with Paul's polemic not only in questioning the reduction of the law to its "spirit" (in the "temptation to encapsulate Judaism in a few 'spiritual' principles," it is hard not to hear an allusion to Jesus' celebrated reduction of the Ten Commandments to the principle of love,[11] the proof text for Paul's critique of the literality of Jewish law), but also in its affirmation of the very reasoning that Paul criticizes under the joint headings of "Greek wisdom" and "Jewish signs." However, this inattention to anything like the Voice is crucial to Lévinas's reading.

He notes that "Judaism has always been aware . . . of elements within it which cannot be immediately internalized. Alongside the *mishpatim*, the laws that we can all recognize as just, there are the *hukkim*, those unjustifiable laws in which Satan delights when he mocks the Torah" (219): the ritual of the red heifer, the arcane alimentary prohibitions, and even the act of circumcision itself. But despite their absurdity, Lévinas argues that we cannot dismiss these sometimes incomprehensible adherences as unnecessary or irrelevant compared to the general adherence to the "spirit" of the law. This is because the letter of the law offers a necessary check on what he calls the "angelic essence" of the Law, its purely spiritual dimension.

JACOB'S STRUGGLE WITH THE ANGEL

Lévinas then glosses the biblical story of Jacob's struggle with the angel (Genesis 32)[12] as a cautionary tale about the dangers of succumbing too readily to the "angelism" of the Law. He writes:

There is a constant struggle within us between our two adherences; to the spirit and to what is known as the letter. Both are equally indispensable, which is why two separate acts are discerned in the acceptance of the Torah. Jacob's struggle with the Angel has the same meaning: the overcoming, in the existence of Israel, of the angelism or other-worldliness of pure interiority. Look at the effort with which this victory is won! But is it really won? There is no victor. And when the Angel's clasp is released it is Jacob's religion which remains, a little bruised.

(220)

The angel represents "spirit." But it also represents the lure of "pure interiority," of an identification with the Law in which it would cease to be other. Thus it is important to Lévinas's reading that the being with whom Jacob wrestles is not God, as Jacob himself believes, but an angel. As a "purely spiritual being," the angel is a "principle of generosity, but no more than a principle. Of course, generosity demands an adherence. But the adherence to a principle is not enough; it brings temptation with it, and requires us to be wary and on our guard" (220). What, exactly, is the temptation? That general principles, and even generous principles, can be inverted in the course of their application. As he puts it, "all generous thought is threatened by its own Stalinism" (220).

This threat is acknowledged in the rabbis' creation of the oral law, or Talmud. According to Lévinas, the oral law "is concerned with the passage from the principle embodied in the Law to its possible execution, its concrete effects. If this passage were simply deducible, the Law, in its particular form, would not have demanded a separate adherence" (220). Talmudic casuistry "tries to identify the precise moment when the general principle is at risk of turning into its opposite; it surveys the general from the standpoint of the particular"; in this way, says Lévinas, it "preserves us from ideology" (220). In short, "the Talmud is the struggle with the Angel" (220): the struggle not to "recognize" the angel, or not to presume one is familiar with its essence. But at the same time, it is the admonition to struggle against a danger that presents itself under the guise of generosity, and perhaps even love.

Jean-François Lyotard suggests that Paul interrupts this struggle with his appeal to the mystery of the incarnation: "The Word was made flesh and came among us: is this not to announce that the Voice voices itself by itself, and to say that it asks not so much to be scrupulously examined, interpreted, understood and acted so as to make justice reign, but loved?"[13] The struggle that defines Jewish ethics is inverted, such that it is no longer the "angelism" of the voice one must struggle against, but the letter of the law that limits its euphoric insistence. The voice demands not to be examined and acted, but "loved."

What, then, is the meaning of the "freedom" Paul proclaims, a freedom revealed to him by the Voice? On the one hand, it involves a freedom *from the Law* in its proscriptive formulations, while on the other it implies an identification with a principle *behind* the law that both fulfills it and renders it obsolete.

In this sense Paul is very much the ancestor of Kant, since, as Hannah Arendt observes, "Kant's spirit demands that man go beyond the mere call of obedience and identify his own will with the principle behind the law—the source from which the Law sprang."[14] In Kant, as in Paul, this "principle" is closely linked to the voice (or what Kant calls the "voice of conscience"), which acts as a moral compass for the subject in the absence of any recourse to positive or prescriptive laws. But they are also quite different, in that for Kant this "inner voice" is the voice of practical reason, while for Paul it is the voice of divine revelation. As he writes in the first epistle to the Corinthians,

> "What no eye has seen, nor ear heard, nor the heart of man conceived, what God has prepared for those who love him," God has revealed to us through the Spirit. . . . And we impart this in words not taught by human wisdom, but taught by the Spirit, interpreting spiritual truth to those who possess the Spirit. The unspiritual man does not receive the gifts of the Spirit of God, for they are folly to him, and he is not able to understand them because they are spiritually discerned. The spiritual man judges all things, but is himself to be judged by no one.
>
> (1 Corinthians 2:9–10, 13–15)

In Paul's claim that the mystery can only be "discerned spiritually," without ever passing through speech, we see the insistence of what Lévinas calls the "angelism" of the law, which appeals to a spiritual principle "behind" the law that underlies—but also supersedes—its authority. As Lyotard argues, "neither Jewish signs nor Greek proofs will be offered. Every intermediary is bypassed. You will hear the incarnation only if the incarnated Voice speaks to *you*, speaks through you, in you" (*The Hyphen* 23).

Mladen Dolar, in *A Voice and Nothing More*, notes that while a long tradition of ethical reflection has taken as its guideline the "voice of conscience," its invocation tends to bring with it an implicit opposition between, on the one hand, "the voice, its pure injunction, its imperative resonance," and, on the other, "discursivity, argument, particular prescriptions or prohibitions or moral judgments."[15] Implied in this figure is thus

> a certain view of morality where the signifying chain cannot be sustained by itself; it needs a footing, an anchorage, a root in something which is not a signifier. Ethics requires a voice, but a voice which ultimately does not say anything, being by virtue of that all the louder, an absolute convocation which one cannot escape. . . . The voice appears as the non-signifying, meaningless foundation of ethics. But what kind of foundation? If it is conceived as the divine voice—infallible because divine, and thus a firm guarantee—then it would turn into a positivity which would relegate the subject to a passive stance of carrying out orders—a pitfall one can avoid only if one conceives the voice as a pure call which commands nothing and offers no guarantee.
>
> (A Voice 98)

In Kant's account of the moral law, the "voice of conscience" is the voice of practical reason, and thus the voice of an ethical call that is not only without specific content, but without any external guarantee. As such, it "implies a dimension of the Other which offers no guarantee and circumscribes its lack" (101). But when the voice is conceived as "divine" and therefore infallible, it takes on a substantiality—and is invested with a demand—that is lacking in the "ethical voice" of practical reason. Psychoanalysis identifies this insistent, positivized voice with the psychical agency of the superego, that source of demanding and sometimes cruel injunctions and imperatives that is not only endowed with a voice (the "inner voice" of conscience), but itself derived from "things heard": in Freud's words, "it is as impossible for the super-ego as for the ego to disclaim its origin from things heard [*seine Herkunft aus Gehörtem*]" (cited in *A Voice* 99). This is why Lacan stresses that "the superego, in its intimate imperative, is indeed 'the voice of conscience,' that is, a voice first and foremost, a vocal one at that, and without any authority other than that of being a loud voice [*sans plus d'autorité que d'être la grosse voix*]."[16] The authority of this "loud voice" (*grosse voix*, literally "fat voice") inheres not in what it says, but in the demand implicit in the vacancy of an enunciation without statement, a vocality not limited by or inscribed in speech.

Juliet Flower MacCannell explores the consequences of this superegoic vocality in a reading of Adolf Eichmann, the architect of Hitler's Final Solution, who claimed to be guided in his moral conduct by Kant's categorical imperative. Developing Hannah Arendt's insight into Eichmann's professed "Kantianism,"[17] MacCannell suggests that the "principle behind the law" with which he identified was not practical reason, but the will of the Führer, incarnated in his voice.[18] She assimilates his position to the structure of perversion, which Lacan defines as "a response . . . to the jouissance of the Other as *voice*, rather than to the Other as *speech*" (69). For Lacan, speech is defined classically as the field of the symbolic pact, "the social contract that divides us from each other as mutual aggressors" (69). But "*Voice* is already *object a*; the embodiment or bearer of a 'principle behind the law.' It took shape in Lacan's discourse as one of the four fundamental *objects a* (gaze, voice, breast, feces) around which the fantasy that structures drive circulates" (70). Whereas speech, as the field of the signifier, works to limit the deadly enjoyment that insists within fantasy by erecting barriers against it, the Voice is the bearer of that jouissance: hence Lacan's description of the voice as an "object fallen from the organ of speech,"[19] the material support of the superego that takes shape in demand. MacCannell sees Eichmann as a subject who has decided to forgo this symbolic mediation, identifying his own "voice of conscience" with the "will" materialized in the Führer's voice, above and beyond the specific orders and directives he issues.

When Lacan remarks that "the superego is at the same time the law and its destruction,"[20] he suggests how his analysis of the voice as the support of the superego might relate not only to the Kantian moral law, but to Freud's totemic myth. "In this underside of the law," writes Dolar,

> we can hear an echo of the primal father, the shadow of which would always follow and haunt the law. If in Freud's scenario the law was instituted by the murder of the primal father, if it was the law of the dead father, that is, of his name, then the trouble is that the father was never quite dead—he survived as the voice (this was the function of the shofar). The voice appears as the part of the father which is not quite dead; it evokes the figure of enjoyment, and thus adumbrates the slide to the destruction of the law based on his name.
>
> (101–2)

The voice of the primal father is the "source" of law, the ground of an unlimited authority that the law in its function as pact was supposed to defend against by debarring the exceptional jouissance that defined the father's position with respect to the brothers of the horde. In substituting the law of the father's name for this unlimited authority (of which the father's voice might be the ultimate embodiment), the Mosaic law made the father's death or absence—and thus the quieting or withdrawal of that voice—the condition of the symbolic order of law.

In his seminar on anxiety Lacan offers an extended reading of the shofar, the ram's horn whose singular blast is sounded whenever it is a matter of renewing the covenant with God, not only in the historical narratives of the Bible, but also at festivals of remembrance and solemn moments of judgment.[21] Its function, he suggests, is to "model the site of our anxiety" with respect to the Other (*L'angoisse* 320), and thereby present the voice in an exemplary form that reveals its function as an essential object of fantasy. What provokes anxiety is that the "voice" is without content; it does not demand or prescribe. As the "affect that corresponds to the desire of the Other," anxiety confronts us with the unknowability of the Other's desire, the lack (of presence, of authority, of demand, and so on) implied in the law of the father's name. In the last chapter, I referenced Lacan's analysis of the Hebraic religion as concerned with "the desire of a God who is the God of Moses" (*Television* 90), a desire that differs from demand in confronting the adherents of the religion with a lack in the Other that cannot be satisfied and thus with the necessity of assuming responsibility for their acts. In Lacan's reading, the function of the shofar is to be understood against this background. The anxiety provoked by this disembodied "voice" presents the Israelites with a choice: are they going to live with the unknowability of God's desire and the responsibility it implies, or will they choose instead to "respond" to the voice, to substantialize it as demand, or even to make sacrifices to it in order to not confront this desire? When he describes sacrifice as a "specific response to the anxiety provoked by the voice as object a" (*Television* 85), Lacan suggests that the compulsion to sacrifice should be understood not as a demand imposed by an all-powerful God, but as a refusal of the lack in the Other that attributes an insatiable demand to the Other so as not to confront its inconsistency.

The crucial point is that the domain of ethics confronts us with what Dolar calls *enunciation without a statement*, that is, the voice understood not merely as enunciation *in excess* of statement, its material support or invisible internal surplus, but as not bound to a statement and the signifying order it supposes. When enunciation is severed from statement altogether (as in the case of Eichmann), we veer in the direction of the superego and its unlimited injunctions. In contrast, Kant shows us the difference between a voice completely severed from speech and an ethical voice that, while "empty" in the sense of preceding any possible statement, nonetheless necessitates a continuation in speech. In Dolar's words,

The voice is enunciation, and we have to supply the statement ourselves. The moral law is like a suspended sentence, a sentence left in suspense, confined to pure enunciation, but a sentence demanding a continuation, a sentence to be completed by the subject, by his or her moral decision, by the act. The enunciation is there, but the subject has to deliver the statement and thus assume the enunciation, respond to it and take it on his or her shoulders. The voice does not command or prohibit, but it nonetheless necessitates a continuation, it compels a sequel.

(98–99)

Kant listens to a voice that is situated "beyond the law," in the sense that it is not limited by positive prescriptions, but it is nonetheless not antithetical to speech. To the contrary, the voice must be voiced in speech. The moral imperative supposes that the subject complete the enunciation (in the form of the moral maxim he authors himself), and above all that he assume responsibility for it in the absence of any guarantee. It supposes the lack of any guarantor or source for the moral imperative other than the subject him or herself. The Kantian "voice of conscience" is not a fantasy object, therefore, but something already belonging to speech, "circumscribing its lack" in Dolar's formulation. (Here it is worth noting that Eichmann, despite his professed Kantianism, never actually formulates a moral maxim. In Arendt's words, the implicit imperative guiding his conduct is to "act in such a way that the Führer, if he knew of your action, might approve it" [*Eichmann* 136], a "maxim" that substitutes the superegoic demands imputed to another person for the voice of reason. It is not an instance of the moral law, therefore, but an abdication of the responsibility it requires.)[22]

In the Hebraic legal traditions to which Lévinas refers, the responsibility to "complete the enunciation" is the responsibility implied in the literal practices that found the study of Talmud, which require the subject to take upon himself the act of enunciation. If the "angelism" of the law—its "spirit" or voice—is for Lévinas a *part* of the law, but no more than a part, it is because the subject must take upon himself the responsibility for deciphering it in the absence of any guarantee.[23]

It is no doubt significant that Lévinas's reading of the angelism of the law appears in a commentary on a Talmud passage concerning the handing down of the law at Sinai, which implies a very different conception of the Voice than we find in Paul, one that explicitly stresses its violent or superegoic character. In his commentary on the Hebrew Decalogue, which is introduced by the verse "and God spoke all of these words [all together]" (Exodus 20:1), the medieval French rabbi Rashi suggests that the voice of God took the form of a single, terrifying utterance,[24] so unbearable that the people of Israel begged Moses to shield them from God's voice by speaking the commandments for them, mediating its awesome force.[25] This gloss contests the stock reading according to which Judaism is marked by the tragedy of God's absence, the withdrawal of his living voice from the "dead" letter of the law. Rashi makes clear that the Israelites' relation to God is marked by a profound dread of the unmediated voice, and not simply by the mourning of a lost presence or plenitude. He suggests that Hebraic legalism responds to that voice not only by calling upon the human subject to "supply the statement" in the form of a spoken enunciation, but through recourse to the symbolic *limits* implied in speech, and writing in particular.

Lacan expresses something similar in his own reading of the Ten Commandments, which he understands precisely as a writing—and thus as a committing to the order of speech or language—of what the superegoic voice of God transmits only as an inchoate noise or murmur.

In his words, the "loud voice" (*grosse voix*) of the superego is "the voice that at least one text in the Bible tells us was heard by the people parked around Mount Sinai. This artifice even suggests that its enunciation echoed back to them their own murmur, the Tables of the Law being nonetheless necessary in order for them to know what it enunciated. Now, for those who know how to read, what is written on those tables is nothing but the laws of Speech itself."[26] The Tables of the Law (which importantly are inscribed by the human hand of Moses) constitute the enunciation lacking in the voice itself, and thus the emergence of a symbolic dimension of law that is limited by what can be articulated in speech. The written laws of speech do not simply allow the Israelites to "know what the voice enunciated," however, but to quiet—or at least to hold at a distance—the "loud voice" that in its superegoic materiality enunciates nothing in particular, only a pure demand. If the commandments are the "very laws of speech," it is because the condition sine qua non of speech is "distance between the subject and *das Ding*,"[27] the fantasy object (of which the voice is one of the most important exemplars) that gives consistency to the Other's will or jouissance. (If for Lacan speech as pact is understood as a protection against violence, this development suggests that what it defends against is not only the possible aggression of other people—the neighbor who might covet my goods or the criminal who might make an attempt on my life—but the aggression of the Voice itself.)

In some respects Paul is recognizably the heir of this tradition. His criticism of the Corinthians' attraction to the phenomenon of "speaking in tongues," for example, attests to a suspicion of any vocality that is not inscribed in speech or argument, and its potential to lead the young spiritual community away from the core tenets of Christ's Gospel. Paul's response to the "voice of conscience" diverges from Eichmann's not only in avoiding a complete surrender to the authority of the superego (even if those elements are arguably also present in his discourse, and notably in the anti-Semitism that is the inescapable underside of his "new covenant"), but in giving rise to new institutions, to new spiritual practices, and perhaps most importantly to his commitment to transcribe his fidelity to the Voice in writing, to transmit it in the form of open, public letters to the members of the new communities that spring up in response to the Gospel. His relation to the voice is therefore extremely complex: on the one hand, it is constrained by writing, has a public address, and even seeks to circumscribe the lure of an irrational "spiritualism"; and on the other, it develops a vengeful and persecutory relation to Judaism and to the letter of the law.

But while Paul himself may not *speak* in tongues, he does claim to *hear* the substantial and positivized voice that the Jewish law displaces. When Freud argues that Paul's gospel of salvation represents the ultimate culmination of the totemic trajectory resulting from the father's murder, in which the murdered father reasserts his rights by appearing unambiguously as omniscient and omnivoyant, he suggests that the "voice of conscience" resurfaces in Christianity in a particularly invasive form, explicitly identified with divine omnipotence. As Paul's polemic makes clear, it also represents the repeal of law in its dimension as speech or pact. If in the Hebraic tradition the voice of conscience is simultaneously committed to words and held at bay in its superegoic force by the foregrounding of the letter at the expense of the voice, that superegoic dimension is arguably what resurfaces with Paul's proclamation of the letter's obsolescence, and the return of the Thing itself in the form of the living Voice.

The "distance" between the law and its object that Lacan sees as the condition of speech is precisely what Paul complains of, in his notorious argument that to live under the law is to live with the impossibility of ever fulfilling the law, since one would have to fulfill the precepts in their entirety, something the flesh can never do (Galatians 3:10). But what is behind this impulse to "fulfill" the law, or more properly the voice that both grounds and destroys it? While Kant listens to a voice that is situated "beyond the law" but that is nonetheless not antithetical to speech, Paul attunes his ear to a Voice *beyond* speech, a voice whose call is never expressed discursively as an argument or prescription, and is therefore not limited by the word. It does not call upon the subject to supply the enunciation, as in Kant's moral philosophy, but rather demands its fidelity or allegiance.

Paul, we will recall, claims that the spiritual man "judges all things, but is himself to be judged by no one." From what exactly does he escape judgment, then? Of course the spiritual man is not subject to the judgment of the law, which is wielded by those who are "jealous" of his freedom. This is not just a matter of getting off without judgment, however. The cost of eluding judgment by the law is *profoundly delivering himself over to the violence of the Other*, in the form of the absolute authority of the Voice. As Paul says again and again, "I was freed to the law so that I might become a slave to Christ" (Romans 6; see also Romans 1:1; 1 Corinthians 9:16–18). After the event of Damascus, the Acts of the Apostles attributes to Jesus the words: "I myself will show him how much he must suffer for the sake of my name" (Acts 9:16). Slavoj Žižek has argued that the most horrifying, superegoic dimension of God is witnessed not in Judaism, as is often maintained, but in Christian love itself.[28] Remarkably, Paul makes exposure to this superegoic violence the very basis of ethics, identifying not simply a hermeneutic error or a lack of faith but a severe ethical failing or cowardice in the refusal to open oneself to the Voice, not just in its love, but in its violence. Perhaps this is what Lacan meant when he said that "Christianity ended up inventing a God who enjoys,"[29] a God of limitless jouissance. Israel, on the other hand, is not always eager to surrender to this enjoyment. As Rashi makes clear, she has reservations about exposing herself to the "love" of God without any protections, an insight that casts in a different light the stakes of the Jewish law and the nature of its own violence.

In a provocative essay on the problem of sacrifice, Frank Vande Veire notes that one of the core innovations of early Judaism with respect to its antecedents was the shift from ritual human sacrifice to law-based observance, whose biblical proof text is God's intercession on behalf of Isaac at the moment when Abraham prepares to kill his son.[30] But the corollary of this shift, he claims, is that it is no longer possible to manage divine terror: God cannot be seduced or appeased with gifts. The result is a "spiritualization" of sacrifice, which now takes the form of unconditional respect for the law. In this sense, he argues, the nonsacrifice of Isaac corresponds to a demand for totally uneconomic, unconditional sacrifice, a sacrifice that can be required at any moment, without advance warning. He cites as an example the infamous episode from the Book of Exodus where God, after having called Moses to be his prophet, suddenly decides to kill him. Moses is saved only by the ingenious ruse of his wife Zipporah, who quickly circumcises their infant son and touches the bloody foreskin to Moses' "feet" (his own genitals), in effect circumcising him by proxy and so warding off the demonic attack (Exodus 4:24–26). Vande Veire interprets the impromptu circumcision as a reminder that God can strike at any time with his insatiable demands. In this reading, the act of circumcision is less a protection against divine terror than an extension of it, a mark of the Israelites' profound subjection to the destructive force of divine wrath.

I would interpret this episode differently. For me it is the passage that best expresses the stakes of circumcision in the Mosaic tradition; it is a barrier *against* the deity that is intimately related to the function of speech as a limit against the Voice. The act of circumcision is not just a submission to the deity's exorbitant demands, but a talismanic protection against them. It is a purely symbolic sacrifice that is ultimately rather modest, and serves to ward off something more radical. Having verified Moses' circumcision, God is no longer at liberty to strike against the mere mortal who stands helpless before him; he cannot go on to demand an arm, a leg, and so forth. As the act that seals the covenant with God, circumcision is not just a demand imposed from without, but a pact. Most obviously, it is a mark of election that identifies the subject of the covenant as under God's protection. But more importantly, it protects its subject against the unmediated wrath of God himself.[31] Israel's covenant with God is a mutually binding contract, one that commits both parties to certain obligations with respect to each other (although there is no denying, as Vande Veire rightly observes, that those obligations are asymmetrical, and that God has a pretty open-ended time frame in which to make good on his promises). In this sense the law limits the satisfaction not only of the subject who submits to it, but of the deity himself.

In contrast, consider the notion of "sinning in the heart" elaborated in Jesus' Sermon on the Mount (Matthew 5), which holds that to think lustful thoughts about another woman is already to commit adultery, even in the absence of an adulterous act. In this logic, it is no longer possible to fulfill the law simply by not transgressing it, or by avoiding the object it designates as abject. As a result, the law loses its function as a protective barrier. The difference between the two ethics can best be illustrated by reference to the commandment against lying, or "bearing false witness." Lacan famously suggests that this may be the cruelest commandment of all, because the subject is potentially inseparable from the ability to lie.[32] But if there is a commandment against lying, it is because, in the context of Hebraic law, it is *possible* to lie; in Judaism there is no supposition of divine omniscience. When Jesus introduces the notion of sinning in the heart, and thus the transparency of the heart to God, he suggests that it is no longer possible even to lie. In the process, he lifts the barrier *against* the deity that is so central to Judaism.[33]

The Gospel of John famously asserts that Christ "dwells in us" (John 1:14). While Christian doctrine tends to emphasize the positive side of this cohabitation (the Christian is not alone, is redeemed from his fallen state, and so on), it also introduces an ominous new possibility, one markedly absent in Judaism: the subject's radical exposure to invasion by the deity. In this sense, the psychotic Dr. Schreber's fantasy of being anally raped by

God is not so much a delusional departure from the logic of Christianity as an intuition of the superegoic violence implicit in the intimate relationship between God and man.[34]

For Badiou, the message of Paul's gospel is that "we *can* overcome our impotence, and rediscover what the law has separated us from."[35] This reading posits the Jewish law as one in which the subject is impotent with respect to the all-powerful Other. But what it does not acknowledge is that this impotence is itself a kind of potency (or at least possibility), in that it carves out a space in which the subject can live by limiting—and thus rendering "impotent"—the Other itself. In other words, what the Mosaic law has "separated us from" is not merely the object that would "complete" or fulfill us, but the superegoic jouissance of the Other.

VOICE AND THE PERSECUTION OF THE LETTER

Paul's treatment of the law really casts a new light on the problem of the pact as a protection against this violence. The stakes of this position become clear in his reversal of the attitude toward the law implied in Jacob's struggle with the angel, a reversal whose implications are far-reaching and sometimes contradictory. I wonder whether Jacob's struggle with the angel is not in some way already implied or encrypted in the event of Damascus, as a heritage it both alludes to and displaces. On the road to Damascus, Paul, like Jacob, is waylaid by the angel of the Lord. Both men are traveling alone in anticipation of a possible confrontation: Jacob with his brother Esau, and Paul with the Christian converts of Damascus. In both cases, the divine intervention results in a wound: Jacob is made lame, and Paul is temporarily blinded. Both men are renamed. And both events result in new covenants: the naming of Israel as the heir to Abraham's promise, and the "new covenant" with the Gentiles that will become Paul's special mission.

The two episodes are almost diametrically opposed, however, in their subjective and hermeneutic implications. In the Jacob story, the renaming that follows the struggle gives birth to the nation of Israel, whose name is traditionally interpreted in one of two ways: "the one who strives with God" or "God strives." Their struggle results in a mutual wounding, in which each strives against and marks the other without managing to prevail over him. Their parting at dawn is really a kind of "mutual nonaggression treaty" in which blessings are exchanged as part of a pact. Significantly, however, the story Lévinas reads as an allegory of the transmission of the law is also a narrative that produces a law: one of the *hukkim*, or "unjustifiable laws," concerning the taboo against eating the sciatic muscle of the hip where Jacob is marked by his opponent. In this sense it also concerns the dangers inherent in trying to "digest" the law, to presume to internalize its spirit.[36] The taboo is a reminder that the encounter with the Other causes the subject to lose some part of himself, the attribution of the name causing something of his being to fall under erasure. Yet in delivering the wound, the angel is also checked, and so made to confess its limitations.[37] The contest is abandoned at the break of dawn, without either party managing to prevail decisively over the other.

The scene of Paul's conversion both recalls and displaces the Genesis story. Paul is stricken with blindness only to be filled with "vision," wounded only to be made whole again. If for Lévinas it is Jacob's "religion" that emerges from the struggle, a little bit wounded, here it is Paul's faith that emerges, whole and intact. Whereas Jacob struggles with an opponent who delivers his blessings without revealing his name or his character, Paul's revelation is complete. Jesus reveals himself to Paul as the living word of God; the voice speaks to him and to him alone, calling him into being out of nothingness. As he tells the Corinthians, "by the grace of God I am who I am" (1 Corinthians 15:10). The vision on the road to Damascus is not the reaffirmation of an existing pact, but a violent rupture: it marks the birth of Paul out of the ashes of Saul, but it also gives rise to Christianity as a displacement and erasure of the Jewish tradition. It represents the overturning of the struggle implied in Israel's relation to the law, in which that struggle is put to rest "once and for all" (Hebrews 10:10) by the advent of the Voice. In the words "why do you persecute me?" it seems that Paul hears a call to end not only the persecution of the Voice, but also the struggle against it.

Paul's polemic does not end there, however. His reading of faith invites not only the "Stalinism" inherent in listening only to the "angelism" of the law, but also a turning of that angelism *against* the Jews. Recall that the Voice that interpellates Paul on the road to Damascus is credited with only one specific enunciation, the question "why are you persecuting me?" It seems to me that Paul understands that question, at least initially, as follows: *Why are you, Saul the Jew, persecuting me, the living Voice, the resurrection, with the Law, the dead letter?* When Paul the Christian invents figural reading, the Voice insists in a new way, in the form of a voice not voiced, with a new question: *Why are you not persecuting the Jews* instead *of me?* Even as it cries out against its own persecution, the Voice demands a sacrifice.[38]

In Augustine's reading of the Jacob story in *City of God*, the angel, understood to be Christ himself, wounds the Jews but spares the Christians. He writes:

> This angel obviously presents a type of Christ. For the fact that Jacob "prevailed over" him (the angel, of course, being a willing loser to symbolize the hidden meaning) represents the passion of Christ, in which the Jews seemed to prevail over him. And yet Jacob obtained a blessing from the very angel whom he had defeated; thus the giving of the name was the blessing. Now "Israel" means "seeing God";[39] and the vision of God will be the reward of all the saints at the end of the world. Moreover, the angel also touched the apparent victor on the broad part of his thigh, and thus made him lame. And so the same man, Jacob, was at the same time blessed and lame—blessed in those who among this same people of Israel have believed in Christ, and crippled in respect of those who do not believe. For the broad part of the thigh represents the general mass of the race. For in fact it is to the majority of that stock that the prophetic statement applies, "They have limped away from their paths."[40]

For Augustine, the Christian is above all the one for whom "wounding" is no longer necessary, because Christ has taken the wound upon himself, "being the willing loser" to assume—and thus preempt—their wounds. For the Jews, however, the angel of God becomes an avenging angel, the angel of the apocalypse. Those who lack faith will be wounded, disinherited, and condemned to slavery.

This reference to Augustine is not as much of a digression as it might appear, since its proof text is Paul's typological reading of Hagar and Sarah as representing the distinction between the "Jerusalem of the flesh," in slavery with her children, and the "Jerusalem above," born free through the promise (Galatians 4:22–31). Paul's reading of the Abraham saga is structured by two oppositions: slavery and freedom, and faith and works. But perhaps more fundamental, and much less commented on, is another opposition, which is implied but never stated directly: faith and *doubt*. Consider Paul's synopsis for the Romans of Genesis 17, where God promises Abraham that he and his barren wife will have a child through the covenant:

> He *did not weaken in faith* when he considered his own body, which was already as good as dead (for he was about a hundred years old), or when he considered the barrenness of Sarah's womb. *No distrust made him waver* concerning the promise of God, but he grew strong in his faith as he gave glory to God, being *fully convinced* that God was able to do what he had promised. That is why his faith was "reckoned to him as righteousness."
>
> (Romans 4:19–22, my emphases)

In the text of Genesis, however, Abraham greets God's words very differently: "Abraham fell upon his face and laughed, and said to himself, 'Can a child be born to a man who is a hundred years old?'" (Genesis 17:17). When the same promise is made to Sarah in the following chapter, the same incredulous laughter erupts once more. Now, this laughter has been interpreted in many ways.[41] But it would be difficult, I think, to read it as an expression of simple faith. Certainly the God of Genesis does not read it that way. Immediately following Sarah's outburst, he says to Abraham, "Why did Sarah laugh, and say, 'Shall I indeed bear a child, now that I am old? Is anything too wonderful for the LORD?'" At these words, the text reads, "Sarah denied, saying 'I did not laugh,' for she was afraid." To which God replies, "Oh yes, you did laugh" (Genesis 18:13–14).[42]

God clearly reads the laughter as a sign of doubt or disbelief. But importantly, he does not punish it. His rebuke of Sarah is more comical than truly stern, anticipating the patience and even fondness with which he will later entertain Abraham's doubts when he questions the soundness of making the righteous few of Sodom and Gomorrah perish with the sinners. So why, for Paul, must this doubting laughter be foreclosed? I think it is because Abraham's distrust of the words of God introduces the possibility that the Voice itself might be castrated, that in having to pass through the signifier it must necessarily lose something of his power. In this sense, Augustine's characterization of the Jew's lack of belief as a "wound" is a displacement, where what must not be acknowledged is doubt, the doubt that points to a wound *in God himself.*

We are all familiar with Paul's rereading of circumcision as a "circumcision of the heart," in which the cutting of the flesh is replaced by the internal mark of faith (Romans 2:25–29). But how does Paul have to circumcise the Hebrew Bible to arrive at his vision of faith? What has to be cut off or trimmed away? In my view it is not only the "letter" of the law, but also the doubt it sustains, in other words, whatever undercuts or disbelieves the authority of the Voice. In the Voice that interpellates him on the road to Damascus, I think Paul hears another question: *Why are you not persecuting and prosecuting the doubt that stands in the way of love, that doubt that seeks to castrate the Voice?* Perhaps this is what Lyotard means when he writes that "Paul's suffering, his own passion, consists in having to kill the father of his own tradition, or at least having to pronounce him dead" (*The Hyphen* 16), that is, in having to kill the doubt that defines Abraham in the Jewish tradition.

4

THE GAP IN THE WRITTEN LAW
AND THE UNWRITABLE ACT
OF DECISION

Carl Schmitt's *Political Theology*

WHEN WE JUXTAPOSE the two polemics that in many ways book-end the long history of political theology—Paul's polemic against the Jewish law and Carl Schmitt's critique of constitutional liberalism—it becomes apparent that both authors challenge spatial notions of law that establish a boundary between an "inside" and an "outside" by topologizing "inside" and "outside" as continuous: through the "fulfillment of the law" in Paul, and through the strategy of sovereign exception in Schmitt. In his mission to the Gentiles, Paul argues that the covenant with the Israelites does not define the borders of the kingdom of God; the "new covenant" (which is importantly not formalized in laws or practices) universalizes the promise by "including what was excluded," inscribing or integrating what was once "outside." Schmitt, on the other hand, suggests that the sovereign is the one who "decides on the exception," determining when the constitution needs to be suspended in its entirety in order to address an extreme threat that falls outside the bounds of ordinary legal prescriptions. The exception is thus defined by "unlimited authority," a breaching of the borders of the law that allows the sovereign to bring the exception under the authority of state power. Schmitt even describes sovereignty as a "border concept," a *Grenzbegriff*: a concept that pertains to borderline cases, but perhaps at the same time a concept *of* the border, one that proposes a particular interpretation of the border and its logical function.

THE UNWRITABLE BORDER
AS FULFILLMENT OF THE LAW

In his book *Political Theology*, published in 1922, Schmitt observes that there is a "gap" in the law, which corresponds to the place of the exception. He asserts that the concept "legal order" is made out of two independent and autonomous elements, norm and decision, which together constitute the juristic sphere. In a normal situation, "the autonomous moment of the decision recedes to a minimum"; the existing law is simply applied.[1] But the law cannot deal with a true exception, since an ordinary legal prescription is merely the representation of a general norm, an existing state of affairs; by definition, an exceptional situation is one that falls outside the norm (6). Since "the exception . . . is not codified in the existing legal order," it "can at best be characterized as a case of extreme peril, a danger to the existence of the state" (6).

In such an extreme case, the sovereign is defined as "he who decides on the exception" (5), intervening to act in the absence of any legal guideline. Initially Schmitt defined norm and decision as two autonomous elements of the legal order. Decision never entirely disappears, even when norms prevail; but in an exceptional situation, Schmitt now specifies that "the norm is destroyed" altogether (12). Decision alone comes to encompass the entirety of the juridical order, displacing the supposedly "autonomous" sphere of norm.[2] In practical terms, the sovereign suspends the constitution in order to preserve the state. Nevertheless, Schmitt insists that the legal order does not disappear with the suspension of the constitution; instead, it is temporarily transferred to the person of the sovereign so that it may endure. The "legal order" is therefore something distinct from law itself; indeed, the primary function of the exceptional decision is to uphold the *order of law* by temporarily suspending the *application* of law. Once the exceptional situation is brought under his power and order is restored, the sovereign alone determines when the constitution can be reinstated. In Schmitt's words, "there exists no norm that is applicable to chaos. For a legal order to make sense, a normal situation must exist, and he is sovereign who definitely decides whether this normal situation actually exists" (13).

The problem with the law is therefore a problem of representation: since the law does not create new situations but merely "describes" a situation that is already in place, it is always secondary with respect to the legal order. Citing the words of Gerhard Anschütz, Schmitt writes: "There is not only a *gap in the law*, that is, in the text of the constitution, but moreover *in law as a whole*, which can in no way be filled by juristic conceptual operations. Here is where public law stops" (15, my emphases). Schmitt's initial gloss of this "gap in the law" considers the law as the representation of a norm, one that can either be applied to a given object or situation or be found to be inapplicable, as in the exceptional case. But when he follows Anschütz in claiming that there is a gap not only in the *text* of the constitution but "in law as a whole," Schmitt extends his critique from the problem of representation or naming (the gap between what the law foresees and the exceptional case) to a more structural problem. The law as such, the whole of law, contains a gap: one that "can in no way be filled." Or, more accurately, the gap structurally internal to law means that there is no such thing as a "whole of law," because the law "as a whole" is structured by a gap that prevents it from achieving totalization or closure. To the critique of law as secondary representation, he therefore adds an implicit critique of law as *limit*, as what suspends or puts a stop to juridical authority.

Unlike Anschütz, however, Schmitt asserts that the gap in the law can indeed be filled: not only the gap in the text of the constitution, but the gap in the "law as a whole." The decision on the exception fills this gap by substituting the embodied power of the sovereign for the suspension or gap internal to the law. The sovereign is the one who is not limited by the limit, and who therefore *suspends the suspension introduced by the law*. In Schmitt's words,

What characterizes an exception is principally *unlimited authority*, which means *the suspension of the entire existing order*. In such a situation it is clear that *the state remains, whereas law recedes*. Because the exception is different from anarchy and chaos, order in the juristic sense still prevails, even if it is not of the ordinary kind. The existence of the state is undoubted proof of its superiority over the validity of the legal norm. The decision frees itself from all normative ties and becomes in the true sense absolute. *The state suspends the law in the exception on the basis of its right of self-preservation, as one would say.*

(12, my emphases)

When Schmitt writes that "the state remains, whereas law recedes," he makes clear that the "order of law" is really an order *without* law, which differs from law in that it excludes the "gap." The basic tension is between law as the *mediation* of an authority—an authority it simultaneously represents and limits—and the unmediated character of the sovereign decision that "embodies" law, allowing the legal order to coincide with authority or power. According to Schmitt, "The exception reveals most clearly the essence of the state's authority. The decision parts here from the legal norm, and (to formulate it paradoxically) *authority proves that to produce law it need not be based on law*" (13).

Let us now return to Schmitt's initial definition of the sovereign as "he who decides on the exception" (5) and the peculiar understanding of the border it advances. Schmitt writes,

Only this definition can do justice to a borderline concept [*Grenzbegriff*]. Contrary to the imprecise terminology that is found in popular literature, a borderline concept is not a vague concept, but one pertaining to the outermost sphere. This definition of sovereignty must therefore be associated with a borderline case and not with routine. It will soon become clear that the exception . . . refer[s] to a general concept in the theory of the state, and not merely to a construct applied to any emergency decree or state of siege.

(5)

Sovereignty relates to "borderline cases," those at the edge of the law's juris-diction. But at the same time, sovereignty is *itself* a border case, since the sovereign is neither internal nor external to the legal order. To describe his place, Schmitt resorts to an oxymoronic formulation: "Although the sover-eign stands outside [*steht außerhalb*] of the normally valid juridical order, he nevertheless belongs [*gehört*] to it, for it is he who must decide whether the constitution needs to be suspended in its entirety" (7, translated modi-fied). When we try to represent logically the different moments or positions implied in this figure, it becomes clear that three different understandings of the border are in play.

The first diagram (figure 4.1) might describe the simple case of "belong-ing to" the juridical order. In the binary rules of classical logic, either a thing is or it is not. P and –P are complementary and mutually exclusive, meaning that together they cover all possible cases. This is the "law of the excluded middle," which excludes any consideration of the border case. The border is simply disregarded. In the terms of Schmitt's argument, P is the "juridical order" or *nomos*, and –P is the anomic situation that threatens its existence. The sovereign belongs to the juridical order.

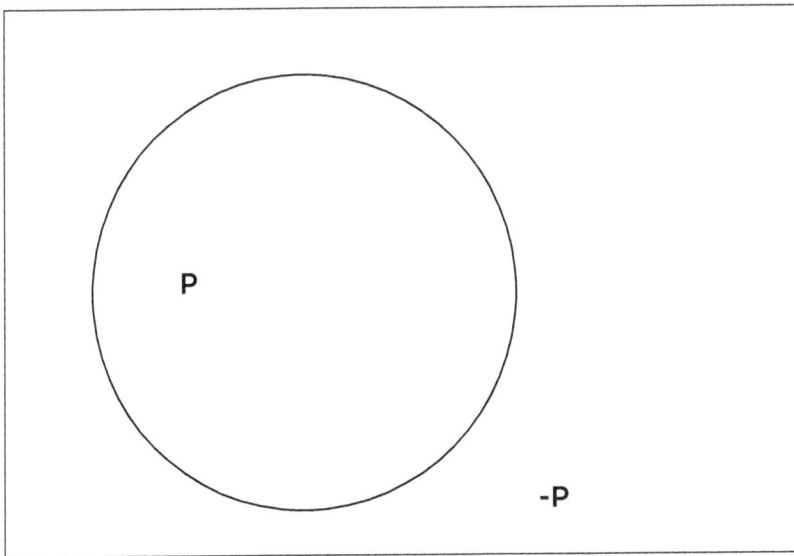

FIGURE 4.1. Classical Logic

In the second diagram (figure 4.2), which corresponds to the case of "standing outside" the juridical order, the border has its own status. This is constructive logic, where the "law of the excluded middle" is not a theorem. P and –P are still mutually exclusive; however, a new "boundary case" arises which is written as a border. If we define the two regions that were previously mutually exclusive as "yes" and "no," the border would correspond to something like "maybe" or "we do not know yet": a case whose position with respect to the opposition of P and –P has not yet been decided. In Schmitt's terms, the definition of sovereignty is associated with a "borderline case"; the decision on the exception does not belong to the "*normally valid* juridical order" ("yes"), and the exception must therefore be brought within it by the act of sovereign decision.

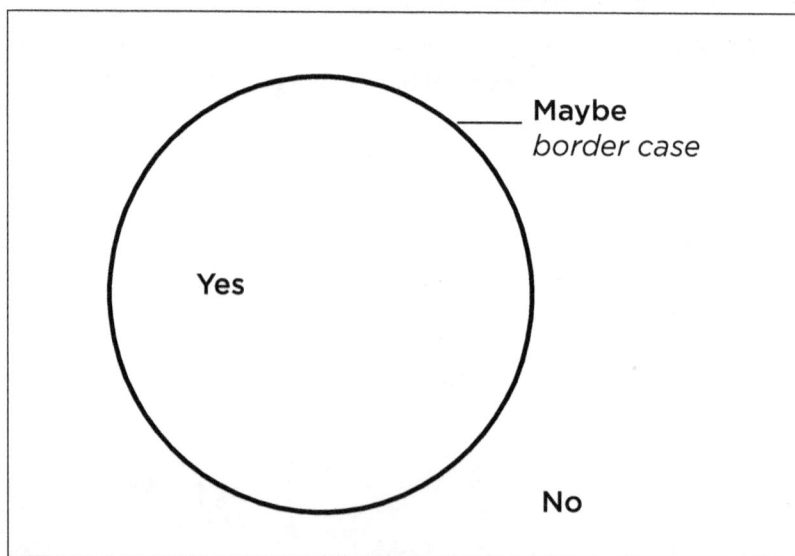

FIGURE 4.2. Constructive Logic

The third diagram (figure 4.3) corresponds to the figure of "standing outside, yet belonging." The sovereign decides whether the constitution needs to be suspended in its entirety, in order to bring the anomic situation under

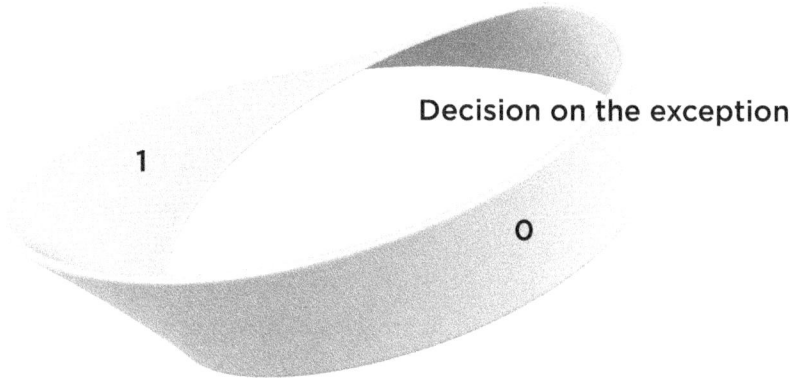

Decision on the exception

1

0

FIGURE 4.3. Topology

the control of the legal order, the state. In so doing, he inaugurates an exceptional situation defined by "unlimited authority," in which "authority proves that to make law it need not be based on law." In this case it is no longer possible to distinguish between "inside" and "outside," "yes" and "no," *nomos* or anomie. If we were to evoke it topologically, for example, as a moebius strip, the border would become a twisted, two-sided circular band, making inside (1) and outside (0) continuous. With respect to the first two diagrams, the border is neither a mere line of demarcation (as in figure 4.1) nor a distinct case (as in figure 4.2), but the articulation and integration of previously distinct spheres (the juridical order and the exception). The sovereign embodies the state, and there is nothing outside his authority.

My point in presenting these different treatments of the border is to show that while each of these cases can be written logically, there is no way to write the movement from one to the next: each implies an interpretation of the border that is incompatible with the others. The incompatibility inheres in their different treatments of negation. In the first case, P negates –P and vice versa. In the second case, "maybe" does not negate "yes" or "no," even if it does not belong to either of them; but "yes" and "no" are still mutually exclusive.

In the third case, this possibility of negation is eliminated altogether. It is an understanding of the border from which the notion of the limit has been excluded. *(In other words, although one can use a line to draw a moebius strip, this writing does not have the same logical function as in the first two cases: it merely allows for an imaginary representation of a figure that cannot be "written" at all, insofar as writing is aligned logically with the limit or negation.)*

With respect to Schmitt, the upshot is that it is impossible to write the place of the *act*, the decision that articulates these different articulations of the legal order. In his claim that sovereignty is a "border concept," Schmitt's contribution to the logical problem of the border is thus to claim that the border is not of the order of a writing, but a "miracle" that is by nature unwritten and unwritable (if not, indeed, antinomial to writing). The border is now an "act," whose function is to close the gap in the law by *transforming* the set it intervenes in: the juridical order defined by norms becomes the "legal order" embodied by the sovereign. (In figure 4.3, the space that corresponded to "yes" in figure 4.2, the space of the "normally valid legal order" or law, is in the process of being "destroyed" by the exception, such that the border representing the decision comes to encompass the whole juridical order.) While the law both erects boundaries and is itself bound by a writing, neither condition applies to the juridical order. The result is that not only the decision but the juridical order itself cannot be written in logic.

This is what Schmitt aptly terms the "miracle" of the theologico-political, in his famous claim that "the exception in jurisprudence is analogous to the miracle in theology" (36). The model for the sovereign's "direct intervention in a legal order" is the "transgression of the laws of nature through an exception brought about by direct intervention, as is found in the idea of a miracle" (36).[3] When Schmitt claims that "all significant concepts of the modern theory of the state are secularized theological concepts" (36), he reveals his debt not only to the early modern Catholic theologians he discusses at some length, but more profoundly to the political theology of Paul. Most immediately, his conception of the state as unbounded or unwritable recalls Paul's famous distinction between the two Jerusalems: the "Jerusalem of the flesh," who lives in slavery to the law, and the unbounded "Jerusalem above," born free through the promise (Galatians 4:22–31).

More specifically, Schmitt's argument reproduces almost exactly Paul's interpretation of the "fulfillment of the law" introduced by Jesus. This fulfillment takes a paradoxical dual form, which anticipates the fraught topology of the exception. On the one hand, Jesus realizes or completes the law, bringing it to fruition by making good on its promises and animating its living spirit; but on the other, he voids the law, renders it obsolete, in much the same way that the fulfillment of a legal contract renders it null and void. As the ultimate example of the sovereign exception, Christ is the model for the paradoxical logic of "being outside, yet belonging" that for Schmitt defines the sovereign's place with respect to the juridical order: because he embodies the law, he can suspend the law.

Importantly, Schmitt takes from Paul not only a theory of sovereign action, but a critique of the written law as a mediating representation. Paul's famous polemic against the Jewish law is structured by a distinction between two orders of law: the "law of God" and the "law of sin." The first is associated with the intelligible "spirit" of the law, which is "written in the heart," and the second with the prescriptive "letter" of the law, which compromises or corrupts the first by binding it to a particular representation and consigning it to written form. His polemic is directed not just at any law, but at one of the commandments of the Hebrew Decalogue. In his letter to the Romans, Paul writes:

If it had not been for the law, I should not have known sin. I should not have known what it is to covet if the law had not said, "You shall not covet." But sin, finding opportunity in the commandment, wrought in me all kinds of covetousness. Apart from the law sin lies dead. I was once alive apart from the law, but when the commandment came, sin revived and I died; the very commandment which promised life proved to be death to me. For sin, finding opportunity in the commandment, deceived me and by it killed me. . . . So I find it to be a law that when I want to do right, evil lies close at hand. For I delight in the law of God, in my inmost self, but I see in my members another law at war with the law of my mind and making me captive to the law of sin which dwells in my members.

(Romans 7:7–11, 21–23)

In prohibiting, the law incites transgression by representing to the imagination an object of desire.[4] The commandment is thus the vehicle through which sin and death insinuate themselves into the Jewish law, perverting or derailing our quest for the law of God.

Paul's solution is to bypass the law, to bypass representation and perhaps even language itself. Law as we know it—the prescriptive "letter" of the Jewish law—must be subordinated to and sublated by the law of the spirit:

My brethren, you have died to the law through the body of Christ, so that you may belong to another, to him who has been raised from the dead in order that we may bear fruit for God. While we were living in the flesh, our sinful passions, aroused by the law, were at work in our members to bear fruit for death. But now we are discharged from the law, dead to that which held us captive, so that we serve not under the old written code but in the new life of the Spirit.

(Romans 7:4–6)

As the living embodiment of God's law, Christ is the "sovereign exception" who upholds the spirit of the law by "fulfilling"—and so rendering obsolete—its written form. In the same way, the result of the sovereign exception theorized by Schmitt is that we no longer obey the law, but the sovereign who introduces a new order through its suspension. In both cases the attempt to extend the order of the *nomos* takes the paradoxical form of a fulfillment or eradication of the law as such, in favor of the "order of law" embodied by the sovereign himself.

This argument reveals something further about the nature of the "gap in the law" bemoaned by Schmitt, which the decision is supposed to fill. The gap in the law is a problem internal to the law as representation, which does not simply fail to anticipate anomic situations, but structurally stands in the way of fulfillment because it introduces a detour or distance with respect to the Good. As Paul puts it, "I find it to be a law that when I want to do right, evil lies close at hand"; this is because "the commandment that promised life proved to be death to me." In other words, the commandment that promised access to the good deceived me with representations that derailed my quest, leading me astray from my aim.

In Schmitt's terms, the law binds us to a "normal" situation: it has no transcendent dimension or capacity for "miracle." Only the sovereign exception can inscribe the good within the juristic sphere, by suspending the law that introduces a gap between the legal order and the general good to which everyone aspires: "Everyone agrees that whenever antagonisms appear within a state, every party wants the general good—therein resides after all the *bellum omnium contra omnes*. But sovereignty (and thus the state itself) resides in deciding this controversy, that is, in determining definitively what constitutes public order and security, in determining when they are disturbed, and so on" (9). The decision is what closes the "gap" between representation and the good, bringing it within reach. Importantly, though, Schmitt makes clear that "the good" has no specific content, not even something as abstract as "equal opportunity" or "life, liberty, and the pursuit of happiness." In deciding on the good, the sovereign simply determines "what constitutes public order and security." This suggests that the "general good" is really just a synonym for the preservation of the state, whose continued existence is secured by bringing under its power the forces that seek to limit its authority through violence or other subversive actions.[5]

Schmitt's contemporary Walter Benjamin offers what may still be the most trenchant critique of this argument when he questions the form (or lack of form) this "good" takes. In his *Theses on the Concept of History*, Benjamin writes: "the tradition of the oppressed teaches us that the 'state of exception' in which we live is the rule. We must attain to a concept of history that accords with this fact. Then we will clearly see that it is our task to bring about a real state of exception, to improve our position in the struggle against fascism."[6] In suggesting that the state of exception has become the rule, Benjamin contests Schmitt's account of the exception by suggesting that the sovereign's suspension of the law may not be temporary, as Schmitt claims, but endure indefinitely. This is his assessment of the state of exception in the Weimar period, where the state of emergency declared by the Nazi Reich was never repealed.[7] Benjamin's notion of a "state of exception become the rule" is not specific to modern totalitarianism, however, but could even function as a possible definition of the kingdom of Christ, within Paul's understanding of the fulfillment of the law.[8] Since for Paul the law impedes access to the Good, it follows that the fulfillment of the law must involve a permanent suspension: one that "becomes the rule."

What would a state of exception become the rule look like? Glossing Benjamin's remarks, Giorgio Agamben proposes that in such a case, "every fiction of a nexus between violence and law disappears"; what remains is "nothing but a zone of anomie, in which *violence works without juridical clothing of any kind.*"[9] Schmitt himself specifies that "the state intervenes everywhere," acting with "unlimited authority":[10]

> There always exists the same inexplicable identity: lawgiver, executive power, police, pardoner, welfare institution. Thus to an observer who takes the trouble to look at the total picture of contemporary jurisprudence, there appears a huge cloak-and-dagger drama, in which the state acts in many disguises but always as the same invisible person. The "omnipotence" of the modern lawgiver . . . is not only linguistically derived from theology.
>
> (38)

Even in Paul, for whom the fulfillment of the law ushers in the reign of the holy "law of the spirit," this state of exception tends to sound uncannily like a police state. This is because the "spirit of the law" takes the form of an internal "voice of conscience" that is distinctly superegoic in character, and fundamentally opposed to the "letter" as limit. The result of Paul's logic is that the subject is not only "freed" from law in its prescriptions, but delivered over to another authority: as he tells the Romans, "you have died to the law through the body of Christ, so that you may belong to another." What Agamben describes as an "anomic zone where violence works without juridical clothing of any kind" could be assimilated to the unarticulated, invisible "force of law" that animates Christianity. The Christian is a "law unto himself," but only insofar as he is possessed by a "force of law" that works without "juridical clothing." In Paul's words, "Christ judges the secret thoughts of all" (Romans 2:1), bypassing speech in order to penetrate the subject's consciousness.

THE GAP IN THE LAW
AND THE FUNCTION OF THE SYMBOLIC

In his seminar *The Ethics of Psychoanalysis*, Jacques Lacan offers a different approach to the problem of the Sovereign Good, which attempts to account for the superegoic character of any ethics that seeks to bypass the function of the law. He begins with Freud's account of the incest prohibition that excludes the mother as a possible object of sexual fulfillment. What it reveals, says Lacan, is that "the Sovereign Good, which is *das Ding*, which is the mother, is also the object of incest, is a forbidden good, and there is no other good. Such is the foundation of the moral law as turned on its head by Freud."[11] The incest prohibition reveals that the law does not lead to the Good. Instead, its function is to lead us away from this Good, to debar it or put it under erasure. The mother is marked as the Good that one must not have, because to possess it would mean the effacement of the subject, its absorption by the Other.

Lacan defines *das Ding*, "the Thing," as the guiding pole of our desire. At the level of unconscious experience, *das Ding* presents itself as that which "makes the law" (73): a "capricious and arbitrary law ... in which the subject receives no guarantee from anywhere, a law in relation to which he has no [security]" (73). This is the law of the death drive, of the repetition compulsion that causes the subject to pursue its pleasure on the very paths that have the potential to cause it the most pain.

While *das Ding* is experienced as "making the law" at the level of the unconscious, driving the subject in ways he cannot control, the role of the law as *prohibition* is to limit its insistence. Its function can be understood with respect to what Freud calls the pleasure principle, the psychic regulatory mechanism that maintains equilibrium by keeping the Thing at a distance. Lacan sums up its function in a paradoxical formula: "the pleasure principle governs the search for the object and imposes the detours which maintain the distance in relation to its end" (58). From this perspective, "*das Ding* is at the center only in the sense that it is excluded" (71). It is the horizon of the pleasure principle, its "aim"; and yet it is an aim that it can only approach indirectly, by detouring around it. What we call "pleasure" is really nothing more than a detour away from the ultimate "fulfillment," the Thing that cannot be born and that, when the subject gets too close, is experienced as the most unbearable pain. This is why Lacan says of *das Ding* that "if he is to follow the path of his pleasure, man must go around it" (95).[12]

The law functions to erect a barrier against *das Ding* in two ways: it holds it at a distance by introducing a gap or space between the subject and his good, and it proposes representations that evoke *das Ding* indirectly or in a distorted form. Lacan develops the first point through an account of the creation ex nihilo. Like the potter who fashions a vase, the mythical creator starts with a hole (121). In the biblical myth, the first act of creation is really a *negation*, the division of the primordial unity into earth and sky, land and water: a series of cuts or oppositions that create a space where *something is missing*, a space in which life becomes possible. What it demonstrates is that "the fashioning of the signifier and the introduction of a gap or a hole in the real are identical" (121).

Lacan famously claims that "nothing is missing from the real." But if the real can be defined most simply as an uninterrupted unity or presence, this means not only that the real is complete, but that nothing *is missing* from the real: the real includes everything except the nothing. In other words, what is missing from the real is the "no," the barrier or prohibition that opens up a space for the subject by negating some part of the real, interrupting this original unity: for example, the paternal prohibition that separates the original dyad of mother and child, allowing the child to pursue an independent life of desire. Lacan defines *das Ding* as "that which, in the real, suffers from the signifier" (118). But this "suffering" is necessary, since if *it* does not suffer *we* do.[13]

The operation of the pleasure principle is therefore associated with a certain comfort or well-being. But Lacan argues that when the moral law introduces the Good as its aim, it disrupts this sense of well-being (72–73). The remark occurs in a commentary on the revolution in ethics introduced by Paul and developed by Kant. I would argue that it applies not only to Paul's understanding of the "fulfillment of the law," however, but to Schmitt's account of the exception. For Schmitt, "nothing is missing" is really the ideal of the legal order embodied by the sovereign: the decision on the exception includes what was excluded, closing the gap in the law. Both authors could be understood as collapsing the defenses introduced by the law, attempting to reconnect the order of the law to its excluded center. What Benjamin describes as a "state of exception become the rule" is really the intrusion of the real associated with the breaching of the law as barrier, the collapsing of this symbolic space.[14]

Lacan's understanding of law as introducing a gap or distance with respect to *das Ding* introduces another way of thinking about representation as well. He argues that law on the model of the pleasure principle makes use of representation to "evoke the good *das Ding* brings with it" (72), but on the condition that it be evoked only indirectly or in distorted form.[15] In the example of the incest prohibition, the law not only proposes the mother as forbidden Good as a representation of *das Ding*, but introduces a further detour with respect to its aim by proposing women who are *like* the mother as substitutes for the mother herself. In Lacan's words, "Freud's use of the good can be summed up in the notion that it keeps us a long way from our jouissance," from the ultimate fulfillment represented by *das Ding* as the Good (185).

With respect to the distinction we find in Paul and Schmitt between the written law as mediation and the embodied law of the sovereign, Lacan proposes a different understanding of the law as representation, whose function is symbolic rather than imaginary. It emphasizes a different kind of distance than the one implied in description or imitation, as a greater or lesser resemblance to the thing represented.

Paradoxically, Lacan will also identify this symbolic function of the law with the lie. But whereas Paul conceives of the written law as a deceitful (mis)representation of the Good, Lacan suggests that the law consists in "lying about evil." Because the subject cannot stand the extreme good that *das Ding* may bring him, he must defend himself against it; human defense, says Lacan, "takes place by means of something that has a name, which is . . . lying about evil. At the level of the unconscious, the subject lies. And this lie is his way of telling the truth of the matter" (73). What, then, is meant by "lying about evil," and how does it differ from the modality of lying indicted by Paul?

Lacan clarifies it through a discussion of one of Freud's patients, a woman who has a phobia of going into stores because she is afraid people will make fun of her clothes. He summarizes her case in the following terms:

> Everything is related to an early memory. At the age of twelve she went into a store and the shop assistants apparently laughed at her clothes. One of them attracted her and even stirred her in some way in her emerging puberty. Behind that we find a causal memory, that of an act of aggression she suffered in a shop at the hands of a *Greis*, . . . an elderly man, who pinched her under her dress in a very direct manner. This memory thus echoes the idea of a sexual attraction experienced in the other.
>
> All that remains in the symptom is attached to the clothes, to the mockery of her clothes. But the path of truth is suggested in a masked form, in the deceiving *Vorstellung* of her clothes. In an opaque way, there is an allusion to something that did not happen on the occasion of the first memory, but on the second. Something that wasn't apprehended in the beginning is apprehended retroactively, by means of the deceitful transformation.
>
> (74)

The "deceitful *Vorstellung*" of the clothes is a "lie," a displacement or distortion of what is really at stake; but it also leads to it, indirectly.[16] In the terms of Lacan's earlier argument, representation introduces a distance with respect to *das Ding*, and so "lies about evil"; but in lying, it also allows it to be represented indirectly, by means of detours that maintain it at a certain distance.

The choice of clothing as a "deceitful *Vorstellung*" is further important in that the mode of representation is metonymic and not metaphoric. In other words, the substitution is commanded by a spatial logic of contiguity, rather than a logic of resemblance or similarity. It recalls the logic of the fetish, a representation that functions as a metonymic substitute for the unbearable truth of the mother's castration. Analyzing the frequency with which feminine underclothes occur as fetishes, Freud suggests that the choice of the fetish is determined not by resemblance to the expected organ, but by spatial contiguity: it is the last thing the child sees before discovering the lack of the mother's penis. The fetish is therefore a representation without an imitative function, not only because it represents something that does not even exist, that is of the order of a hallucination, but because it stands in for the unthinkable truth of castration. Its function is to *clothe the unrepresentable in a representation.*

While Paul and Lacan are in agreement that the law "lies about evil," they interpret this lie in two different ways, which bring into relief a fundamental distinction between the *imaginary or "representational" function* of law (where the law attempts to represent the Good, but always falls short of its goal) and the *symbolic or "barrier" function.* Where Paul maintains that the law as representation is inevitably a mis-representation, a superficial or misleading depiction of an ideal or truth, Lacan suggests that the "failure" of representation is part of the point, since the function of law on the model of the pleasure principle is to represent inaccurately or in distorted form, and thereby maintain at a distance.[17] In other words, he asserts that the lie has a symbolic function, as well as an imaginary one. It does not merely conjure up a (false) image, but introduces a space that was not there before.

The interdependence of these two modalities of "lying" is nowhere more obvious than in the Hebrew Decalogue, which Lacan reads as an exemplary articulation of the structure of law. The Decalogue is divided into two tablets, whose commandments are often broadly interpreted as concerning God and the neighbor, respectively.

Commandments concerning God	Commandments concerning the neighbor
1. no other gods	6. no murder
2. no idols or images	7. no adultery
3. no misuse of the divine name	8. no theft
4. remember the Sabbath day	9. no bearing false witness
5. honor the mother and father	10. no coveting

The first tablet concerns the Sovereign Good as *das Ding*, as something beyond representation that cannot be depicted or named. The first three commandments—against worshiping other deities, making images of God, or misusing the divine name—evoke the field of *das Ding* in relation to God. Together they establish that the Good that is beyond representation is also a deadly Good, and that we must keep our distance from it. As the book of Exodus never tires of reminding us, to look on the face of God is to die. But while the sublime God of terrible power may be the ultimate representative of *das Ding*, something similar is at stake in the commandment to honor the mother and father. Linking the veneration of the parents to the worship of God, it recalls Lacan's earlier argument concerning the mother as *das Ding*, the forbidden Good named by the incest prohibition. Both must be worshiped or "honored" from an appropriate distance.

In identifying God with a space that cannot be breached or transgressed, the Mosaic law does not simply establish the parameters of religious observance. It articulates something fundamental about the symbolic structure of the law, whose violent spacing of the real undercuts the fantasy of a possible embodiment or incarnation of the Good implicit in Paul's and Schmitt's different accounts of the exception. In early Jewish ritual practice, this negative space is given form in the Holy of Holies, the innermost sanctum of the Israelite tabernacle. It is associated with the deity not as the site of his manifestation or presence, but as a space that must not be entered on pain of death, a "holy hole."

This logic is nowhere better expressed than in the fourth commandment:

Remember the sabbath day, and keep it holy. Six days you shall labor and do all your work. But the seventh day is a sabbath to the LORD your God; you shall not do any work—you, your son or your daughter, your male or female slave, your livestock, or the alien resident in your towns. For in six days the LORD made heaven and earth, the sea, and all that is in them, but rested the seventh day; therefore the LORD blessed the sabbath day and consecrated it.

(Exodus 20:8–11)

According to Lacan, "that suspension, that emptiness, clearly introduces into human life the sign of a gap, a beyond relative to every law of utility" (81). What it remembers or sanctifies is God's creation of the world, which paradoxically concludes with the insertion of a gap. In a rich gloss of Lacan's reading, Julia Lupton and Ken Reinhard write that "God completes the world by subtracting something from it, namely his own activity. . . . The sublime emptiness of the seventh day marks the close of the process of creation *ex nihilo* that began with God's first utterance, an act, the Kabbalah argues, that required God to diminish himself, to decomplete his own fullness in order to make room for the world."[18] God withdraws to create a place where "something is missing," namely, his own full presence. In this way, the commandment links the emergence of the human subject to the negation of the fullness of the real, the unmediated presence of *das Ding*. In the words of Lupton and Reinhard, "the subject of religion . . . only emerges in the decompletion of the symbolic universe, through the positive addition to the cosmos of an instance of negation."[19]

Turning to the second tablet, we might say that the commandments concerning the neighbor propose substitutions for what is at stake in the first tablet, "translating" *das Ding* into a different order of "things": the objects and interpersonal relations regulated by the juridical sphere. Lacan notes that German contains two words for the thing, both of which relate to the juridical context: *die Sache* and *das Ding*. *Die Sache* is "the thing that is juridically questioned," which marks "the transition to the symbolic order of a conflict between men" (44). In Freud's usage, *die Sache* is intimately linked to representation in speech: hence the close connection in his theory of the unconscious between *Sachevorstellung*, "the representation of things," and *Wortvorstellung*, "the representation of words." But while "*Sache* and *Wort* . . . form a couple, *das Ding* is found somewhere else" (45). It is "the true secret" (46), the Thing at stake in the law only in the sense that is excluded by it (71). At the level of what it names or represents, the law is concerned with the objects at stake in conflicts between men; but these objects assume their true significance only in their secret relation to *das Ding*, the excluded center around which the law circulates.

Drawing on this analysis, we might say that the second tablet concerns *goods* as substitutes for *the Good*, recalling the function of the "deceiving *Vorstellung*" analyzed by Lacan. The law "lies about evil," and this is its chief virtue: it proposes objects that "represent" or substitute for *das Ding*, thereby keeping it at a distance. (Now it is a matter of women, slaves, and donkeys as mere commodities or things, and not *the Thing*.) In relation to the first tablet, we could say that the law provides us with representations, but only on the condition that the depiction of the Good be strictly outlawed: something else, some other thing, must be represented in its place.

Lacan illustrates his point using the same example commented on by Paul—the commandment against coveting the neighbor's goods—but with a different conclusion. In the wording of the commandment, says Lacan, "the covetousness that is in question is not addressed to anything that I might desire but to a thing that is my neighbor's Thing" (*Ethics* 83). In other words, the subject's Thing is evoked in displaced form, metonymically, through reference to the neighbor's wife and goods. What the commandment is *really* saying is that I must not covet my own Thing, that I must keep it at a distance; but it expresses this by attributing that Thing to the neighbor. (This suggests that the fifth and tenth commandments might together express what is at stake in the incest prohibition: the neighbor's forbidden wife both partakes of the allure of the mother as *das Ding* and holds it at a distance by means of displacement.) In the "deceitful *Vorstellung*" of the neighbor as a metonymic substitute for the self, the moral law "lies about evil" by suggesting that the Thing that must be avoided is my neighbor's

Thing, and that it is a question of protecting the neighbor from my aggression. In this example, the "lie" consists not in distorting or misrepresenting, but in holding at a distance; in other words, it represents the thing, but in such a way as to put it *over there*.

The ninth commandment, against bearing false witness, is related to this. It concerns testimony, the use of speech in the juridical situation. Noting that the word "testimony" derives from the Latin *testes*, Lacan implies that testimony always concerns what is most intimately at stake for the one who speaks, regardless of what he is talking about. Even when he is speaking about the neighbor, in other words, it is always his own testicles that are on the line. The earlier discussion of the law as "lying about evil" also allows for a more ironic reading of the commandment: do not give false testimony against the neighbor, *but by all means lie about das Ding*, in part by pretending that it is the neighbor you are really talking about.

Taken together, the first and second tablets delineate the two functions of the signifier: negation and representation. The first tablet involves the introduction of a gap where "something is missing," a violent spacing that disrupts the unity of the real, causing it to "suffer." The second tablet concerns speech as representation or evocation: on the one hand, the "imaginary" function of the law indicted by Paul (where the law conjures up objects that incite transgression, deceiving us with images), and on the other, the function of representing indirectly, by substituting goods for the Good.

This is all very well, you might be saying, but what does it have to do with Schmitt? One could reasonably object to everything I have just said that Lacan is talking specifically about the function of the moral law, which concerns the problem of ethics in its relation to the Good, whereas Schmitt is dealing with the more concrete concerns of constitutional law and of the juridical sphere as such. But what the logic of the Ten Commandments makes clear is that the "everyday" law that adjudicates disputes between persons and things, assigning responsibilities and regulating conduct, cannot be considered in isolation from the structural function of the law as the introduction of a space or gap. In terms of Hebraic law, it makes clear that the second tablet, which anticipates and in some ways condenses the 613 specific laws that follow, cannot be severed from the first. This insight is the specific innovation of the Mosaic law, a heritage that has been sidelined or forgotten as the commandment tradition has been integrated into Western jurisprudence. Even as the commandments of the second tablet became the foundation of property and tort law, the commandments of the first tablet were largely been abandoned by subsequent legal traditions.

This forgetting really begins with Paul himself, who directs his polemic at one of the commandments from the second tablet, but never confronts the logic implied in the first. His critique of the law represents a turning point with respect to this understanding of law as barrier, since it supposes that the point is to get to the aim, to accede directly to the Good. In the letter to the Galatians, he argues that to live under the law is to live with the impossibility of ever fulfilling the law, since one would have to fulfill the precepts in their entirety, something the flesh can never do (Galatians 3:10). In essence, Paul's conclusion is that if we aspire to reach the Good by way of the law, we will never get there.

In insisting on the logic of the first tablet, Lacan's analysis of the Hebraic law does not so much dispute Paul's conclusion as affirm it. When Paul complains that the law introduces a detour with respect to the Good, Lacan's response is to say, in effect, *Exactly! That is what the law is for! We are not trying to use the law to get to the Good, but to protect us from a Good that cannot be born.* Lacan would surely not dispute Paul's charge that the Hebraic law cannot be "fulfilled." But to the extent that one lives within its borders, it nonetheless functions as a protection or barrier against something that is considerably more difficult to live with, the unmediated insistence of *das Ding*.

Paul's polemic against the Jewish law draws upon Jesus' Sermon on the Mount (Matthew 5:1–7:27), which condenses the Ten Commandments to two fundamental principles: love of God and love of the neighbor. This condensation effaces the distinction between the two tablets of the Decalogue that is of such importance in Judaism, with the result that God and man are now understood as occupying the "same" space. The result is that the symbolic function of space (as the introduction of a gap) is replaced by an imaginary unity.[20] There is no longer any direct theorization of what Lacan calls *das Ding*, nor is there any emphasis on the function of the symbolic as such or of the role of the signifier in limiting *das Ding*. In fact, one could even argue that the imaginary replaces the symbolic altogether, rendering it obsolete.[21]

While the Mosaic law suggests that I must fear God and keep my distance from him, Jesus says that we must *love* God: a fearsome and even inconceivable prospect for the Jew. Now the commandments concerning the neighbor and the neighbor's things are understood not as *substitutes* for what is at stake in the commandments concerning God (representations that hold *das Ding* at a distance by evoking it in distorted form), but as fundamentally identical. Moreover, the neighbor is understood not as the uncanny or even menacing figure Freud describes (from whom I would do well to keep my distance),[22] but as someone whom I am invited to identify with and to love as I love "myself." The link between the subject and the neighbor implicit in Lacan's reading of the Decalogue (where the neighbor is a displaced figure for the subject and the neighbor's Thing is fundamentally *my* Thing) is brought out into the open. The result is that the "lying about evil" that defines the operation of the law is no longer allowed: the border between the subject and the neighbor, or between the subject and *das Ding*, is breached.

POLITICAL THEOLOGY AND THE QUESTION
OF THE BORDER

Despite its emphasis on God as something that must be held at a distance, Lacan's analysis of the law does not abandon the frame of political theology, but rather deploys it in a different way. Of course, it is important to Lacan's analysis that the God of the Decalogue is a *negative* God, defined by his absence or withdrawal from the world, and not the positive God of the miracle whose transformation of the legal order completes what was incomplete. Whereas Schmitt asserts that "all significant concepts of the modern theory of the *state* are theological concepts," what Lacan finds in the Hebraic tradition is really a theory of *law* as distinct from the state (what Schmitt calls the "legal order") or from sovereign power. This theory of law is "theological" not because it derives the law from divine authority, but because it theorizes the divine in negative terms or in relation to the function of negation.

As we saw earlier, Schmitt equates the sovereign's direct intervention in a valid legal order with the *transgression* of the laws of nature implied in the theological concept of the miracle. Implicit in Paul's and Schmitt's respective treatments of the law is the question: where does the law belong in relation to "what is"? Both link the law to an existing order, a current state of affairs, and imagine the exception as a suspension or "transgression" of that order, one that brings about a "new kingdom." In contrast, the Hebraic tradition posits that the *law itself* represents a break with "what is," a break that does not bring about a "new order" by substituting one state of affairs for another, but rather that carves out a negative space identified as the space of the subject, in other words, what by definition cannot be captured in the "order" of law or state, because it is located solely in speech. This is the miracle not of sovereignty, but of the signifier, which first transgresses the laws of nature by introducing a gap at the center of the real, creating a space where "something is missing."[23] The act as conceived by Paul not only rejects this logic, but involves a reinscription of the very space that was opened up by the Hebraic law, such that the "fulfillment of the law" really amounts to a canceling or undoing of this first act.

Earlier I suggested that in his claim that sovereignty is a "border concept," Schmitt's contribution to the logical problem of law as border is to claim that the border need not be written, that the sovereign exception is not of the order of a writing but of a "miracle" that is by nature unwritten and unwritable. We see something similar in Paul, who famously wrote of his own conversion experience, "I know a man in Christ who fourteen years ago was caught up to the third heaven—whether in the body or out of the body I do not know, God knows. And I know that this man was caught up into Paradise, . . . and he heard things that cannot be told, which man may not utter" (2 Corinthians 12:2–4). In thrall to the event, Paul is neither in the body nor out of it, but "outside-in."[24] His conversion experience is no more "logical" than Schmitt's topology of sovereignty, but like Schmitt he makes no apologies about it. There is something that is more than a little bit mad about these miracles, but that in no way undercuts their force or fascination—to the contrary.

No one has embraced this dimension of Paul's discourse more profoundly than Alain Badiou, who demonstrates that Paul's letters must be read not as the adumbration of a theology, but as a theory of the event. Schmitt is in many ways Paul's most faithful heir in this endeavor, demonstrating that the only response to the event of the exception is an act, an act that is necessarily as unwritable as the event itself. I would even argue that the aim of such an ethics is to demonstrate the superiority or vigor of the act with respect to the written, understood as a binding limit or normative constraint. It is surely not a coincidence, then, that the political-theological discourse of the act is invariably structured as a polemic against the written law, one that leaves us to choose between a constraining norm and an explosive act.

5

THE EVENT OF THE LETTER

Two Approaches to the Law and Its Real

A LAIN BADIOU HAS made numerous and important contributions to the problem of the symbolic, including but not limited to the elaboration of what might be called a symbolic dimension to his theory of the event.[1] Strikingly, however, his work appears to leave no room for a symbolic understanding of *law*. Almost invariably, it is reduced to the imaginary function of representing the "situation" or "world" where the event intervenes.[2] Indeed, Badiou's work might even be read as an attempt to rehabilitate the concept of the symbolic precisely by purging it of law. It tends to reinforce an understanding of the law as nothing more than the "dead letter," a normative representation of a "situation" that can be decisively transformed only through the intervention of an explosive event. In a presentation to a symposium on "Law and Event" titled "The Three Negations," for example, Badiou argues that "the field of law is always a concrete world or a concrete situation; but the event has a negative relationship to the laws of the world."[3]

In Badiou's treatment of law (and of Judaic legal traditions in particular), I see a consistent denigration of the written that places him within a political-theological tradition that opposes "law" and "decision" (or "representation" and "act"), and that therefore tends to overlook—if not outright deny—the symbolic dimensions of law that are so richly elaborated by these traditions. While Lacan insists that the symbolic is by no means reducible to the law, but also that there is a symbolic dimension of law that must be distinguished from its imaginary character (the field of "representation," including the representation of norms, contents, and predicates), Badiou consistently opposes "law" and "event." Here I wish to examine the debt of his formulation to Paul's polemic and question its centrality to Badiou's theory of the event, arguing that it overlooks the way in which the Mosaic law can itself be understood as an "event" by elaborating the evental understanding of the law implicit in Pierre Legendre's writings on Jewish law and Romano-Canonical juridicism and Freud's *Moses and Monotheism*.

ALAIN BADIOU ON LAW: SAINT PAUL AND USES OF THE WORD "JEW"

In *Saint Paul: The Foundation of Universalism*, published in 1997, Alain Badiou offers his fullest exploration of the relationship between his theory of the event and questions of law. This book offers not only a comprehensive discussion of the event of universalism as theorized by Paul, but more specifically a reflection on the event's relation to its site. The construction of truth is in a particular situation, a particular world; it is made of particular material. But the result, in the form of an accomplished truth, is universal.[4] In *Saint Paul*, the site of the Christ event is the discourse of Jewish legalism; its effect is to liberate the faithful subject from obedience to law and expose him to the universal called "grace."

Badiou's reading underscores the novelty of Paul's discourse with respect to the positions of "Jew" and "Greek," which he understands not as ethnic or religious designations, but as the two dominant discourses of subjectivity with which Paul has to contend in his invention of Christianity. Both discourses are instances of what Badiou calls "particularity," since they are organized around obedience to worldly objects that function as traits of identification. In Jewish discourse, the object is election, the exceptional alliance between God and his people; observance of the law cements it.[5]

In Greek discourse, the object is the finite cosmic totality as the domain of thought (56), mastered through the cultivation of wisdom. The discourses of "Jew" and "Greek" are thus symptomatic for Paul of the "worldly proliferation of alterities," in which each position believes that it alone holds the key to salvation. In contrast, Christian discourse declares that the object-identifications that cement worldly identity and promise mastery of the universe are indifferent to salvation.

The Christian discourse implies an "absolutely new relation to its object" (55), because it must be an "indifferent traversal of worldly differences, avoiding the casuistry of customs" (99). The most important manifestation of this indifference is the overcoming of the law in its particularity. The counterpart of Paul's denunciation of the Jews' enslavement to the law—and to the sinful objects and rites it both prohibits and brings to life as objects of desire—is the affirmation of a love born of the resurrection event, which Badiou reads as a liberation of the subject from the repetition-compulsion of desire, and thus from subservience to worldly objects and ritual practice (79). To the "multiplicity of legal prescriptions, whose objects fuel the mortifying autonomy of desire," Paul opposes "a sole maxim, affirmative and not tied to an object, that would not solicit the infinity of desire with the transgression of the interdiction" (89). For Badiou, "love" (or what was long translated as *caritas* or "charity") is Paul's name for the universal address of the truth whose process the Christian sustains. It implies the "existence of a trans-literal law, a law of the spirit" that supersedes the authority of all particular laws (87). For the New Man, therefore, love is the "law of his break with the law" (89).

One of the most distinctive features of Badiou's thought is the critique of particularity as a kind of rigid uniformity and the corresponding revaluation of universality not as an imposed unity or unification (which would imply the imposition of a communal predicate and thus a particularism), but as a truth that *traverses* particular positions without either absorbing or being absorbed by them. For Badiou, "every particularity is an instance of conformity" (110), rooted in a unary trait that defines identity. In contrast, Pauline universalism consists in an *address to all* in which universality "must expose itself to all the differences and show, in the trial of their sharing, that they can welcome the truth that traverses them" (106). "In the eyes of Paul the Jew, the weakness of Jewish discourse is that its logic of the exceptional sign is only valid *for* the Greek cosmic totality. The Jew is in exception to the Greek" (42). As a result, "neither of the two discourses can be universal, because each supposes the persistence of the other"; their respective forms of mastery "divide humanity in two (the Jew *and* the Greek), thereby blocking the universality of the Announcement" (42). In contrast, universality "*produces* a Sameness and an Equality" (109). In the famous declaration that Badiou reads as the foundation of universalism, Paul declares: "There is neither Jew nor Greek, there is neither slave nor freeman, there is neither man nor woman; for you are all one person in Christ Jesus" (Galatians 3:15).

More recently, Badiou has made a similar argument in a series of texts concerned with contemporary politics, which are critical of the identity politics and minoritarian discourses that stand in the way of a viable solution to the Middle East crisis. Here, too, the discourse around the word "Jew" is a central theme. In a series of short essays and interviews collected under the title *Uses of the Word "Jew"* (published in English in the collection titled *Polemics*), Badiou examines how the word "Jew" and its overdetermined connections with the Holocaust have been deployed in political debates over the Middle East to justify the policies of Israel and its allies with respect to the Palestinian crisis, arguing that the exceptional or even sacred signification often ascribed to the word stands in the way of a fair and equal settlement of political disputes.

This recent collection was vigorously attacked when it was published in France, and was even accused by a few critics of fomenting anti-Semitism by lending it philosophical credibility.[6] This charge is misplaced, since Badiou's stated goal is really to loosen the proprietary claim to the word "Jew" in certain right-wing or Zionist discourses, arguing that such a use ultimately fuels anti-Semitism instead of finding a solution to it. Certainly it would be hard to deny that Israel and its allies have made strategic use of the Holocaust to justify illegal and colonial incursions into Palestinian lands and to deny the civil rights of dissenting Jews and non-Jews in the process. Moreover, I think Badiou is right to suspect that Western support of Israeli policy is driven by something other than a love or respect of the Jewish people themselves; anti-Semitism continues to thrive in all of these countries even as they remain steadfast in their support of Israeli policies.

However, I do feel for very different reasons that his treatment of the word "Jew" reveals a limitation in his treatment of the universal: namely, a tendency to reduce to "particularism" or to identity claims what are really very structural questions of law, the symbolic, and even the signifier or speech more broadly. The remarks that follow pertain less to the recent collection than to Badiou's earlier book on Saint Paul. Nevertheless, the following passage from the introduction to this recent work offers a succinct formulation of the issues I want to address. The collection was inspired, writes Badiou, by the need to examine

> whether or not, in the general field of public intellectual discussion, the word "Jew" constitutes an exceptional signifier, exceptional to the point that it becomes admissible to treat it is as a final, or even sacred, signifier. It is clear that we do not approach the process of eradicating anti-Semitic forms of consciousness in the same way when we think they are essentially distinct from all other forms of racial discrimination . . . as when . . . we consider that all forms of racist consciousness call for the same kinds of reactions: egalitarian and universalist. Further, this shared repugnance of anti-Semitism must be distinguished from a certain philo-Semitism which claims not only that attacking Jews as such amounts to criminal baseness but that the word "Jew," and the community claiming to stand for it, must be placed in a paradigmatic position with respect to the field of values, cultural hierarchies, and in evaluating the politics of states.[7]

When he argues that anti-Semitism should not be viewed as "distinct from all other forms of racial discrimination," my question is to what extent Badiou himself accepts—even in proposing a different approach to it— that the word "Jew" is first and foremost a collective predicate identifying a people or a discourse, and thus the name of one "particularism" among others. While it may function in these registers among others, is the historical, legal, and political-theological import of the word "Jew" tied to the logic of particularism? Are these identitarian connotations adequate to account either for what makes "Jew" an exceptional signifier, or for the logic of anti-Semitism? Or, in particular, to account for why poststructuralist thought—one object of Badiou's critique of "philo-Semitism" that could hardly be said to be motivated by Israeli politics or right-wing ideology—has found such a rich resource in Jewish legalism and textual practice, or why it has functioned as such a powerful alternative to a broadly Hegelian mode of reflection on the political?

If "Jew" is understood as a marker of identity, I think it becomes impossible to understand why, for two thousand years, the word "Jew" has come to embody such an exceptional point of resistance to universalism, or why, in particular, Paul's conception of the universal is inseparable from the polemic with the Jewish law out of which it emerges. This question is important not only because the "egalitarian and universalist" reaction Badiou proposes as a response to anti-Semitism is modeled on the Pauline declaration he reads as the foundation of universalism ("There is neither Jew nor Greek . . ."), but because the exceptional status of the word "Jew" is closely linked to the question of law on two levels: first because the history of anti-Semitism is inseparable from debates about the function and meaning of law, and second because the form Jewish "particularism" takes in Badiou's *Saint Paul* is adherence to the literal tradition and obedience to law.

It seems fair to say that for Badiou the Jewish discourse is very much on the side of the "law" or concrete situation (a "particular world") and never on the side of the event. (As Peter Goodrich observes, "law" and "event" could be written within the classical logic so dear to Badiou as "P" and "–P.")[8] It generally appears in Badiou's work either as the "site" or "worldly situation" where the event erupts (an event that breaks with that situation and allows for the emergence of something new) or as a "particularist" or identitarian resistance to universality. He understands Paul as a Jew sited in a Jewish discourse, for whom the Christ event interrupts and transforms that site, allowing for the emergence of a subject whose only fidelity is to the truth he declares. But while Badiou identifies the resurrection event and the anti-law of love at the heart of Christian discourse with subjectivation, he tends to diminish the subjective dimension of Jewish discourse by describing it pejoratively as a mere "obedience" or "enslavement" to "what is," aligning it with the conservation or persistence of an existing situation and its worldly adherences.

In focusing on these texts, my aim is not so much to evaluate Badiou's analysis of Jewish discourse as to consider what these arguments reveal about his conception of law. More broadly, then, the question I want to address is whether the notion of "particularism" is adequate to account for what is at stake in law. With respect to Badiou's own framing of the problem in "The Three Negations," I could rephrase that question in the following terms: Is the field of law always a concrete world or a concrete situation? Is it entirely contained within the intuitionist paradigm? Or is it possible to consider the advent of the letter of the law, particularly as it is framed in Jewish legalism, as itself a kind of event?

In what follows I will put Badiou's work in dialogue with two other authors who have written critically about the exceptional status of the word "Jew," specifically in relation to the theory and history of law: the legal theorist Pierre Legendre and Sigmund Freud. Like Badiou, both authors are interested less in the identitarian question of who the Jew *is* than in what "the Jew" comes to signify in certain political and legal contexts. Freud's approach in particular is close to Badiou's in several important respects, notably in attempting to cut through the myth of Jewish "exceptionalism" or "chosenness" and to consider how this myth functions fantasmatically both within Judaism and in anti-Semitic discourse. However, both authors depart from Badiou in foregrounding the question of *transmission* as what is essential, even as they distinguish it from the transmission of a racial or cultural legacy. And while Badiou argues that the exceptional status imputed to the word "Jew" can and should submit to equal and universal treatment, Legendre and Freud both align it with a way of reading and a modality of transmission that is at odds with, if not completely antinomial to, an "evental" understanding of universalism.

JEWISH LEGALISM
AND THE TRANSMISSION OF WRITING

Legendre links the stakes of the word "Jew" to the transmission at stake in the fictional structure of legalism, which is the transmission of a function rather than a content: "The transmission of what interests us in the space of institutions is not the transmission of material objects nor even of a discourse, in the sense in which discourse signifies the contents of a message. . . . This transmission, however historical it may be, is not that of a content; nor is the content of such transmission what should interest us. . . . What is transmitted, properly speaking, is nothing, the Nothing."[9] The transmission of this "nothing" might be understood as a kind of event in law, one that could be compared in certain respects with Badiou's account of the Void at the center of the event. Both suppose a "voiding of particular identities." But Legendre and Freud imply that the "transmission of nothing" at stake in legalism is concerned first and foremost with the advent of the letter, and more generally with the transmission of the symbolic as a "founding fiction." If the void at stake in the event is tied to the eruption of a real, the "transmission of nothing" is concerned with the mechanisms of the symbolic as distinct both from the imaginary *and* from the real. That is, it concerns the structural function of the letter or signifier as distinct from the law understood as a prohibition, norm, or representation, but also from the event that purports to break with that law.

Legendre outlines an alternative genealogy of anti-Semitism, one that has nothing to do with race but with the tension between two different attitudes toward writing and the letter. "Semite" is after all not a racially specific term, but one that applies to Jews and Arabs alike, lumped together from a Christian or "Western" perspective that views both as impediments to its way of structuring the institutions of law and the symbolic. What they share is a relation to writing and to the text that is fundamentally at odds with the underlying tenets of Western jurisprudence, but also and more importantly, for this discussion, with the Pauline reasoning that allows the

Romano-Christian model of law as a "living writing" to triumph over the Semitic legal traditions (both Jewish *and* Islamic) that link law to castration, or to the fundamental relationship between the body and writing that determines the subject's orientation in relation to the logical place of the Other, or what Legendre calls the "absolute Writing."

He develops his argument through a reading of Emperor Justinian's *Novel 146*, "The Jews indulge in some insane interpretations." Justinian was the first emperor to identify his own political power iconographically with the risen Christ, the first and perhaps best representative of the theologico-political conception of sovereignty that Ernst Kantorowicz would later identify with the doctrine of the "King's two bodies."[10] Not coincidentally, he was also responsible for codifying the Roman law that would subsequently serve as the foundation of Western jurisprudence.

More specifically, Justinian's legal legacy consists in having legislated all kinds of issues involving Jewish religious circles. Among other measures, he outlawed the transmission of Judaism by forbidding the Mishnah and its commentary, the Talmud; and he ordered the Jews, on pain of death, not to contradict the doctrines of the resurrection, the last judgment, or the divine creation of the angels.[11] For Legendre, however, there is nothing particularly exceptional about these acts of repression, which he views as nothing more than the articulation of ordinary political violence, in no way specific to the Jewish question. Moreover, Justinian's rulings concerning the Jews were not exclusively punitive; he also introduced certain protections and rights, and allowed the Jews to be inscribed in the legal order of society in a way they were not previously. What this duality makes clear, writes Legendre, is that

> we must not assume that a problem like anti-Semitism can be resolved simply by abolishing punitive or repressive measures. To the contrary, we can see that *Novel 146* operates on two levels: it enumerates measures of protection of the Jews as well as measures of persecution. . . . If the protection of the Jews is a commodity as ancient as anti-Semitism itself, if these two elements can exist side by side in the same text, it is because

there is something more behind juridical regulation and theological reasoning than simple hostility or benevolence.

("Jews" 102–3)

The real interest of Justinian's ruling lies elsewhere, and involves the mode
of functioning of the text. It concerns what in classical Romano-Christian
language is called "the destruction of the Jewish fables (*Iudaeorum fabulas*)"
("Jews" 100). For Legendre, the Novel is the work of a magistrate, a work
that comes to master for all the signifier "Jew" by making it function according to a Christian logic. Specifically, it foregrounds the question of the Jew
as the *question of the text* ("Jews" 100). At stake are two different and mutually exclusive ways of entering into law and the writing of law: the Romano-
Christian approach, which is founded on the oracles of incarnate power,
and the Jewish approach, founded on the transmissions of the interpreters.

Legendre advances that the Romano-Christian approach to the text is
"founded in a discourse which denies the essential quality of the relation
of the body to writing"; "its basic characteristics can be set out by means
of a fundamental Romano-pontifical maxim: the Emperor carries all the
archives in his breast (*omnia scrinia habet in pectore suo*)" ("Masters" 110, 109).
The understanding of the emperor or the pope as the "living voice of the
law" (*viva vox iuris*) or the "Law that breathes" (*Lex animata*) ("Jews" 105–6)
suggests that "in the imaginary relation to the place that knows, one person
alone is supposed to act on behalf of all the others" ("Masters" 111). A mystically alienated human body—or what Legendre calls the "living writing"—
"stands in the place of the absolute book" (109). The result is a "banalisa-
tion of writing," in which the text is conceived not as an object of love, but
merely as the bearer of a message (111).

In contrast, Legendre observes that "in other legal traditions, most notably the Islamic and Talmudic, our ways of dealing with texts seem like an
imposture" (107–8). In Talmudic law, for example, "circumcision becomes for
each subject the mark of an interpreter and the proof of his allegiance to the
absolute Writing or, in psychoanalytic terms, of the relationship between
the human subject and the logical place of the Other" (110–11). In this

tradition, law is not a description of an existing order or the representation of a lawgiving authority, but a text whose meaning is uncertain. Writing is understood not as the more or less transparent medium of communication, the bearer of a message that originates elsewhere, but as a form of inscription that implicates the subject in a process of interpretation determined from the outset as structurally incomplete. Fidelity to the "absolute Writing" is thus a fidelity to the letter in its undecidable character. In the diaspora context in which the Talmud originates, there is no privileged mediator or interpreter of the law, no court of last recourse. The object of rabbinic commentary is not to fill this vacuum with an authoritative interpretation that would to determine or decide the meaning of the law, however, but to model an approach to religious practice based on the necessity of wrestling with the letter of the text. In the paratactic style typical of Talmudic commentary, many different glosses are presented side by side, without any subordination or synthesis.[12] In its nondecisionist character, the Jewish interpretation of law foregrounds the decompletion of the symbolic, the absence of a final arbiter, including God himself.

This fundamental difference is crucial to the "juridical anti-Semitism" institutionalized by Justinian, which is founded on two implicit charges: the Jews are slaves of the letter, and the Jews interpret the text all the way to castration ("Jews" 107). Because the Jews have neither emperor nor pope to guarantee for them the truth, the signifier functions in a more autonomous and more radical fashion, which explains the significance of fables, of stories with a poetic or metaphoric sense, in the architecture of rabbinic interpretation (107). This is why the Christian authors of antiquity classified the Jewish interpretations of Scripture as *purely human interpretations* (107). That there can be no reconciliation between the two is made clear by Saint Jerome, who distinguishes between what he calls "the Scriptures in the Jewish sense" (*judaico sensu*) and the "study of the Law of God" (*studium Legis Dei*), which is Christian (100).

The Christian system of thought conceives of itself as promoting a spiritual interpretation of the text (111). This mode of interpretation originates with Paul himself, who pioneered the practice of "figural" or "typological" reading: an allegorical mode of exegesis that subordinates the letter of the text to a spiritual meaning. In his famous typological reading of the two wives of Abraham as representing two covenants (which, incidentally, immediately follows the passage that begins "there is neither Jew nor Greek," and is presented as its gloss), Paul explains:

> It is written that Abraham had two sons, one by a slave and one by a free woman. But the son of the slave was born according to the flesh, the son of the free woman through promise. Now this is an allegory: these women are two covenants. One is from Mount Sinai, bearing children for slavery; she is Hagar. Now Hagar is Mount Sinai in Arabia; she corresponds to the present Jerusalem, for she is in slavery with her children. But the Jerusalem above is free, and she is our mother. . . . Now we, brethren, like Isaac, are children of promise. But as at that time he who was born according to the flesh persecuted him who was born according to the Spirit, so it is now. But what does scripture say? "Cast out the slave and her son, for the son of the slave shall not inherit with the son of the free woman."
>
> (Galatians 4:22–30)

The Jews are slaves to the flesh, slaves to a purely corporeal interpretation of the covenant as a covenant with the flesh and blood of Abraham. But they are also slaves to the letter, slaves to a practice of reading that focuses on the "flesh" of the letter to the exclusion of its allegorical meaning.

In the Letter to the Romans, Paul will associate the letter of the law with "sinful flesh," the Law of God with the spirit: as fleshly beings, we are delivered over to sin by the very law that tells us to do good, because we interpret it according to the flesh. But Christ delivers us from sin by delivering us from the written law:

> While we were living in the flesh, our sinful passions, aroused by the law, were at work in our members to bear fruit for death. But now we are discharged from the law, dead to that which held us captive, so that we serve not under the old written code but in the new life of the Spirit. . . . For the law of the Spirit of life in Christ Jesus has set me free from the

law of sin and death. For God has done what the law, weakened by the flesh, could not do: sending his own Son in the likeness of sinful flesh and for sin, he condemned sin in the flesh, in order that the just requirement of the law might be fulfilled in us, who walk not according to the flesh but according to the Spirit. For those who live according to the flesh set their minds on the things of the flesh, but those who live according to the Spirit set their minds on the things of the Spirit. To set the mind on the flesh is death, but to set the mind on the Spirit is life and peace. For the mind that is set on the flesh is hostile to God; it does not submit to God's law, indeed it cannot; and those who are in the flesh cannot please God.

(Romans 7:5–6; 8:2–8)

Access to the truth is by means of the spirit alone; the fleshly letter leads only to falsehood, and thus to sin and death. In Legendre's words,

If the Jews are the slaves of the letter, if they turn their backs on Reason, it is because, in the words of the patristic formula, they have a *corporeal interpretation of the text*. The proof is that they call themselves the sons of Abraham. They are, but only "according to the flesh" [*secundum carnem*]. The flesh deceives us, and the Jews deceive us as well: the children of Abraham are the "children according to faith" [*imitatio fidei*]: in other words, the faith at stake in the Christian reading of the text.[13]

("Jews" 108)

Justinian translates Paul's reasoning into the language of juridicism, where "spirit" and "letter" found the juridical notions of truth and falsehood. He thereby recuperates as a legal judgment the traditional claim that the Jews are the "sons of the devil" because they "speak falsely" (97). This accusation implies that "to speak is to speak the truth, to give voice to the truth of the text. To speak truly is to speak within a genealogy of texts. In other words, legally" (97). With respect to this model, the Jewish approach to the letter can only appear as "insane" or diabolical, a deviation from truth: "The Jews are the sons of the devil, the sons of the deceiver, because their genealogy is false: false *according to the truth of the text*. The Jews are false because they are juridically false, the false heirs of Abraham; they have misunderstood the text and misconstrued the meaning of the formula "the children of Abraham" (*Abraham et semen eius*) (97).

In charging that "the Jews indulge in some insane interpretations"—interpretations whose transmission must henceforth be forbidden—Justinian reveals a blind spot of occidental jurisprudence, which pertains to the space of incarnated power: only one can respond, only one can guarantee. It supposes the "telescoping of a human body with the absolute Other, an ultimate Other who guarantees everything, telescoping a body with the divine signifiers, or with God himself" (99).[14] If the transmission of Judaism is a threat to the legal order of the Roman Empire, it is because the autonomous operation of the signifier is not subordinated to truth, and so must be censured. In questioning or failing to recognize the spiritual equivalences that found power, the Jewish relation to the text breaks the allegorical link between state and spiritual kingdom (Paul's "Jerusalem above"), Emperor and God.

This relation to the text is not unique to Judaism, however. Rather, it is an approach to the letter that Legendre will identify with a variety of different reading practices, and psychoanalysis in particular. "If there's something fundamentally Jewish about psychoanalysis," he writes, "it is not for the purely anecdotal reason that Freud happened to be a Jew. I would say it goes much further than that, and that psychoanalysis is much more Jewish than one imagines." The real link between psychoanalysis and Judaism is the practice on which Freud's system of thought is based, namely, "the unraveling of the logic of interpretations that had until then been inscribed in a single legitimating authority, and the signaling of another logic: the play of texts in the space of the unconscious, the space of castration itself" (98). This is why, says Legendre, psychoanalysis is not conceivable in Christian or Roman terms: "if madness is something that causes reason to malfunction, then psychoanalysis, as a Jewish fable or folly, a madness identified legally within a system of thought that is juridically and politically guaranteed, can only function as a rupture within this system of thought" (104).[15]

In both cases, the relationship between writing and the body is understood as the writing of a limit that precludes any notion of a "living writing" or the "telescoping of a human body with the Absolute Other."[16]

This limit or impasse is what is at stake in the charge that the Jews "interpret the text all the way to castration." Legendre notes that the Christian exegesis of the law is born out of the rulings of the Jerusalem Council on the question of circumcision, a council in which Paul participated and in which his own theological writings on circumcision played a determining role: namely, his distinction in Romans between the law of faith and the law of circumcision.[17] When Paul declares that "real circumcision is a matter of the heart, spiritual and not literal" (Romans 2:29), he implies that the importance ascribed to the rite of circumcision in Jewish practice is the index and symptom of a literalism that stands in the way of spiritual truth. More than that, however, Legendre argues that circumcision is the mark of an allegiance to what he calls the "absolute Writing," a writing that foregrounds the decompletion of the symbolic because it cannot be sublated into the living law of the spirit.

The tension between these two attitudes toward the text is one of the central preoccupations of typological reading, crucial to the interpretation of who inherits the covenant. In chapter 3 we saw that Augustine, in *City of God*, draws on Paul's typological distinction between the children of slavery and the children of the promise in his gloss of another key biblical episode, the naming of Israel through Jacob's struggle with the angel. The contest ends with the angel striking Jacob on the hip, causing him to limp on one foot. Augustine interprets the wound to mean that the angel, understood to be Christ himself, wounds the Jews but spares the Christians:

> This angel obviously presents a type of Christ. For the fact that Jacob "prevailed over" him (the angel, of course, being a willing loser to symbolize the hidden meaning) represents the passion of Christ, in which the Jews seemed to prevail over him. And yet Jacob obtained a blessing from the very angel whom he had defeated; thus the giving of the name was the blessing. Now "Israel" means "seeing God";[18] and the vision of God will be the reward of all the saints at the end of the world. Moreover, the

THE EVENT OF THE LETTER

angel also touched the apparent victor on the broad part of his thigh, and thus made him lame. And so the same man, Jacob, was at the same time blessed and lame—blessed in those who among this same people of Israel have believed in Christ, and crippled in respect of those who do not believe. For the broad part of the thigh represents the general mass of the race. For in fact it is to the majority of that stock that the prophetic statement applies, "They have limped away from their paths."[19]

For Augustine, the Christian is above all the one for whom "wounding" is no longer necessary, because Christ has taken the wound upon himself, "being the willing loser" to assume—and thus preempt—their wounds. Christ not only guarantees truth against lies, therefore, but makes it possible to overcome the subjection of the body to writing and the wounding it effects. Or as Badiou puts it, the message of Paul's gospel is that "we *can* overcome our impotence, and rediscover what the law has separated us from."[20] It is otherwise, however, for the "general mass of the race," the Jews who lack faith. Paul and Augustine both make clear that the wound (like the "literal" circumcision that is its sign) will not disappear altogether, but will henceforth be borne entirely by the Jews.

This wound is important for our topic in that it is tied to the Jews' inability to recognize the event. In his gloss of Genesis 25 (where Jacob steals the blessing intended for his brother Esau by wrapping himself in goat skin to deceive their blind father, Isaac), Augustine, like Paul, suggests that the younger brother's theft of the blessing foreshadows the Christians' ascendance over their elder brothers, the Jews. But he also takes this Pauline interpretation further by suggesting that the error of the Jews consists not merely in failing to recognize and accept Christ, but in adhering so closely to the letter that they are blinded to the event of the Messiah:

The blessing of Jacob is the proclamation of Christ among all nations. Isaac is the Law and the Prophets; and Christ is blessed by the Law and the Prophets, even by the lips of Jews, as by someone who does not know what he is doing, because the Law and the Prophets are themselves not understood. . . . Our Christ, I repeat, is blessed, that is, he is truly spoken of, even by the lips of Jews who, although in error, still chant the Law and the Prophets: and they suppose that another is being blessed, the Messiah who is still awaited by them, in their error.

(City of God 16:37)

Like the blind Isaac fooled by Jacob's clothing, the Jews are unable to see beyond the letter of the text to its concealed meaning. In contrast, figural reading allows the Christian to lift the veil of the letter, to see the revealed truth of the text in its full splendor.

In implying that a commitment to the letter precludes openness to the Christ event, Paul and Augustine also reveal that the "event" paradigm is itself inseparable from the logic of "spiritual" or typological interpretation. The question of faith stages the tension between fidelity to the letter and fidelity to an event figured as "beyond" the letter, its spiritual truth. This point is crucial to Badiou's own reading of Paul as well. He notes that after the conversion event of Damascus, Paul turns away from "all authority other than that of the Voice that personally summoned him to his becoming-subject" (*Saint Paul* 18). The authority of the Voice is opposed to Greek wisdom and Jewish signs, embodying a mysterious "demonstration of the spirit" that forgoes any appeal to the letter or even to rational argumentation: "For Jews demand signs and Greeks desire wisdom, but we proclaim Christ crucified, a scandal for the Jews and folly for the Gentiles" (1 Corinthians 1:22–23). Christ reveals himself to Paul as the living word of God, the Voice speaks to him and to him alone, calling him into being out of nothingness: as he tells the Corinthians, "by the grace of God I am who I am" (1 Corinthians 15:10).

Why, then, is the general mass of the Jews unable or unwilling to hear the Christ event and the Voice that proclaims it? Paul explains, "we impart this in words not taught by human wisdom, but taught by the Spirit, interpreting spiritual truth to those who possess the Spirit. The unspiritual man does not receive the gifts of the Spirit of God, for they are folly to him, and he is not able to understand them because they are spiritually discerned. The spiritual man judges all things, but is himself to be judged by no one" (1 Corinthians 2:9–10, 13–15). There is a kind of "election" implied in the tautology of the spiritual model: the spiritual man discerns spiritual truth because he has received the gift of the spirit. What Paul and Augustine both suggest is that the true heir of the promise—the Christian—is the one who receives the gift of the spirit and hears the Christ event (whether Jew or Gentile according to the flesh), while a Jew who remains with the "general mass" is deaf to the event and disinherited by virtue of that deafness.

THE UNIVERSAL AS AN "ADDRESS TO ALL"

In emphasizing his universalism, Badiou argues for a different reading of Paul than the one institutionalized by such figures as Augustine and Justinian, and attempts to extract the essence of Paul's contribution from the many traditional—and especially doctrinal—recuperations that have long obscured what he considers to be the more profound stakes of his declaration. Badiou proposes to read Paul "as an atheist" (*Saint Paul* 3), and is less interested in Paul's interpretive authority and role in shaping Christian theology than in the subjective dimension of his discourse. He reads Paul's conversion experience as attesting to the liberatory potential of the event he calls "resurrection," which culminates in the production of a "New Man" who declares his emancipation from law and fidelity to a subjective truth procedure. Badiou describes the resurrection as a "fable," concerned less with an eschatology of salvation than with a singular process of subjectivation. According to this reading, there is no group election or communal resurrection; Paul is concerned not with figuring out who will inherit the promise, but only with declaring his fidelity to the subjectivation—or "grace"—that results from his own experience of the Christ event.

If Paul is the founder of universalism, it is not because he paved the way for the global expansion of the Christ religion by bringing the Gospel to the Gentiles, but because he declares fidelity to a truth procedure whose consequences are addressed to everyone. For Badiou universalism is not an imperialist or hegemonic phenomenon, therefore, but a singularity that is entirely subjective in nature. In his "Eight Theses on the Universal" (1998), roughly contemporaneous with the publication of *Saint Paul*, Badiou describes his own conception of the universal in the following terms:

"Thesis 1: The proper element of the universal is thought," and all true thought operates at the limits of available knowledge. Nothing objective is universal.

"Thesis 2: Every universal is a singularity." The universal cannot be directly articulated with any recognizable particularity, grouping, or identity.

"Thesis 3: Every universal has its origin in an event, and the event is intransitive to the particularity of the situation." A universal is always unpredictable, incalculable, and so in a certain sense "unconscious."

"Thesis 4: A universal appears at first as the decision of an undecidable or the valorization of something without value," that is, as a decision concerning the reality of those elements collected in a situation's evental site.

"Thesis 5: The universal has an implicative or consequential structure." The universal is the consequence of a decision, visible only to those who share in making the decision.

"Thesis 6: The universal is univocal." The universal is a matter of fidelity to the consequences of a truth, and not of the interpretation of its meaning(s).

"Thesis 7: Every universal singularity is unfinishable, or open." The universal is indifferent to our mortality or fragility.

"Thesis 8: Universality is nothing other than the faithful construction of an infinite generic multiplicity." Universal is properly an adjective that applies to a certain "status of being" (being assembled according to the criteria of its pure being as being, i.e., through the mechanics of a truth procedure) rather than to a category of judgment or knowledge.[21]

If Badiou goes so far as to identify Paul (a relative latecomer) with the *foundation* of universalism, it is because Paul is an "*antiphilosophical theoretician of universality*" who "assigns his thought to a singular event, rather than a set of conceptual generalities" (108, emphases in original). Paul's fundamental contribution to universality is thus to have revealed that something is "universal" not as a class or as a predicate (something held in common), but because it is proposed and addressed to everyone.[22]

There is no denying that Badiou has made a major contribution to our understanding of Paul by focusing on the subjective dimension of his discourse and offering an original new interpretation of the stakes of "resurrection." While I am convinced by much of what Badiou has to say, my aim in drawing upon Legendre's analysis is to show that Badiou's postulation of universality as a consequence of the event is undermined by his failure to account for the extent to which the event and its consequences are defined polemically within Pauline hermeneutics as an objective, rather than subjective, truth. My reservations can be grouped into three major concerns.

(1) The real blind spot of Badiou's otherwise remarkable reading of Paul is the lack of any consideration not only of his importance for Christian and Nazi anti-Semitism (a silence that was justly criticized by many readers at the time of its publication), but more importantly of the strategy of typological or "spiritual" interpretation that makes it possible. Paul is not only the inventor of universalism, but the originator of the argument against the Jewish relation to the letter that will lead to its censuring and gradual foreclosure from Western legalism, and thus arguably the inventor of anti-Semitism in its fullest sense.

The sidestepping of this question results in a misreading both of the Jewish relation to the letter and of Paul's response to it. Recall that for Badiou, the Jewish and Greek discourses are both instances of "particularity," since they are centered on obedience to worldly objects that function as unary traits of identification (law and ritual practice for the Jew, wisdom for the Greek). The corollary of this particularism is that each discourse supposes that the key to salvation can be found in the universe: through "direct mastery of the totality" in the case of Greek wisdom, and through "mastery of the literal tradition and the deciphering of signs" in the case of Jewish prophecy (*Saint Paul* 42). Conversely, Paul's discourse ties salvation to the event in which the subject is called forth as a subject: "By the grace of God I am what I am," as Paul puts it (17).

However, Badiou's description of the Jewish discourse as a "discourse of the sign" and its deciphering actually applies better to Paul than to Jewish textual practice. He writes: "What is Jewish discourse? The subjective figure constituted by it is that of the prophet. But a prophet is one who abides in the requisition of signs, one who signals, testifying to transcendence by exposing the obscure to its deciphering. Thus, Jewish discourse will be held to be, above all, the discourse of the sign" (41). As we have just seen, however, neither Paul nor his theological or juridical heirs associates Judaism with "mastery of the literal tradition" or with an ability to decipher the obscure: to the contrary, they insistently underscore the failings of Jewish interpretation, its "merely human" quality, its inability to attain complete revelation. On this point Badiou's interpretation of Paul's discourse is impossible to justify either historically or hermeneutically. Indeed, the "deciphering" of Scripture as an encoded revelation originates with New Testament sources, and has no obvious antecedent in Jewish textual practice.[23] Jesus invariably frames his own actions and teachings with references to prophetic sayings that seem to foretell his own advent and mission, presenting himself as the messianic fulfillment of the law. But it is Paul himself who really radicalizes and systematizes this mode of interpretation. Jesus' appeals to Scripture could be understood primarily as attempts to confirm his identity as the Messiah, and to situate his actions within a recognizable theological framework. Paul's celebrated readings of the Abraham cycle, on the other hand, suggest that even the patriarchal and historical narratives of the Hebrew Bible are encoded prefigurations of the Gospel and its message of resurrection, whose concealed meaning can be deciphered by those who have the gift of the spirit. The generic formula that introduces these typological readings, "as it is written," is one of the most frequently repeated phrases in the New Testament, occurring more than forty times in the synoptic Gospels and more than fifty times in Paul's letters.[24]

Badiou's reading arguably inverts the positions of mastery and nonmastery by failing to consider the extent to which the "gift" of spiritual interpretation itself implies a kind of *absolute mastery*, a mastery with respect to which Jewish interpretation is represented as completely impotent, irreparably "wounded" or "blinded." In his sixth thesis on the universal, Badiou writes that the universal is "univocal," a "matter of fidelity to the consequences of a truth, and not the interpretation of its meaning(s)." To what extent, however, is this univocity already bound up in interpretation and, in particular, a spiritualist interpretation with respect to which the letter is nothing more than a "veil" to be penetrated?

Badiou has offered a self-criticism of his book on Paul that intersects to some extent with the reservations I have just expressed. He proposes that the title is not a good one, for two reasons. First, because Paul's letters are less the "foundation" of universalism (a formula that implies a kind of temporal and conceptual priority) than one example or instance among others. And second, because Paul's "universalism" is itself equivocal, a *universalism without universality.* This is because the resurrection is a fable or fiction, and not a creation of something universal. In other words, Paul provides a *new explanation of what is universal,* but does not create a *new universal proposition.*[25] In emphasizing Paul's explanatory power as the crux of his innovation, I think Badiou offers an implicit acknowledgment of the significance of interpretation in Paul's account of the Christ event, even if he stops short of considering its full hermeneutic and political consequences. But I would further extend this critique by arguing that the resurrection is not so much a new "explanation of what is universal" as a new definition of *who is addressed by the promise* (the heir according to faith) and of *what it means to inherit the promise* ("resurrection," which Badiou interprets nonliterally as a figure of subjective renewal and rebirth). Badiou's reading of the second question is absolutely stunning, a virtuosic (and, I think, definitive) treatment of this problem. But I believe he obscures what is at stake in the first not only when he credits Paul with founding universalism, but even in the more restricted claim that Paul's letters offer a new "explanation of what is universal."

(2) Importantly, Paul does not so much "universalize" the promise as argue that it concerns a *different* addressee: not the children of Abraham "according to the flesh," but the children of Abraham "according to faith." While Badiou argues that a truth is universal only to the extent that it is addressed to everyone and for everyone, the preceding analysis suggests that

Paul does not enlarge or generalize the possible addressees of the covenant so much as substitute one set of addressees for another. The logic of Paul's polemic is thus at odds with the way Badiou wants to read "there is neither Jew nor Greek, there is neither slave nor freeman, there is neither man nor woman." While for Paul any of these terms *may* be included in the promise, it is only on the condition that they "hear" the event; the "true" addressee is not anyone and everyone, therefore, but only those who welcome Christ into their hearts. Tellingly, Badiou never glosses (or for that matter even cites) the last part of the sentence: "for you are all one person [εἰζ] in Christ Jesus." The Jew who accedes to the universal, who is "one in Christ Jesus," is the Jew who hears the event, and who renounces the flesh of the letter in favor of its spirit: in other words, a Christian. In this sense, Paul's declaration is less the "faithful construction of an infinite generic multiplicity" (Thesis 8) than the construction of a community organized around a new predicate, the acceptance of Christ as the sovereign mediator or "living voice" of the law. This also raises the possibility that Paul's letters are less an opening onto the universal than a polemical privileging of one "particularism" over another.[26]

The universal Paul founds is a *partisan universal*, and it is precisely in this respect that it is important for Badiou. Indeed, one of the most original contributions of Badiou's conception of the universal is to reveal that it is always and necessarily partisan. His "Eight Theses" make this point explicit in stating that "the universal is the consequence of a decision, visible only to those who share in making the decision" (Thesis 5). The more hegemonic or coercive side of this claim comes out in *Uses of the Word "Jew"* where Badiou argues not only that the word "Jew" should be wrested free from the Zionist and other political discourses that have attempted to control its signification, but that it must submit to universalizing treatment. Even Badiou's call to find new significations for the word "Jew" arguably participates in the typology that undergirds Paul's reading of the promise by treating the word "Jew" as a "particularism" (a bit of flesh?) that must give way to a "spiritual" (or generic) interpretation. In arguing that the word "Jew" should succumb to egalitarian and universalizing approaches, is Badiou not making that signifier function according to a Christian logic, just like Paul and Justinian?

At the very least, Badiou is silent about the extent to which a real sacrifice is going on here, and not just an "emancipation," a transcendence of "mere particularities" or of "enslavement to an object." This sacrifice is at work in the affirmation of the event itself, since the condition of accepting the event is sacrificing the letter. If the Jews' refusal to recognize and receive the event is such an irritant for Paul, for Western legalism, and now even for a purely philosophical approach to the event, I would suggest that it is not because it makes a unique identity claim in excess of equality, but because it represents a relation to writing, language, and the symbolic for which a system predicated on the event leaves no place. This is why the word "Jew" is not just the index of one "particularism" among others, but a paradigmatic point of resistance to the logic of universalism as such, for Paul and Badiou alike.

(3) Finally, does the affirmation of the "event" repeat the logic of political theology or the polemical opposition of spirit to letter, exception to norm, decision to deliberation? This question has two main vectors. First, to what extent does the "decision of an undecidable" imply a spiritual interpretation of the political act, or what Legendre describes as the "telescoping of a human body with the absolute Other?"

Second, to what extent does the privileging of univocity tend toward decisionism or even dictatorship? Simon Critchley has expressed a similar reservation in charging that Badiou's work promotes a "heroism of the decision."[27] He locates it in Badiou's claim that "dictatorship is the natural form of organization of political will,"[28] even if what Badiou has in mind is not the power of a sovereign executive, but something more akin to the self-authorizing, collective dictatorship implied in Marx's notion of a "dictatorship of the proletariat." I would add to this criticism a comment about how the repudiation of writing or the letter functions within the decisionist paradigm. From Paul to Schmitt, the political-theological discourse of the decisive act is invariably structured as a polemic against writing, against the logic of the letter itself, and not just against "rote norms." It promotes a banalization of writing by conceiving of law as nothing more than a "dead letter," with respect to which the unscripted act, dictatorial decision, or explosive "event" represents the only possibility for a dynamic transformation of the situation. In Schmitt's terms, the institutions of law are displaced by what he calls the "order of law," an order that under certain exceptional circumstances is "embodied" in miraculous fashion by the sovereign who suspends the constitution to preserve the existence of the state. What Legendre describes as a "living writing" is substituted for the logical space of written law, the space of an absolute Writing that cannot be completed "spiritually."

THE EVENT OF THE MOSAIC LAW

Sigmund Freud's analysis of law in *Moses and Monotheism* responds to this very point, showing how the Mosaic law constitutes a critique of the "living writing" by foregrounding the symbolic dimension of the written law and opposing it to the real. In the process, he offers a novel approach to the relation between law and event by considering the advent of the letter of the law as itself a kind of event.

The Mosaic law is really *the* event for Freud, the first true rupture with the underlying assumptions of totemism. In Lacanian terms, I have suggested that the key innovation of the Mosaic tradition is the invention of the symbolic as distinct either from the real (the exceptional jouissance of the primal father) or from the imaginary (the father, but also the norms and prohibitions that take the father's place in the logic of the fraternal pact). As the "laws of speech,"[29] the commandments institute a break not only with every previous understanding of law, but also with the "law of the spirit" at stake in Paul. They are understood not as mere representations or as placeholders of a force or authority figured as "beyond" the law—"our custodian until faith came," as Paul puts it—but as the articulation of a symbolic structure whose spacing or negation of the real undercuts the fantasy of an incarnate law implicit in Paul's and Schmitt's different accounts of the exception. With respect to the Mosaic law, Freud suggests that Paul's innovation is less a novel, emancipatory "event" than a *restoration*. This is because "Paul, by developing the Jewish religion further, became its destroyer."[30] What is destroyed is the symbolic function of the Mosaic law itself, the object of Paul's polemic to which he opposes the spiritual authority of the Voice.

In Badiou's reading of Paul, the Christ event is conceived as something "outside" or "beyond" law; it confronts the law with its limitations, contests its ordering of reality, and in the process radically transforms or even annihilates the law as such. Freud takes a different tack by considering the advent of the letter of the law as itself a kind of event. More broadly, he raises the question of whether there is something evental about the symbolic itself. In his account of the Mosaic law, it is not the event of the real that comes to "liberate" the Jews from the letter, but the letter itself that comes to liberate them from enslavement to the real.

This development leads me back to question I asked at the beginning of this chapter: is the field of law concerned merely with an existing situation or a concrete world? Following Freud, we might say that Badiou's account of the event as having "a negative relationship to the laws of the world" could apply not only to the resurrection event described by Paul, but to the Mosaic law itself. Martin Buber suggests that the defining characteristic of early Judaism is its break with the worship of nature, symbolized by the gap introduced into the solar and lunar cycles of day and month by the commandment to honor the Sabbath day.[31] In the context of the ancient Mediterranean, Yahweh is the only God who is not part of his own creation; but more than that, his function is linked to a negation of the world of existence. In this sense, the advent of the "negative" laws of the Decalogue could itself be understood as an event of subjectivation, one that liberates the Jews from obedience to a concrete situation. Freud takes this analysis further, suggesting that the Mosaic law is the first true break not only with the laws of the natural world, but also with the imaginary laws of the totemic order. This event is repressed by the event of Pauline universalism, which in reinterpreting the event of the law actually effaces it.[32]

The shift from the Mosaic law to Paul could be understood as a shift from a paradigm that privileges the event of the signifier to one that privileges the event of the real, or from a legal structure based on what Legendre calls the "transmission of nothing" to what Badiou describes as the void of the event. When Legendre argues that legalism is concerned with the "transmission of nothing, of the Nothing," he makes clear that the stakes of this transmission cannot be appreciated if it is confused with the transmission of a content, whether that content is an interpretation, a bloodline, a cultural history, or anything else. Like Badiou's own account of the void at the center of the event, the "transmission of the Nothing" supposes a voiding of particular identities. But while the theory of the event supposes that the subject is the by-product of a real, the "Nothing" supposes that the subject is the effect of a signifier, the originary inscription that Legendre calls the "absolute Writing" and that Lacan will identify with the commandments as the "laws of speech."

In affirming the event of the signifier, it is important to stress that neither Legendre nor Freud is promoting anything like "particularism." Freud in particular has no interest in promoting the Jewish *religion* or in arguing for the singularity of the Jewish people. The Jewishness of the Jews (if this is understood to inhere in their racial bloodline or lived cultural history) is completely indifferent to this transmission, which after all originates in Egypt. If the Jews have cause to be proud of their history, it is simply because they have managed to transmit this Mosaic legacy, however imperfectly and whether or not the broad mass of the people have any fidelity to it at all. In other words, it is quite clear to Freud that the vast majority of the Jews continue to inhabit the totemic logic, just as the vast majority of Christians do; there is absolutely no notion, in Freud's reading, of Jewish "exceptionalism," if this is understood to be a special feature of the race. This is a dimension of his argument that I imagine Badiou would also affirm: neither author has any love for the cult of "particularism." Where they do differ is that Freud insists on the exceptional quality of the *transmission*, of the legal structure itself and in particular its status as a symbolic fiction. The site of this transmission is not the Jewish race or religion, but Jewish *legalism*. As long as this symbolic innovation is dismissed merely as a feature of "particularism," it becomes impossible to take stock of what is at stake in this transmission, and what it would mean to close ourselves to it.

I appreciate fully that in affirming the importance of universalism and the vigor of the event, Badiou is in no way espousing a hegemonic or imperialist idea of universalism, or a group psychology of nation or party. Fundamentally, he is advocating a respect for the human subject in its emptiness, as a purely formal supposition that must be subtracted from any communal predication of identity. But Legendre and Freud both suggest that respect for the human subject is inseparable from a respect of the letter, or the radically autonomous operation of the signifier that defines the relation between writing and the body: a logic that is necessarily "insane" and "sophistic" from the vantage point of an event that presents itself as a break with or as a liberation from the letter.

* * *

Even if the event of the real and the event of the letter could both be considered as "events" without diluting the stakes of the concept, it does seem that they are of fundamentally different registers, and that fidelity to one is incompatible—indeed even mutually exclusive—with fidelity to the other. Paul understands this very well in positing a complete antinomy between an attitude of openness to the event and an attitude of fidelity to law. His original contribution is simply that this antinomy is not situated at the level of racial birthright, ritual initiation (circumcision), or history (the transmission of a tradition).[33] In essence, one could understand Paul as saying to the Jews: it is not your blood or your circumcision that makes you a Jew, but your relation to the text. But while your blood and your circumcision are indifferent to the covenant (neither guaranteeing participation nor precluding it), your relation to the text excludes you from the covenant because it prevents you from hearing the Voice, from receiving the living law in its full revealed splendor.

This interpretation, while remarkably dismissive and even damning, arguably also helped Judaism to become what it is, by causing it to emphasize increasingly the textual practices that would give rise to the Talmud and to abandon or vastly minimize the messianic impulse that had become increasingly important during the prophetic period. When this tendency was drained off by the small sect of Jesus' followers who would later break off to found a new religion, it no longer occupied a central place in mainstream

Judaism. Judaism is not the same after Paul, and it owes as much to this polemic as Christianity does. Nevertheless, the polemic undeniably polarizes the two terms, and makes impossible any reconciliation between them. In founding Christian practice as a break with Judaism (something that Jesus himself does not do), Paul founds a new religion and a radically new relation to the law. But it is not clear that this amounts either to a founding of universalism or even (as in Badiou's self-criticism) to a new explanation of what is universal. I would propose that the contemporaneity of Paul has to do less with his universalism than with having introduced and formalized a polemic that is as much in play today as it was in his own time.

This polemic, however, cannot persist as a confrontation of two positions if the differend at stake in their respective attitudes toward the letter or writing is either suppressed or decided in such a way that one position is declared "true" and the other "false." Paul arguably opts for "deciding" the polemic, for christening the "children of faith" as the true heirs of the promise. But should not the role of the philosopher be to *think* the polemic, rather than decide it? In opting for the latter, I think that Badiou breaks with his own very powerful understanding of the philosopher's task as that of thinking the event and its consequences, a task that is arguably compromised if one simply declares fidelity to the event and attempts to win over adherents as if to a political cause.

In the debate surrounding Badiou's recent writings on the word "Jew"— a debate that has quickly devolved into the mutual flinging of accusations ("You're an anti-Semite!" "Well, you're against equality!")—it seems that there is no place to recognize and examine a real difference, a real differend, one whose resistance to "equal" or "universal" treatment may be neither a limitation nor a virtue, but a fact worth considering in its own right. Just as it is preposterous for Eric Marty to claim that Badiou is a fascist and a hater of Jews simply because he has dedicated his life to promoting the universalism for which he feels so deep a conviction, so it may be unreasonable to call for the Jewish tradition to make its peace with that universalism and to hear the "address to all," or, more broadly, to accuse anyone who questions that universalism of being antiegalitarian or a right-wing ideologue.

6

THE COMMANDMENT
AGAINST THE LAW

Writing and Divine Justice
in Walter Benjamin's "Critique of Violence"
and Immanuel Kant's *Critique of Judgment*

ALTER BENJAMIN'S EARLY writings on law from the Weimar period model another, more productive way of thinking about the written law. They cast a critical eye on any account of the political sphere that upholds the unwriteability of the act as its chief virtue, or attempts to reduce the function of law to the status of a secondary representation. Benjamin, who was at once a harsh critic of the failures of parliamentary democracy, a committed proponent of revolutionary class struggle, and a grudging admirer of "the fascist public law theorist" Carl Schmitt,[1] might seem an unlikely source to appeal to for a more generous understanding of law. His "Critique of Violence" is one of the most scathing treatments of law imaginable, offering a blistering critique of the violence perpetrated in the name of law and arguing eloquently for its annihilation through anarchy. Remarkably, however, Benjamin manages to advance an analysis of law and a critique of its mediating function that not only refuses the familiar terms of the Pauline dialectic, but subverts its most fundamental presuppositions. His analysis can be read as both anticipating and enriching Jacques Lacan's distinction between the imaginary and symbolic dimensions of law, which he elaborates in the context of a political and juridical theory of violence.

Central to the novelty of Benjamin's approach is a profound appreciation of the structural function of the written law (and more generally of what he calls the "symbolic side of language") as an alternative both to the lawmaking violence of dictatorship and to the decadence and ineffectualness of parliamentary democracy. While he joins with many other voices in denouncing the failures and limitations of law, Benjamin is careful to distinguish law in its representational or "mediate" function (or what Schmitt places under the heading of "norm") from what he calls "language as pure means," the structural function of language as a limit to violence and power that he identifies with the historic innovation represented by the advent of the written law. In the process, he offers an original and compelling defense of the indispensable role of language in the resolution of human conflicts.

Like his predecessor and likely source of inspiration in this argument, Immanuel Kant (whose *Critique of Judgment* will be discussed at the end of this chapter), Benjamin draws attention to the absence of any serious meditation on the symbolic function of the *written* law in the traditional critique of law as norm, and invites us to consider the specific function of the law's *writtenness* as distinct from whatever content it might communicate. Significantly, both authors appeal to the commandments of the Hebrew Decalogue to illustrate the indispensable role of the written law in resisting the lure of the imaginary and the blind submission to power it encourages. This focus on the commandment form is especially provocative with respect to Paul's polemic, since for Paul the commandment is not just one example among others of the defect in the written law, but absolutely exemplary of the problems internal to the written law as a distorting mediation. Paul is careful to specify that the holy commandment is not the law of sin. Nevertheless, he asserts that the law of sin "finds opportunity in the commandment": "I should not have known what it is to covet if the law had not said, 'you shall not covet'" (Romans 7:7). In prohibiting, the law incites transgression by offering up to the imagination an object of desire. The commandment is thus the vehicle through which sin and death insinuate themselves into the Jewish law, perverting or derailing our quest for the purely spiritual law of God. In short, Paul understands the commandment as nothing more than a *representation* of divine law, corrupted by the mediation of the letter that consigns it either to a rote normativity devoid of spiritual meaning or to a transgressive seduction by the imagination.

In contrast, Benjamin and Kant both distinguish the precepts and norms of positive law from the commandment form, understood neither as a positive prescription nor as an empty "principle," but as a *limit* with which one must struggle that is conditioned by its writtenness without functioning to mediate or represent the "spirit" of the law. While the commandments of the Hebrew Decalogue are exemplary in each case, neither author strictly follows Jewish tradition. Instead, each locates in the need to struggle with the commandment the possibility of subjective freedom and liberation from tyranny. If they call this possibility "divine," it is not to appeal to a "mystical foundation of authority" that would have the force of law,[2] but rather to invoke a justice that cannot be represented or embodied, but that nonetheless involves an encounter with a specific limit.

This more nuanced understanding of the commandment is central to Benjamin's essay "Critique of Violence," published in 1921, which concludes with his notoriously elliptical distinction between "mythic" and "divine" violence, or between the founding violence that makes the law and the destructive violence that annihilates law. The essay mounts an exhaustive critique of the mythic order of law, understood as the site of a "tyrannical" violence whose only function is to guarantee the perpetuation of its own power. But in the midst of this withering critique of law, Benjamin nonetheless advances a very strong argument in favor of the written commandment in its relation to justice. In essence, Benjamin inverts the usual Pauline logic by associating the pernicious lawmaking function of mythic violence with what he calls the "tyranny of spirit," which is linked to an absence of writing. At the same time, he recovers the function of writing as something distinct from—or even opposed to—the function of law as a representation or mediation of a higher authority. Where Paul opposes the intelligible to the sensible and the divine to the human, Benjamin's essay links divine justice to the letter of the commandment and makes it the affair of men.

"CRITIQUE OF VIOLENCE"

"Mythic violence in its archetypal form," writes Benjamin, "is a mere manifestation of the gods. Not a means to their ends, scarcely a manifestation of their will, but primarily a manifestation of their existence."[3] The violence at stake in mythic manifestations sheds light on all lawmaking violence, revealing that lawmaking is *powermaking*, and that the object of retribution is always "mere life." Benjamin cites as an example the legend of the Theban queen Niobe, who refuses to show deference to the gods and boasts that she is more worthy of admiration than the goddess Latona because she has given birth to fourteen beautiful children as compared to the goddess's two. In response, Apollo avenges his immortal mother by felling Niobe's children one by one with his arrows, until the city of Thebes is soaked with their blood. The grieving Niobe is not killed, however, but stripped of the power of speech and frozen in a block of stone, where she is doomed to suffer in silence for all eternity.

For Benjamin, the interest of the legend is that it reveals mythic violence to be a *lawmaking violence*: "Niobe's arrogance calls down fate upon her not because her arrogance offends against the law but because it challenges fate—to a fight in which fate must triumph and can bring to light a law only in its triumph" (248). This is why, he writes, mythic violence "establishes a law far more than it punishes the infringement of a law that already exists" (248). Its capricious character reveals the essence of the mythic order, in which violence appears to be "crowned by fate":

> However unluckily it may befall its unsuspecting victim, its occurrence is, in the understanding of the law, not chance, but fate showing itself once again in its deliberate ambiguity. Herman Cohen, in a brief reflection on the ancients' conception of fate, has spoken of the "inescapable

realization" that "it is fate's orders themselves that seem to cause and bring about this infringement, this offense." Even the modern principle that ignorance of a law is not protection against punishment testifies to this *spirit of law*.

(249, my emphases)

Benjamin notes that "laws and circumcized frontiers are also, at least in primeval times, *unwritten laws*," which means that "a man can unwittingly infringe upon them, and so incur retribution" (249, my emphases). As distinct from punishment, which implies the violation of a law that is published and known, retribution is always "provoked by an offense against the unwritten and unknown law."

Even in its occult character, however, mythic violence is "boundary preserving." Benjamin gives as an example the establishment of frontiers after a war that secures new territory (249). These frontiers are "laws" only in the sense that they circumscribe a territory, identifying a sphere of operation of power. One could also cite examples from Greek mythology, in which the offenses that provoke the lawmaking violence of the gods are frequently boundary violations: the body steps on taboo ground, incurs the wrath of the gods, and is instantly stricken dead or transformed into an inanimate object.[4] This understanding of law is implicit in the term "trespass," which links the violation of a law to the effraction of a space or territory.[5] A trespass is first of all a territorial breach, a "crime" of the body against a zone of power, and only secondarily and by extension a moral or legal infraction.

The story of Niobe reveals that the "boundary preserving" character of mythic violence is concerned with more than territory, however. "Violence . . . bursts upon Niobe from the uncertain, ambiguous sphere of fate," leaving her behind as an "eternally mute bearer of guilt and as a boundary stone on the frontier [*als Markstein der Grenze*] between men and gods" (248). If she becomes a "boundary stone," it is because there is no real boundary or limit between gods and humans, only a "sign" of the former's absolute and unbounded power. This lack of boundary is implied not only in the absence of written laws, but in the silencing of speech, which deprives Niobe of her only means of defying the gods or protesting their violence.

In the modern state, the "spirit" of mythic violence tends toward dictatorship as its logical limit, with the police function as its most ubiquitous and ambivalent manifestation. Both make the "spirit" of law synonymous with the perpetuation of the legal order itself, and not the securing of just ends. Benjamin advances a similar argument in his book on the German mourning play, where he shows that the *Trauerspiel* is concerned with a manifestation of spirit that shows itself to the outside under the form of power, as the faculty to exercise dictatorship: "Spirit [*Geist*]—such was the thesis of the age—shows itself in power; spirit is the capacity to exercise dictatorship."[6] In the words of Jacques Derrida, Benjamin understands dictatorship as an "instituting decision that, by definition, does not have to justify its sovereignty before any preexisting law and only . . . utters itself as a series of orders, edicts, and prescriptive dictations or dictatory performatives."[7]

The spirit of mythic violence is not limited to autocratic rule, however. Its insidious presence pervades even the democratic state, where its clearest manifestation is the police function. Benjamin describes it as a melding of two types of violence—lawmaking and law-preserving—"in a kind of spectral mixture" (242). What he denounces in the police is not only the formlessness of its power, its "ghostly presence" (*gespenstische Erscheinung*), but its "spirit" (*Geist*), which betrays "the greatest conceivable degeneration of violence" (243). The police are everywhere; there is nothing "outside" their authority; their use of such invasive tactics as surveillance and wiretapping reveals that mythic violence inevitably breaches its boundaries in order to maintain them, extending the reach of state power in the name of "securing" its borders. In both cases, "spirit" expresses not the ultimate end of law, its highest aim or underlying principle, but rather the unbounded nature of mythic power.

While he identifies unlimited authority as the most troubling manifestation of mythic violence, Benjamin is equally pessimistic about the capacity of "preexisting laws"—or even constitutional protections—to contain or control it. The legal rights of individuals cannot be opposed to the pervasive power of the state, since the legal order grants those rights with the sole aim of preserving its own existence: "the law's interest in a monopoly of violence vis-à-vis individuals is explained not by the intention of preserving legal ends but, rather, by the intention of preserving the law itself" (239). What state power most fears is not the legal rights of individuals, but their potential for exercising extralegal violence. This is because "violence, when not in the hands of the law, threatens it not only by the ends that it may pursue but by its mere existence outside the law" (239). He gives as an example the workers' guaranteed right to strike. The state concedes to organized labor a legal right to strike, a right that would seem to contradict its own interests, because it forestalls the violent actions the state fears, such as workers' engaging in sabotage or setting fire to factories (245). The legal violence of the strikers is not a means to a natural or just end, therefore, but already inscribed in the law-preserving function of mythic violence: the state authorizes the legal violence of means only in order to suppress a violence that might spell the end of its own monopoly on power.

The only solution, then, is to oppose violence with violence. But which violence? Not a lawmaking violence or a legal violence of means, but a "different kind of violence" than that imagined by legal theory:

> Among all the forms of violence permitted by both natural law and positive law, not one is free of the gravely problematic nature, already indicated, of all legal violence. Since, however, every conceivable solution to human problems . . . remains impossible if violence is totally excluded in principle, the question necessarily arises as to what kinds of violence exist other than all those envisaged by legal theory. . . . How would it be, therefore, if all the violence imposed by fate, using justified means, were of itself in irreconcilable conflict with just ends, and if at the same time a different kind of violence arose that certainly could be either the justified or the unjustified means to those ends but was not related to them as means at all but in some different way?
>
> (247)

This "different kind of violence" is what Benjamin calls "divine violence," which alone is capable of securing just ends. Whereas "power [is] the principle of all mythic lawmaking," writes Benjamin, "justice is the principle of all divine endmaking" (248). If mythic violence is concerned with boundary violations, and itself involves the breaching of the subject's boundaries, then divine violence will "call a halt to mythic violence" by erecting a different kind of boundary, making the barrier against the "spirit of mythic states" the necessary condition of justice:

> Far from inaugurating a purer sphere, the mythic manifestation of immediate violence shows itself fundamentally identical with all legal violence, and turns suspicion concerning the latter into certainty of the perniciousness of its historical function, the destruction of which thus becomes obligatory. This very task of destruction poses again, ultimately, the question of a *pure immediate violence that might be able to call a halt to mythic violence.* Just as in all spheres God opposes myth, mythic violence is confronted by the divine. And the latter constitutes its antithesis in all respects. If mythic violence is lawmaking, divine violence is law-destroying; if the former sets boundaries, the latter boundlessly destroys them; if mythic violence brings at once guilt and retribution, divine power only expiates; if the former threatens, the latter strikes; if the former is bloody, the latter is lethal without spilling blood. The legend of Niobe may be contrasted with God's judgment on the company of Korah as an example of such violence. God's judgment strikes privileged Levites, strikes without warning, without threat, and does not stop short of annihilation. But in annihilating it also expiates, and a profound connection between the lack of bloodshed and the expiatory character of this violence is unmistakable. . . . *Mythic violence is bloody power over mere life for its own sake; divine violence is pure power over all life for the sake of the living.*[8]
>
> (249–50, my emphases)

While the mythic power of the gods of antiquity finds its modern equivalents in dictatorship and the police function, Benjamin identifies the expiatory violence of the Hebrew God with the transformative violence of revolutionary class struggle. He describes revolutionary violence as the "highest manifestation of pure violence by man" (252), and illustrates its "law-destroying" character by reference to Sorel's distinction between the political strike and the proletarian general strike. The political strike, which supposes a set of demands addressed to authority, ultimately involves the strengthening of state power, since it functions merely to modify (and so maintain) the existing order (246). It illustrates the law-preserving function of violence as means. But the proletarian (or revolutionary) general strike demonstrates that under certain conditions—for example, in the context of class struggle—strikes can be seen as "pure means" (245). This is because the revolutionary general strike makes no demands, but instead sets itself the sole task of destroying state power. It reveals its indifference to material gain by declaring its intention to abolish the state as such, as the basis of the existence of the ruling group that exploits the public (246). It is no longer a matter of modifying the legal order, or even of founding a new law, but of "calling a halt" to the order of law and so inaugurating a new epoch.

Although the revolutionary strike is annihilating with respect to the state, Sorel argues that such a rigorous conception of the general strike is capable of diminishing the incidence of actual violence in revolutions (246). The paradoxical conclusion Benjamin draws from his argument is that a method of solution that is beyond all legal systems is therefore also beyond violence:

> Whereas the first form of interruption of work is violent, since it causes only an external modification of labor conditions, the second, as a pure means [*als ein reines Mittel*], is nonviolent. For it takes place not in readiness to resume work following external concessions and this or that modification of working conditions, but in the *determination to resume only a wholly transformed work, no longer enforced by the state, an upheaval that this kind of strike not so much causes as consummates.* For this reason, the first of these undertakings is lawmaking but the second anarchistic. Taking up occasional statements by Marx, Sorel rejects every kind of program, of utopia—in a word, of lawmaking—for the revolutionary movement: "*With the general strike, all these fine things disappear,* the revolution appears as a clear, simple revolt, and no place is reserved either for the sociologists or for the elegant amateurs of social reforms or for the intellectuals who have made it their profession to think for the proletariat."
>
> (246, my emphases)

In the "consummating" quality of the general strike, we find the expiatory violence characteristic of the divine. While it causes the legal order to "disappear," anarchistic or revolutionary violence does not necessarily require the spilling of blood; it is lethal to the legal order, but not lethal to life.

Given Benjamin's overarching interest in revolutionary violence as an alternative to the tyranny of dictatorship and the decadence of parliamentary democracy, it is perhaps surprising that what he opposes to the corrupt "mythic spirit" of the modern state is "divine" violence. While the biblical story of God's judgment against Korah may serve as a paradigmatic instance of such violence, the allusion is fleeting and its import ambiguous.[9] Since the defiance of mythic power is most obvious in the example of the proletarian general strike, why does Benjamin not call the expiatory violence of just ends a "revolutionary" or "anarchistic" violence? As the "highest manifestation of pure violence by man," is revolutionary violence meant to embody fully the expiatory power of divine violence? Or is it to be understood merely as a more limited or imperfect manifestation of a violence that God alone can wield with complete justice?

Readers of Benjamin are essentially split between those who insist on the historical context of the essay to argue that it is really concerned with the proletarian general strike as an instrument of class struggle (and who are therefore somewhat embarrassed or perplexed by the reference to the "divine"), and those who suggest that the reference to the divine couches an implicit appeal to a transcendent authority that arguably undercuts any application to proletarian struggle. Benjamin certainly does little to dispel this second hypothesis, especially in his discussion of the irreconcilable conflict between means and ends: "it is never reason that decides on the justification of means and the justness of ends: fate-imposed violence decides on the former, and God on the latter" (247). In this statement and in many others, the antagonism between the "mythic" and the "divine" seems to derive from the confrontation of two different conceptions of divinity, or of two equally theophanic accounts of violence: polytheist versus monotheist, Greek versus Jewish, sacrificial versus exalting of life, and so forth. Does the distinction between the mythic and the divine ultimately come down to an opposition between a polytheist world order and a monotheist transcendence, or between the manifest and the ineffable? Is God being invoked as the transcendent guarantor of justice, of a Law beyond the laws?[10]

This debate really comes down to what Benjamin means when he indicts lawmaking violence as a corrupt or distorting mediation of pure violence. In his words,

> Only mythic violence, not divine, will be recognizable as such with any certainty, . . . because the expiatory power of violence is invisible to men. Once again all the eternal forms are open to pure divine violence, which myth bastardized with law. . . . All mythic, lawmaking violence, which we may call "executive," is pernicious. Pernicious, too, is the law-preserving, "administrative" violence that serves it. Divine violence, which is the sign and seal but never the means of sacred dispatch, may be called "sovereign" [*mag die waltende heissen*].
>
> (252)

Mythic violence "bastardizes" divine violence by rendering visible, and so reducing to a fixed manifestation, what is fundamentally invisible: the expiatory power of divine violence. It concerns the imaginary, the sensible, what manifests itself or makes itself seen. This imaginary order is not limited to signs or manifestations of power, but extends even to the lawmaking character of programs, agendas, and ideals: for example, the utopian political projects of the intellectuals and "amateurs of social reform" that recede, in Sorel's conception of the proletarian general strike, before the consummating force of the revolutionary movement ("with the general strike, all these fine things disappear").

If divine violence is a law-destroying violence, what it destroys *in* law is thus its mediate character. How, then, are we to understand the stakes of mediation? Is the "pure" merely the ineffable or the transcendent? More specifically, what is the relation of language to violence and power? Is the medium of language complicit in what is corrupt in law? What are the consequences for the letter or for writing?

In placing the "divine" on the side of the intelligible or invisible (or what he calls the "eternal forms") and the "mythic" (as a "bastardization" of law) on the side of representation, Benjamin's analysis would seem in many respects to accord seamlessly with Paul's neo-Platonic distinction between an intelligible truth and its mediating representation, or between the transcendent "spirit" of the law and its compromising letter. However, his own account of mythic violence as promulgated by "unwritten laws" interferes with this translation. The recognizability of mythic violence is not necessarily mediated by language or writing, since what is made visible is the manifestation of power itself. Conversely, divine justice has nothing to do with the "spirit" of the law, which Benjamin will associate with the "tyranny of mythic states."

LANGUAGE AS "PURE MEANS"

This problematic goes to the heart of a distinction that structures much of the essay, between "language as mediation" and "language as pure means." Benjamin associates language as mediation with mythic violence, and language as "pure means" with the nonviolent elimination of conflicts. But what is meant by "language as pure means," and what is its relation to divine justice? In what sense are its means "pure," and how do they avoid the pitfalls of mediation or of violence as means?

Jacques Derrida has provided the most influential reading of this problem. He argues that for Benjamin, language as mediation is identified with the problematic of the "sign," which is always understood as a means toward an end ("Force" 285). This is what we find in mythic violence, where the speechless Niobe is left behind as a "boundary stone" on the frontier between men and the gods, a warning sign to anyone who would challenge fate. When Benjamin calls for a "different kind of violence" that might combat the mythic order, a violence that is "not related to [ends] as means at all but in some different way" (247), Derrida hypothesizes that this question must open onto "another dimension of language, beyond mediation and thus beyond language as sign" (285).

What is this "other dimension of language," and what is its relation to divine justice? For Derrida, it would be the immediate language of presence, associated with the divine power of naming. He cites as evidence Benjamin's essay "On Language as Such and on the Language of Man," published in 1916, which defines original sin as the fall into a language of mediate communication where words have become means ("Force" 286). What Benjamin opposes to it is the "pure immediate" language of the name before the fall, identified with the divine power of naming as an "immediate communication of the concrete."[11] Reading through the lens of this earlier essay, Derrida hypothesizes that divine violence is fundamentally related to the sovereign power to name. He finds further evidence in the final line of "Critique of Violence," which invokes the power of naming in relation to sovereignty: "Divine violence, which is the sign and seal but never the means of sacred dispatch, may be called 'sovereign'" (*mag die waltende heissen*) (252). Derrida argues that the verb *heissen*, which means not only "to be called," but "to name," establishes a fundamental link between divine violence and the sovereign power to name.[12] It implies that divine violence is what *names* the sovereign, what *calls itself* sovereign, what is sovereign because it can call itself or because it can name: "But who signs? It is God, the Wholly Other, as always. Divine violence will always have preceded but will also have given all the first names. God is the name of this pure violence—and just in essence: there is no other, there is none prior to it and before which it has to justify itself. Authority, justice, power, and violence are all one in him" (293). Derrida thus identifies in the figure of divine violence an implicit recourse to what he calls (following Pascal) a "mystical foundation of authority" (285), in which the divine "signature," as the pure presence of authority with the name, alone seals justice. God is present with his signature, and his signature is presence itself: what it concerns is "nothing less than the origin of language in its relation to truth" (285). For Derrida, then, the invocation of "divine violence" constitutes an appeal to an authority that is just as boundless and omnipotent as what Benjamin indicts in mythic violence.[13]

The problem with this conclusion, in my view, is that in linking "language as pure means" to the secret and unspoken "immediate language of presence," and thus to the intelligible or ineffable, Derrida attributes to Benjamin the very Pauline logic that I read him as trying to dismantle. While Derrida is absolutely right to underscore the link between divine violence and language as pure means, he relates them in a way that conflates pure means with divine *authority* (the signature or seal) and thus with an onto-theological conception of sovereignty. That it is not a question of a "mystical foundation of authority" is clearly attested to by the examples Benjamin provides of "pure means," which are concerned less with naming or presence, I would argue, than with the function of the limit or barrier, and thus with the violent spacing that is the signature of writing.

THE SYMBOLIC FUNCTION OF LANGUAGE

From his earliest critical writings, Benjamin insists on a third understanding of language, which can be assimilated neither to "language as mediation" nor to "language as pure presence." While "On Language as Such" is often read as promoting an understanding of "pure" language as unmediated presence, the essay actually concludes with Benjamin distinguishing between language as "sign" and what he calls the "symbolic side of language," which concerns something else altogether: "For language is in every case not only communication of the communicable but also, at the same time, a symbol of the noncommunicable. This symbolic side of language is connected to its relation to signs, but extends more widely—for example, in certain respects to name and judgment. These have not only a communicating function, but . . . also a closely connected symbolic function."[14] This essay suggests that language is not simply inadequate to the task of communication because it is mediate or sensual, as Paul might argue; it is also valuable in communicating the *incommunicable*, its resistance to communication, that is, in underscoring a limit. I would argue that the "symbolic side" of language sheds light on what Benjamin understands by "language as pure means" and suggests that the latter is "pure" not because it gives access to the "origin of language in its relation to truth," but because it resists the lure of communication, the fantasy of unbounded access or transparency.[15]

In "Critique of Violence," this "symbolic side of language" is implicit in Benjamin's account of language as "wholly inaccessible to violence" (245). Asking whether a nonviolent resolution to conflict is possible, Benjamin responds in the affirmative. He notes that we find "pure means [*reine Mittel*] of agreement" in relationships among private persons and in the conference as a technique of civil agreement (244, translation modified). Agreement is a process of negotiation in which there is no final arbiter. As the medium in which this negotiation takes place, language allows for a decision without recourse to a final authority, and thus to an enforcing violence. We find something similar in the example of education, which Benjamin cites as a modern instance of "divine power." In its perfected form, the educative power stands "outside the law" (250). Like the revolutionary general strike, education illustrates how the "pure immediate violence" of divine power often appears as nonviolent. But what it shares with other examples of divine violence is not merely bloodless expiation and the absence of lawmaking, but a reliance on language as its privileged medium.

The clearest evidence of the function of language as pure means, however, is the fact that historically, "no legislation on earth" originally stipulated a sanction for lying (244). Benjamin interprets the absence of any such sanction as an exclusion of violence. What it demonstrates is that "there is a sphere of human agreement that is nonviolent to the extent that it is *wholly inaccessible to violence*: the proper sphere of 'understanding,' language" (244–45, my emphases). Essential to this possibility of language is not communication or representation (giving expression to what "really happened" or what one "really thinks"), but the creation of a space that is immune to the tyranny of the mythic order. Lying is a use of language whose function is to limit the intrusion of the other. To lie is, among other things, to erect a barrier, to stave off the other's knowledge of—and power over—one's interiority. In this sense the lie is diametrically opposed to all "communication," which aims at the complete transparency of the mind. With respect to Derrida's argument, it is significant that Benjamin's key example of language as "pure means" concerns the lie—an instance of *false* naming—and not the sovereign power to name *truly* ("the origin of language in its relation to truth") that Derrida wants to identify with divine violence.

Indeed, the relatively late preoccupation of legal systems with truth and lies is for Benjamin the very hallmark of mythic violence. He identifies it with the penalty placed on fraud, but also with such abuses of legal power as surveillance and the use of force to extract testimony. In these practices, the subject's ability to lie comes under attack, with the result that the barrier against state power is eroded. Importantly, though, this violence against the legal subject is first and foremost a violence against language in its symbolic function. In the penalty placed on fraud and other forms of lying, Benjamin remarks, language itself is "penetrated by legal violence" (244), such that it can no longer function as a protective barrier.[16]

Derrida himself suggests that Benjamin's critique of the formless, intangible, "ghostly presence" of the police should be read as a more general indictment of the invasive, superegoic character of *Geist*, or "spirit."[17] Earlier we saw that Benjamin defined spirit as "the capacity to exercise dictatorship."[18] The corollary is that "dictatorship, which is the essence of power as violence, is of spiritual essence."[19] Importantly, though, this "spiritual" character is also linked to a refusal of language in its limiting function and, in particular, of writing. Benjamin specifies that mythic violence is promulgated by "unwritten laws," orders that take the form of fated decrees or dictatorial pronouncements that do not have to justify their sovereignty before existing laws. This contempt for the written is structural to dictatorship. Etymologically, the dictator (from the Latin *dicere*, "to say" or "to speak") is the one who speaks, whose sovereignty inheres in the performative authority of the voice. (As Adolf Eichmann famously said of Hitler, "the words of the Führer have the force of law." Importantly, though, these sovereign words were almost never recorded or written down. Eichmann speaks at length of the distrust of written orders among the Nazi elite, and the corresponding valuation of the voice and of spoken commands as expressing more fully the "spirit" of the law, a spirit inseparable from the authority of the Führer himself.)[20]

In his discussion of the "unwritten" laws that define the mythic order, Benjamin suggests that "the struggle over written law in the early period of the ancient Greek communities should be understood as a rebellion against the spirit of mythic states" (249). In other words, men appeal to the concreteness of the written law—and even the punishment it incurs when violated—as a defense against the "spirit" of the unwritten law, whose retributive character is inevitably tyrannical. When Benjamin describes the mute and frozen Niobe as a "boundary stone on the frontier between men and gods," he suggests that the mythic "sign of power" is one kind of boundary marker, while the written law is another: the first is a mere sign or emblem of the gods' absolute power over human life, while the second demarcates the sphere of the human as off-limits to the capricious, retributive violence of the mythic order.[21] If mythic violence is a violence *against* the symbolic, then divine violence is a violence *of* the symbolic.

Samuel Weber, in an essay on "Critique of Violence" titled "Deconstruction Before the Name," suggests a link between the sovereignty of divine justice and its symbolic character. Commenting on the final line of the essay, "divine violence . . . may be called sovereign," Weber notes that the term translated as "sovereign," *die waltende*, means not only "ruling" or "prevailing," but also "protecting": "*die waltende* prevails and protects, but only by demarcating itself from its other: *die schaltende*—the 'switching,' 'shifting' movement—that marks mythical force."[22] This "protecting violence" is the violence of the symbolic, which demarcates and differentiates; what it protects against is the unmarked, unwritten, "shifting" character of the mythic.

In foregrounding the function of language as pure means (and written language in particular) as a limit to power, Benjamin effectively introduces a chiasmus with respect to Paul's critique of the Jewish law by identifying the unwritten "spirit" of the law with the mythic and the function of language with the divine. In essence, he identifies an antinomy between mythic violence and the symbolic function of language, which in turn explains the antithetical relation of divine justice to mythic power. The antinomy inheres in the fact that mythic violence concerns unmarked boundaries and is thus hostile to language in its function as protective barrier. In other words, mythic violence is simultaneously *imaginary*, insofar as it is linked to the manifestation of power, and *unmarked*, in the sense that the boundaries, like the laws themselves, are not inscribed. Even as it is "boundary maintaining," it allows no limits or barriers to its power. The symbolic function of language is a threat to mythic power in that it erects just such a barrier, one that Benjamin will align with the function of writing.

WRITING AND DIVINE JUSTICE

If the written law of the Greeks is presented as the first defense against the "spirit" of mythic violence, can we then infer that divine violence, which "calls a halt" to mythic violence, has some necessary or structural relation to writing? Benjamin suggests as much in his discussion of the Hebrew Decalogue, which relates the commandment form to the possibility of divine justice.

Benjamin is careful to specify that the commandment is not a "representation" of divine justice; the commandment is *related* to justice, but not as its representation. In this respect the commandment is not a law at all, at least in the terms of Benjamin's definition of law in the first part of the essay: a mediate representation of a force or violence.[23] Most obviously, the commandment is not identified with a state or power. But more importantly, it is not even identified with God, to the extent that God is understood as the source or sovereign authority "behind" the law. The antinomy between the divine and the mythic does not simply oppose the just laws of the almighty God to the unjust laws of man or to the capricious whims of the gods of antiquity. Instead, it opposes the written commandment, understood as an ethical "guideline" or constraint, to the unwritten law understood as a manifestation of power.

After emphasizing the "annihilating" character of divine violence, Benjamin asks: does this argument, if taken to its logical conclusion, confer on all men lethal power against one another? The answer is no. This is because "the question 'May I kill?' meets its irreducible answer in the commandment, 'Thou shalt not kill.' This commandment precedes the deed, just as God was 'preventing' the deed" (250). However, Benjamin stresses that "no *judgment* of the deed can be derived from the commandment" (250, my emphasis). He explains,

> Those who base a condemnation of all violent killing of one person by another on the commandment are therefore mistaken. It exists not as a criterion of judgment, but as a guideline for the actions of persons or

communities who have to wrestle with it in solitude [*als Richtschnur des Handelns für die handelnde Person oder Gemeinschaft, die mit ihm in ihrer Einsamkeit sich auseinanderzusetzen*] and, in exceptional cases, to take on themselves the responsibility of ignoring it. Thus it was understood by Judaism, which expressly rejected the condemnation of killing in self-defense.

(250)

Divine judgment does not "prescribe" or tell us what to do; it has nothing to do with "representation," even the representation of actions or conduct. This is why, says Benjamin, "neither the divine judgment nor the grounds for this judgment can be known in advance" (250). If one can deliberately ignore the commandment without necessarily fearing death, it is because the commandment addresses the ethical subject and the justice that is its principle, and not bare life. In this respect, Benjamin's account of the commandment cannot be reduced either to the Pauline take on the written law (according to which the commandment is no more than a mediate representation of a divine law that is itself "beyond" language) or to Derrida's account of the divine signature, according to which the sovereignty of God signs, seals, or authorizes "in secret" (where the emphasis is on the *power* implicit in this nomination, this secrecy).

At the same time, Benjamin's analysis of language makes clear that the tension between the mythic and the divine cannot be reduced to the opposition between a tyranny coded "Greek" and a justice coded "Jewish," which is so often read as implicit in the essay. Instead, it suggests that the same antagonism between the mythic and the divine, the unwritten and the written, plays out in both contexts.

In ancient Judaism, for example, the commandment not only does *not* function as a representation of God's power, but in many cases is even opposed to it. In the Hebrew Bible, the introduction of the written commandments of the Mosaic law really marks the transition from one understanding of the deity to another: from God as the embodiment of mythic violence to a divine justice that is not necessarily—or even at all—associated with God's power or will. In the early books of the Bible in particular, God's violence has many "mythic" features: the so-called episodes of demonic attack, where Yahweh suddenly and without provocation attempts to kill his own people, including Moses himself; the ban on entering sacred spaces on pain of death; the significance of blood and blood sacrifice; and so forth. But while the early manifestations of Yahweh are primarily "mythic," the post-Decalogue manifestations are primarily "divine," most obviously, the fiery manifestations of the hot-tempered volcano deity give way to the sublimely invisible God of supreme justice.[24] In this respect, one might even argue that the first "mythic violence" opposed by the written law is the mythic violence of God himself.

WRESTLING WITH THE ANGEL

When Benjamin writes that the commandment is a guideline for those who "have to wrestle with it in solitude," he inflects in a particular way the essay's enigmatic final words: "Divine violence, which is the sign and seal but never the means of sacred dispatch, may be called sovereign" (*mag die waltende heissen*). *Die waltende* can be translated variously as "prevailing," "ruling" or "reigning."[25] The connection to the notion of power or force (*Gewalt*) seems to be the idea of vanquishing or prevailing in battle: *die waltende* is what rules because it is victorious. But what exactly prevails *in* divine violence? Benjamin's argument suggests that it is not some ultimate authority or lawmaking force, but a particular tension or dialectic. The notion of ruling or reigning is potentially qualified by a temporal dimension that makes its dominion provisional or uncertain: for example, a "prevailing trend" or "reigning ideology" is one that rules for the time being, but whose dominion is by no means assured or inevitable.

I cannot help but be struck by the resonances between *die waltende* and the name "Israel," which is often interpreted to mean "God prevails." The name is more than a little ambiguous, however, since as any number of biblical examples serve to illustrate, the Jewish God does not always prevail; it is possible to prevail against him. This is true not only of the many rival gods and forces that Yahweh engages in battle, but also of his own people. Such a possibility is implicit in the episode from which the name emerges, Jacob's struggle with an unidentified "man" of superhuman strength, commonly understood to be the angel of the Lord. According to the text of Genesis,

> When the man saw that he did not prevail against Jacob, he struck him on the hip socket; and Jacob's hip was put out of joint as he wrestled with him. Then he said, "Let me go, for the day is breaking." But Jacob said, "I will not let you go, unless you bless me." So he said to him, "What is your name?" And he said, "Jacob." Then the man said, "You shall no longer be called Jacob, but Israel, for you have striven with God and with humans, and have prevailed." Then Jacob asked him, "Please tell me your name." But he said, "Why is it that you ask my name?" And there he blessed him. So Jacob called the place Peniel, saying, "For I have seen God face to face, and yet my life is preserved."
>
> (Genesis 32:25–30)

The meaning of the name "Israel" is generally interpreted in one of two ways: "the one who struggles with God" or "God prevails." The suffix "-el" generally indicates that God is the subject: hence the interpretation "God prevails." In context, though, Jacob is the subject: the angel explains the name by telling him, "you have striven with God and with humans, and have prevailed." But while Jacob manages to check the angel's power, and thus prevent himself from being annihilated by a superior force, there is no clear victor in the struggle; one cannot say that either party prevails against the other in a decisive way. How, then, should we understand the ambiguity of the name? My own interpretation is that God prevails *in* the struggling of Israel, or, in Benjamin's terms, that *divine justice prevails in the subject's struggle with the commandment.*

In this argument I am drawing on Emmanuel Lévinas's essay "The Pact" (discussed in chapter 3), which reads the Jacob story as an allegory for the relation to the written law that Paul's polemic claims to have rendered obsolete. The Jewish law demands two separate forms of adherence: to its particular form (or "letter") and to its general form (or "spirit"). If adherence to the general "spirit" of the law is not enough, writes Lévinas, it is because "everyone responds to the temptation to encapsulate Judaism in a few 'spiritual' principles. Everyone is seduced by what might be called the *angelic essence of the Torah*, to which many verses and commandments can be reduced."[26] Jacob's struggle with the angel should thus be read as a cautionary tale about the dangers of succumbing to the "angelism" of the Law. The wrestling match reminds us that adherence to a principle is not enough, since "it brings temptation with it, and requires us to be wary and on our guard" (220). The temptation is that general principles can be inverted in their application. This threat is countered by talmudic exegesis and debate, which is "concerned with the passage from the principle embodied in the Law to its possible execution, its concrete effects. If this passage were simply deducible, the Law, in its particular form, would not have demanded a separate adherence." Talmudic casuistry "tries to identify the precise moment when the general principle is at risk of turning into its opposite; it surveys the general from the standpoint of the particular"; in this way, says Lévinas, it "preserves us from ideology." The Talmud is thus "the struggle with the Angel" (220), in which careful scrutiny of the letter of the letter offers a necessary check to the seduction of its "angelic essence," its purely spiritual dimension.

With respect to Benjamin's argument, it is interesting that Jacob receives a bloodless wound to the hip even as he seems to "prevail." What it emblematizes is not the violence against "mere life" that defines mythic violence (whose symbol is the spilling of blood), but a mutual checking that "calls a halt" to violence. The wound is not just a punishment or sign of power, but a mark of God's covenant with Israel. Lévinas calls it "the pact," anticipating the later function of the written commandments as a check on the lawmaking violence of the mythic order. What is checked in the angel is the power implicit in the reign of spirit; what is checked in Jacob is his seduction by that spirit, or his belief in the presence or "face" of God as the source of power (recall that Jacob, taking his leave from the angel, declares, "I have seen God face to face").

The same point is made in a different way in a celebrated passage from the Babylonian Talmud. The passage concerns a dispute between the Sages about whether certain objects are clean or unclean. The great Rabbi Eliezer, who plays a central role in many Talmud discussions, finds himself on the opposite side from the majority. He brings forward every imaginable argument in support of his position, but to no avail. Finally in exasperation he invokes the *halachah* (the system of rabbinic law) and invites it to intervene on his behalf, saying: "If the *halachah* agrees with me, let this carob-tree prove it!" At that very instant the carob tree uproots itself and moves a hundred cubits. Unswayed by this apparent miracle, the other Sages retort: "No proof can be brought from a carob-tree." Again Eliezer declares: "If the *halachah* agrees with me, let the stream of water prove it!" When the stream of water obliges by promptly flowing backward, the Sages again rejoin, "No proof can be brought from a stream of water." This goes on and on, until Eliezer says:

"If the *halachah* agrees with me, let it be proved from Heaven!" Whereupon a Heavenly Voice cried out: "Why do ye dispute with R. Eliezer, seeing that in all matters the *halachah* agrees with him!" But R. Joshua arose and exclaimed: "*It is not in heaven.*" [Deut. 30:12] What did he mean by this?—Said R. Jeremiah: That the Torah had already been given at Mount Sinai; we pay no attention to a Heavenly Voice, because Thou hast long since written in the Torah at Mount Sinai, *After the majority one must incline.* [Exodus 23:2]

R. Nathan met Elijah and asked him: What did the Holy One, Blessed be He, do in that hour?—He laughed [with joy], he replied, saying, "My sons have defeated Me, My sons have defeated Me."[27]

If Eliezer invokes Heaven and solicits miracles to bolster his case, it must be because he himself believes the law to be guaranteed or authorized by God.[28] But the other rabbis rightly interpret the Torah to have its own authority, inseparable from the procedures of interpretation and debate implied in majority rule. How, then, should one interpret the miraculous signs that issue forth at Eliezer's request, and God's own testimony on his behalf? Perhaps these competing authorities are meant to imply that although the written law may indeed be of divine origin, it does not answer to the spiritual authority of the Heavenly Voice. It is an instrument of justice only to the extent that men struggle with it—here collectively—to reach a decision that alone is sovereign.

THE NEGATIVE EXHIBITION OF THE INFINITE

What Lévinas calls the "angelism" of the law is really the danger inherent in the imaginary dimension of law. As a demonic combatant apparently possessed of supernatural powers, the angel supports the illusion that the law incarnates or represents some ultimate authority or seat of judgment that one might either submit to or defy: it gives a face to what is fundamentally invisible. In contrast, the commandment is a writing that works against the imaginary by substituting a "purely negative exhibition" for a positive representation. This function is most evident in the first tablet of the Decalogue, which prohibits worshiping idols, making images of God, or invoking the divine name. According to this reading, the commandments do not assert the sublimely ineffable character of divine authority so much as the necessity of proceeding in the absence of any support for the imaginary.

Immanuel Kant makes a similar argument in a celebrated passage from the *Critique of Judgment*, which discusses the second commandment of the Hebrew Decalogue as an example of the dynamically sublime contemplation of nature as a might.

Nature judged as dynamically sublime arouses fear.[29] When we are confronted with manifestations of natural might, we know that we are no match for them: it is a given that our mere life is nothing in comparison to the awesome power of an erupting volcano, an avalanche, or a tidal wave. Kant specifies that it is impossible to find something sublime if we are truly afraid of it, if we are simply seized by terror (120). Nevertheless, fearful manifestations of natural might may be judged sublime despite their capacity to overwhelm us.[30] This is because they raise the soul's fortitude and allow us to discover in ourselves an *ability to resist* that gives us the courage to believe we could be a match for nature's seeming omnipotence. Even as nature confronts us with our own limitations, we find in our power of reason a standard that has infinity itself under it as a unit; in contrast to this standard, everything in nature is small. We thus discover in our mind a force superior to nature in its immensity, which is the basis of a self-preservation different than the one endangered by the nature outside of us. Reason calls forth a strength that makes our merely natural concerns (property, health, and even life itself) appear as small. It prevents our *humanity* from being degraded, even though a *human being* must inevitably succumb to the dominance of nature. While a man's life may be powerless against natural might, reason affirms that the life of man is to be located not in his empirical existence (or "mere life"), but in the exercise of a capacity for transcendence that raises him above not only his own limitations, but those of nature itself.[31]

Kant then considers as a special case of natural might the power of the almighty God. He admits that it would be foolish and even sacrilegious to imagine our mind superior to the effects produced by such a might, since the dominant feeling incited by God's might is not the sublimity of our own nature, but rather submission, prostration, and impotence. Nonetheless, he argues that a righteous person may *fear* God without being *afraid* of him. The effects of might can arouse in us the idea of God's *sublimity* if we are able to recognize in our own attitude a sublimity commensurate to God, which elevates us above fear of God's wrath.[32]

The analytic ends with a discussion of the second commandment of the Hebrew Decalogue. Kant describes it as the "most sublime passage in the Jewish law," because it facilitates a purely "negative exhibition of the infinite" in which there is no sensible support for the imagination:

Perhaps the most sublime passage in the Jewish Law is the commandment: Thou shalt not make unto thee any graven image, or any likeness of any thing that is in heaven or on earth, or under the earth, etc. This commandment alone can explain the enthusiasm that the Jewish people in its civilized era felt for its religion when it compared itself with other peoples, or can explain the pride that Islam inspires. The same holds also for our presentation of the moral law, and for the predisposition within us for morality. It is indeed a mistake to worry that depriving this presentation of whatever could commend it to the senses will result in its carrying with it no more than a cold and lifeless approval without any moving force or emotion. It is exactly the other way round. For once the senses no longer see anything before them, while yet the unmistakable and indelible idea of morality remains, one would sooner need to temper the momentum of an unbounded imagination so as to keep it from rising to the level of enthusiasm, than to seek to support these ideas with images and childish devices for fear that they would otherwise be powerless. That is also why governments have gladly permitted religion to be amply furnished with such accessories: they were trying to relieve every subject of the trouble, yet also of the ability, to expand his soul's forces beyond the barriers that one can choose to set for him so as to reduce him to mere passivity and so make him more pliable.

On the other hand, this pure, elevating, and merely negative exhibition of morality involves no danger of *fanaticism*, which is the *delusion* [*Wahn*] *of wanting to SEE something beyond all bounds of sensibility*. . . . The exhibition avoids fanaticism precisely because it is merely negative.[33]

In Kant's evocation of the unbounded movement of the soul, I am reminded of Benjamin's distinction between the mythic and the divine: "if the former sets boundaries, the latter boundlessly destroys them" (249–50). Mythic law, like the state-sanctioned religious practices described by Kant, sets up imaginary barriers for the subject, and so deprives it of the trouble— but also the ability—to exercise reason beyond those bounds. The divine would then be aligned with the removal of those barriers and the necessity of "expanding the soul" in the absence of any support for the imagination. This is what we see in Sorel's account of the revolutionary general strike, which refuses the lawmaking character of programs and utopias in favor of an unbounded revolutionary movement that no longer confines itself to any existing ideal or image: "With the general strike, all these fine things disappear; the revolution appears as a clear, simple revolt, and no place is reserved either for the sociologists or for the elegant amateurs of social reforms or for the intellectuals who have made it their profession to think for the proletariat" (246).

Importantly, though, this boundlessness is for Kant inseparable from the function of the written law. The ban on the imaginary is introduced by a commandment, by a writing whose effect is not to bind us to a particular behavior, but rather to *remove* the support it provides. What, then, is the advantage of a purely "negative exhibition" of morality? In what sense is the "thou shalt not" of the written law indispensable to the expansion of the soul and the subjective freedom it makes possible? What prevents the prohibition from becoming another kind of barrier or support, one that is just as confining as the images and accessories of religion and positive law?

The answer is that even as the commandment removes the barriers and supports provided by the imaginary, it introduces a new constraint associated with its "negative" form. The paradox is that in order to experience its own boundlessness, the soul needs to encounter a limit. In the absence of such a limit, the imagination risks tending toward fanaticism, which for Kant is really the lure of the imaginary in its most seductive guise. In "wanting to SEE something beyond all bounds of sensibility," the fanatic may forgo strictly *sensual* representations or images, but nonetheless seeks after a "beyond" that has a distinctly imaginary character (and whose archetypal form may even be the "pure presence" or absolute authority that Derrida identifies with the sovereign power of God). Here the imagination is unbounded, not the reasoning soul. As a "negative exhibition of morality," the written commandment both removes the support of the imaginary *and* offers a constraint that is lacking in fanaticism—it guards against the lure of representation *and* against the lure of the ineffable.

In short, Kant makes clear that the commandment as *constraint* must be distinguished from any positive understanding of law as code, norm, or prescription: it has a unique status, whose function is to replace the imaginary with the "negative exhibition" proper to the symbolic, and so facilitate the unbounded exercise of freedom. I see evidence of this purely symbolic account of law in Kant's assertion that "a righteous [*gerecht*] person" is not afraid of God. A righteous person is not someone who submits to God's authority or obeys his orders. Rather, righteousness or rectitude refers to having law (*Recht*) as a presupposition. In the *Critique of Practical Reason*, Kant specifies that the moral law is not a legal prescription or norm, but the simple commandment *that there be law.* The masses manipulated by religious symbols and the delusional visions of the fanatic are equally without law, since in both cases the imagination encounters no constraint in the form of a "negative exhibition of morality." In contrast, the free and unbounded expansion of the soul in the exercise of reason is evidence for Kant of the self-legislating character of a reasoning faculty that is able to forgo positive law precisely because it has law as a presupposition. To have law as a presupposition is thus different from what Benjamin calls "lawmaking," since the latter inevitably privileges the imaginary to the exclusion of the structural or symbolic constraint implied in a purely "negative exhibition."

This argument may shed some light on Benjamin's apparently paradoxical claim that mythic violence is at once a "lawmaking violence" and a violence that purifies or purges the subject of law: "the dissolution of legal violence stems . . . from the guilt of more natural life, which consigns the living, innocent and unhappy, to a retribution that 'expiates' the guilt of mere life—and doubtless also purifies the guilty, not of guilt, however, but of law. For with mere life, the rule of law over the living ceases" (250). In Kant's terms, to be "purified of law" is no longer to be "righteous," no longer to have law as a presupposition. It is thus to be radically "guilty," subject to the deadly might of a superior power for which the mere life of man is no match when it is not exalted and sustained by a force commensurate to that power.[34]

The corollary is that where the negative exhibition of the law is in play in the form of the pure symbolic, something other than guilt and retribution is at stake. The commandment "purifies the subject of law" in a different way than legal violence, by underscoring that justice cannot be generalized and is always compromised when reduced to a rule or representation.[35] While mythic violence purifies the living of the symbolic and at the same time institutes the rule of mythic law in the form of a manifestation of power, the commandment gives expression to the "law-destroying" function of divine violence by purging the imaginary dimension of mythic law.

The general conclusion I draw from Benjamin's and Kant's respective analyses of the commandment is that the destruction of the *imaginary* dimension of law must not entail the destruction of the *symbolic* or of the structural function of the written law. More precisely, it seems to me that each author is calling for the cultivation of what might be called a *practice of the letter*, which is quite different than respect for the authority of law or adherence to the specific content it transmits. (In the Talmud passage considered earlier, the reliance on such a practice is what emboldens the rabbis not only to legislate on their own without any recourse to a higher authority, but to politely ask the almighty God to butt out of their deliberations.) While for Paul the written law is a distorting representation that impedes access to a higher truth, Benjamin and Kant both imply that the pure symbolic, represented by the commandment as distinct from normative law, is the only possible path to justice: not because it represents the will of God, but because it obliges the subject to "wrestle in solitude" and so assume responsibility for his own freedom.

Although it would be a mistake simply to conflate such a practice with Judaism, Benjamin and Kant both appeal to the Jewish commandment tradition as the site of a specific reflection on the function of the written. The introductory tractate of the Jewish Mishnah concludes with a chapter devoted to the scene of lawgiving at Sinai, which links the inscription of the tablets of the Decalogue to the possibility of human freedom. Commenting on the text of Exodus 32:16, which reads, "The writing was the writing of God, graven (*harut*) upon the Tablets," the Mishnah concludes: "read not *harut*, 'graven,' but *herut*, 'freedom,' for no man is truly free unless he occupies himself with the study of Torah" (Pirke Avot 6.2).[36] While the status of the Torah as a divine inscription might be construed to mean that man is under the power of a higher authority, the rabbis read the line to mean exactly the opposite: God may inscribe the written law, but once the inscription occurs it is incumbent upon men to expound on the law through study and debate, and in the process to expand their own souls beyond the boundaries of the manifest world through struggle with the text.

How would this reading inflect Benjamin's treatment of the revolutionary violence at stake in class struggle as an instance of divine violence? In a letter to Martin Buber written in 1916, Benjamin suggests that political struggle is inseparable from the struggle with writing:

I can understand writing as such as poetic, prophetic, objective in terms of its effect, but in any case only as *magical*, that is as un-*mediated*. Every salutary effect, indeed every effect not inherently devastating, that any writing may have resides in its (the word's, language's) mystery. In however many forms language may prove to be effective, it will not be so through the transmission of content, but rather through the purest disclosure of its dignity and its nature. And if I disregard other effective forms here—aside from poetry and prophecy—it repeatedly seems to me that the crystal-pure elimination of the ineffable in language is the most obvious form given to us to be effective within language and, to that extent, through it. This elimination of the ineffable seems to me to coincide precisely with what is actually the objective and dispassionate manner of writing, and to intimate the relationship between knowledge and action precisely within linguistic magic. My concept of objective and, at the same time, highly political style and writing is this: to awaken interest in what was denied to the word; only where this sphere of speechlessness reveals itself in unutterably pure power can the magic spark leap between the word and the motivating deed, where the unity of these two equally real entities resides. Only the intensive aiming of words into the core of intrinsic silence is truly effective. I do not believe that there is any place where the word would be more distant from the divine than in "real" action. Thus, too, it is incapable of leading into the divine in any way other than through itself and in its own purity. Understood as an instrument, it proliferates.[37]

This letter suggests that Benjamin's investment in the "purity" of language is not a turn away from politics, but political through and through. What political struggle shares with writing is a dedication to the "crystal-pure elimination of the ineffable," or the unmasking of the spiritual power at stake in lawmaking violence.

While Benjamin's account of the revolutionary general strike makes clear that anarchistic violence is mutually exclusive with lawmaking, it also implies that such violence is truly liberatory only when it retains its symbolic character, or its investment in language as a sphere "wholly inaccessible to violence." Although the legal order may "disappear" in the face of revolutionary violence, the symbolic does not. In every instance of divine violence, the operative term is "struggle."[38] Just as Kant reveals the freely self-legislating character of morality to be a struggle with the negative form of the commandment and against the imaginary, Benjamin's reading of the general strike invites us to consider what revolutionary violence struggles *with*, in addition to whatever it struggles *against*. As an instance of divine violence, revolutionary violence is not merely an agonistic struggle between rival classes or an attack on a corrupt legal order, but a struggle with a limit or constraint without which these other struggles could not hope to be successful.

CODA

Toward an Aesthetics
of Symbolic Life

7

FREEDOM THROUGH CONSTRAINTS

On the Question of Will

N A SERIES of recent essays on the will of the people, Peter Hallward finds that the question of will is at best disregarded by contemporary philosophy, at worst feared or rejected by it. In particular, he takes issue with a long genealogy of political philosophy that opposes the negativity of law and limits—or the finitude of lack—to a will understood as an irrational agency that must be circumscribed by laws and constitutional limits or diluted by mediating forms of representation. This is generally read by Hallward as a debasing of the subject, a suspicion concerning its political capacities (especially with regard to popular will), even as a privileging of political elites uniquely "qualified" to govern. He looks for an alternative in frank affirmations of subjective determination that posit will as a force for radical change.

Prominent among these is the political philosophy of Alain Badiou. Badiou rejects any subordination of popular will to law or its mediation through the parliamentarian practice of majority vote, which he understands as a subordination of will to the logic of representation. Just as important, he rejects the historical or natural determinism that so often plagues materialist accounts of the subject, affirming instead a vigorous voluntarism of the act or decision. Yet Hallward also questions to what extent Badiou is really invested in the subject and its will to effect change, and not merely the truth of the event to which he declares his fidelity. This is the problem he sees with Badiou's reading of Saint Paul in particular, where the state of "grace" is defined by a "surrender" to the real of an event that merely befalls the subject, a truth that "induces" its subjects, and not the other way around. "It is a short step from here," he writes, "to the affirmation of a subject as an *essentially* haphazard supplement or interruption, a figure occasioned by chance if not 'grace.'"[1]

Yet even as he identifies the shortcomings of both accounts of will, Hallward leaves unquestioned their shared assumption: that will is, and must be, at odds with constraints.[2] "Will," he affirms with Badiou, is "about positive or affirmative capacity, before it is a theory of negation or constraint."[3] While I share with Hallward an investment in subjective will, I want to suggest that in taking for granted that constraints are invariably opposed to the will, he fails to consider that the repudiation of constraints might go hand in hand with a marginalization of the subject. I want to address the implied antithesis between will and constraint that dominates in both of these accounts, and suggest that free will and constraints are in fact inseparable.

WILL, SUPEREGO, AND THE VOICE OF CONSCIENCE: ARENDT'S *EICHMANN IN JERUSALEM*

What, then, is the function of constraints with respect to the will, and how does it differ from a mere negation or exclusion of will? Let me first turn to what is likely a prime object of Hallward's critique: Hannah Arendt's famous account of political will in *Eichmann in Jerusalem*, which locates in the genocidal program of the Third Reich the insistence of an empty and unconstrained will enabled by the failure of traditional symbolic laws. Covering his Jerusalem trial, Arendt becomes convinced that Eichmann was not just "following orders" when he agreed to implement Hitler's Final Solution, but attempting to identify his own will with the law's *source*. Eichmann tells the court he had always been guided in his conduct by the categorical imperative of Kant's moral law, to "act in such a way that the maxim of your will could always hold at the same time as a principle of universal legislation."[4] Overcoming her initial incredulity, Arendt finally accepts Eichmann's claim, but with the following proviso: "In this household use, all that is left of Kant's spirit is the demand that a man do more than obey the law, that he go beyond the mere call of obedience and *identify his own will with the principle behind the law—the source from which the law sprang*. In Kant's philosophy that source was practical reason; in Eichmann's household use of him, it was the will of the Führer."[5] In Arendt's words, Eichmann's distorted moral maxim is to "act in such a way that the Führer, if he knew of your action, might approve it" (136). As the principle "behind" the law, the Führer's will is further remarkable in that it is never expressed in speech, in specific orders or written directives. Even as he affirms that "the words of the Führer have the force of law," Eichmann finds that he is unable to recall any specific words that Hitler spoke in his presence.[6] Instead, the Führer's will is sustained solely by his voice, underscoring what Juliet Flower Mac-Cannell (in an argument I explored in chapter 3) describes as the "unbearable relation of voice to superegoic law."[7]

In a psychoanalytic elaboration of Arendt's argument, MacCannell argues that this voice should be understood not merely as the phenomenological bearer of Hitler's speech, but as a psychical object—the internalized "voice of conscience" with which Eichmann identifies his own will. She notes that for Lacan, speech is defined classically as the field of the symbolic pact, "the social contract that divides us from each other as mutual aggressors" (69). But "*Voice* is already *object a*; the embodiment or bearer of a 'principle behind the law.' It took shape in Lacan's discourse as one of the four fundamental objects a (gaze, voice, breast, feces) around which the fantasy structuring drive circulates" (70). Whereas speech, as the field of the signifier, works to limit the deadly jouissance that insists within fantasy by erecting barriers against it, the Voice is the bearer of that jouissance—hence Lacan's description of the voice as an "object fallen from the organ of speech,"[8] the material support of the superego that takes shape in demand. MacCannell sees Eichmann as a subject who has decided to forgo this symbolic mediation, identifying his own "voice of conscience" with the "will" materialized in the Führer's voice, above and beyond the specific orders and directives he issues. In Lacan's words, what he demonstrates is that "the superego, in its intimate imperative, is indeed 'the voice of conscience,' that is, a voice first and foremost, a vocal one at that, and without any authority other than that of being a loud voice [*sans plus d'autorité que d'être la grosse voix*]."[9]

In the Third Reich, the ethos of surrendering to the will of Hitler goes hand in hand with a refusal of written laws, and more broadly of the structural function of writing as a limit to the superego and the voice that sustains it. The authority of the voice is not transmitted in writing, and more importantly not restricted by the written word. Eichmann speaks at length of the distrust of written orders among the Nazi elite, and the corresponding valuation of the voice and of spoken commands as expressing more fully the "spirit" of the law, a spirit inseparable from the authority of the Führer himself. In his masterful study of the psychic and political stakes of voice, *A Voice and Nothing More*, Mladen Dolar observes,

> This obscene ("non-universalizable") part of the superego is always entrusted to the voice: we can think of the secret rules and rituals which hold certain communities together—rules of initiation (including the harsh humiliation of newcomers), of belonging to an in-group, the dividing line between insiders and outsiders, and so on. Those rules could never be put down in writing, they have to be whispered, hinted at, and confined to the voice. The voice is ultimately what distinguishes the superego from the law: the law has to be underpinned by the letter, something that is publicly accessible, in principle available at all times, while in contravention and in supplement to the law there are rules entrusted to the voice, the superegoic rules which most often take the form of transgression of the law, but which actually and effectively hold communities together and constitute their invisible glue.[10]

At his Jerusalem trial, Eichmann describes the "language rule" (*Sprachregelung*) that applied to communications within the Nazi regime, according to which "those who were told explicitly of the Führer's order were no longer mere 'bearers of orders,' but were advanced to 'bearers of secrets,' and a special oath was administered to them" (*Eichmann* 84–85). The effect of this rule, MacCannell observes, "was to remake what once, under common civil agreements, had been called 'the lie' into a form of special honorific 'secret' bearing. . . . The 'secret' therefore was, in formal communication terms, also technically 'content free'" ("Facing" 80).

MacCannell assimilates Eichmann's position to the structure of perversion, which Lacan defines as "a response . . . to the jouissance of the Other as *voice*, rather than to the Other as *speech*" (69). In the structure of perversion, the pervert forgoes the protections afforded by the symbolic, instead "identify[ing] himself with the object a in its role as agent of the Jouissance of the Other" (70). In Sade's work, this identification is evident in the libertine's attention to the maternal voice, in the form of the unlimited "voice of Nature" that guides him in his systematic critique of symbolic authority. In Eichmann's discourse, it takes the form of an identification of his own "voice of conscience" with the "will" materialized in the Führer's voice, over and above the specific orders and directives the Führer issues. The subject becomes nothing more than an instrument or support for the voice, a voice that is not "its own."

To counter this impulse, MacCannell calls for a written law that would specifically prohibit genocide, a law that could be adjudicated in an international court, and that "the people" (and not simply the individual actor) would be the subject to (71). In calling for a *written* law, and not simply a moral imperative or societal consensus, she implies that the written law—and in particular the negative form of the prohibition that emphasizes its status as a limit or barrier more than as the representation of an authority—is alone capable of functioning as a constraint to such a superegoic imperative.

MacCannell observes of Eichmann that while he "always acted in accordance with the rules," he also "felt compelled to 'go beyond' the written law, the norms of constraint, beyond the limit. He was the instrument of a will-to-jouissance not necessarily his own" (72). In opposing *rule* and *constraint*, MacCannell draws an implicit distinction between law in its imaginary function as a representation of a lawmaking authority (a description that might apply equally well to executive orders, codified laws, and the unspoken or inchoate commands of a superegoic "will") and the properly symbolic dimension of written law as a limit or constraint. In the absence of explicit written laws, Eichmann (like so many of his fellow citizens) felt not only entitled, but actually *compelled* to obey the unwritten rules of the state: a state whose unspoken norm had become "thou shalt" rather than "thou shalt not" kill (76). In Arendt's words,

> Just as the law in civilized countries assumes that the voice of conscience tells everybody "Thou shalt not kill," even though man's natural desires and inclinations may at times be murderous, so the law of Hitler's land demanded that the voice of conscience tell everybody: "Thou shalt kill," although the organizers of the massacres knew full well that murder is against the normal desires and inclinations of most people. Evil in the Third Reich had lost the quality by which most people recognized it—the quality of temptation. Many Germans and many Nazis, probably an overwhelming majority of them, must have been tempted *not* to murder, *not* to rob, *not* to let their neighbors go off to their doom. . . . But, God knows, they had learned how to resist temptation.
>
> (*Eichmann* 150, cited in "Facing" 83–84, ellipses in original)

While a written law certainly cannot be expected to proscribe a subject's actions, MacCannell implies that it might at least have prevented the German people from giving in so easily to something for which they had no natural inclination, and would have marked their actions as a violation of law rather than its dutiful "fulfillment."

If in Hitler's Germany—as in almost every nation, now as then—there was no written law specifically forbidding genocide, it is clearly not because such a prohibition simply "goes without saying." Indeed, it took the United Nations forty years to finally achieve full ratification of its Convention on the Prevention and Punishment of the Crime of Genocide of 1948, which was introduced in response to the war crimes of Nazi Germany but only gained the full support of the Security Council after the last of its five members—the United States—finally became a party to the treaty in 1988.[11] What, then, accounts for the resistance to putting this prohibition in writing?

In her most provocative and difficult claim, MacCannell actually traces the problem to the attribution of a *will to the people* under modern democracy (71), which ascribes to this will an agency not bound or restricted by law, and in the process betrays the "structural susceptibility to fascism" that is the scandal of modern democracy. "How can a people that rules itself with absolute freedom," she asks, "find itself perpetually threatened with rule by dictatorship?" (75). In Kant's wake, democracy makes *will* or *good will* the principle of Law, rather than the traditional prohibition whose function is to repress a desire (71); in the process, MacCannell argues, it enables the logic of fantasy and the violent (and often sacrificial) law of the superego to which the increasingly common phenomena of ethnic cleansing, religious violence, and the "purging" of political and social dissidents attest with alarming frequency. Her point is not simply that "human nature" is fundamentally violent and aggressive, needing to be contained and limited by the artifices of "civilization." Instead, she suggests that the inchoate character of the "will of the people" supposed to be the foundation of democratic law actually opens the door for a leader, movement, or group who claims to give expression to that popular will ("the people have spoken"), to be guided by the "popular voice," or to act "on the people's behalf" to execute its will (71). This was precisely the position of Eichmann. The Law to which Eichmann's drive and desire responded, MacCannell observes, was not a limit; he was merely the "executor" of the will of the group (77–78). Hence his claim at his Jerusalem trial that he had been "mastered" or "overpowered" by a will greater than his own, and as a result felt absolved of any guilt.

In her argument, the elevation of will to the status of the "principle behind the law" functions not to affirm the free agency of the will, therefore, but rather to buttress the superegoic authority of unspoken norms and imperatives. Genocide is thus a symptom of the transformation of law away from prohibition and toward will, which MacCannell understands as structurally instrumentalizing. Her point is that the "will of the people" must be expressed as a law if it is not to risk being collapsed with this kind of super-egoic imperative. The people, that is, must expressly declare—in the form of publicly accessible written laws—the illegality of the crime of genocide that might otherwise be perpetrated in its name.

In questioning to what extent one's will is ever truly one's own, and characterizing even popular will as an irrational or superegoic force to be contained, negated, or circumscribed by law, Arendt's and MacCannell's respective analyses are no doubt emblematic of the mistrust in will that Hallward indicts. Yet Arendt's argument in particular is very close to Hallward's own criticism of Badiou, in which the event in its spiritualist character supersedes the individual will of the subject it induces. No matter how different its focus and intent, Badiou's account of the event is at least *formally* analogous to what we find in Eichmann: a privileging of a causal "void" stripped of symbolic features. Thus while I affirm Hallward's call for a renewed attention to will—and am sympathetic to his impatience with the tendency of such arguments to reduce will tout court to a destructive and irrational agency that is inherently at odds with civilized life, needing to be contained and diluted by laws and limits—I also feel that his own analysis, like Badiou's, fails to reflect on the psychic dimensions of fantasy, superego, and voice; without addressing these issues, it is difficult simply to dismiss Arendt's critique of will out of hand.

On the other hand, MacCannell's (and to a lesser extent Arendt's) suspicion of "collective will" as inherently unspoken, inarticulate, or "empty"—and therefore susceptible to being ventriloquized—potentially leads to a criminalization of will as such, and allows for no alternative to constitutional legalism as a means of channeling, formalizing, and rendering explicit that will. These respective accounts of will thus seem to present us with a forced choice between will without limits (where the formal similarity between Badiou's account of the "event of Damascus" and Eichmann's "surrender" to the authority of the Voice should at least give us pause), or laws and limits that seek to diminish and contain the force of will as a destructive agency at odds with civilized life. Neither argument really imagines the possibility of a constrained will.

WILL AND CONSTRAINT
IN KANT'S CRITICAL PROJECT

Kant, on the other hand, does imagine this possibility. His solution is neither to repudiate or negate the will nor to affirm its inarticulate "emptiness," but to constrain it, and in the process to show that will and constraint are inseparable. In this claim I depart from MacCannell, who suggests—following Lacan—that this superegoic dimension of will is actually structural to the Kantian moral imperative, which in evacuating all "content" from the law also enabled this fantasy object. "In Kant," she writes, "the Law becomes a formal, empty universality by evacuation of all content. But it does not remain inert in its formal emptiness; instead, the emptiness of its form permits a certain kind of universality to be expressed as universal 'Ought' or pure positive command to duty: 'You must!' rather than 'You must not!'" (71). She follows Lacan in proposing that a "new object" resides in the purity of Kant's formally empty imperative: no longer the pathological object he has ejected from its contents, but the "object" present as the cause in and of all Drive, the *object a* of pure excess or pure lack (72). "By evacuating 'content' from the Law, while avoiding recognition of the emergence of the new, 'non-pathological' object," she writes, "Kant founded ethics on a nonpathological basis—and unwittingly empowered the *Thing* (das Ding)" (72).

In this reading Eichmann would not only "pervert" the categorical imperative, but realize something latent within it: the apathetic, dispassionate "execution" of an imperative in which the subject has no pathological stake, and in which desire has no place. Arendt observes that Eichmann was clearly not the man of savage passions his judges expected, but possessed of an apathy that was actually very idealist:

> When he said in the police examination that he would have sent his own father to death if that had been required, he did not mean merely to stress the extent to which he was under orders, and ready to obey them; he also

meant to show what an "idealist" he had always been. The perfect "idealist," like everybody else, had of course his personal feelings and emotions,
but he would never permit them to interfere with his actions if they came
into conflict with his "idea."

(Eichmann 42, cited in "Facing" 82)

Once Kant excludes any consideration of the subject's own pleasure or pain
as a legitimate basis for a moral maxim (famously declaring pain to be the
affect of the moral law, inasmuch as it indicates that its subject is not driven
by self-interest), MacCannell suggests that he leaves the subject in a gray
area where even suffering, horror, and empathy are unable to serve as limits
to the act.

What prevents us from attributing this logic to Kant, in my view, is the
importance he assigns to the formal mechanism of the constraint, which
anticipates and attempts to solve this potential for a perversion of the moral
law that merely entails a surrender to authority. MacCannell's argument
(following Lacan) offers a very convincing diagnosis of the Critique of Practical Reason, but does not take up the question of how the third critique
complements and completes the second by developing the aesthetic dimension of the moral law, its "negative exhibition."

As we saw in the last chapter, Kant's "Analytic of the Sublime" concludes
by appealing to the second commandment of the Decalogue (the ban on
graven images) to illustrate the role of constraints in resisting the lure of the
imaginary and the blind submission to power it encourages.

He distinguishes the function of the commandment from the "religious
accessories" that state-sanctioned religious practices employ to control the
subject, which in setting up imaginary barriers for the subject deprive it of
the trouble of exercising reason beyond those bounds, but also of the ability
to do so. In contrast, the commandment is aligned with the removal of those
barriers and the necessity of "expanding the soul" in the absence of any support for the imagination. Yet even as the commandment removes the barriers and supports provided by the imaginary, it introduces a new constraint
associated with its "negative" form. To experience its own boundlessness,
the soul needs to encounter a limit. In its absence, the imagination risks

tending toward what Kant calls "fanaticism," which is really the lure of the imaginary in its most seductive guise. As a "negative exhibition of morality," the written commandment both removes the support of the imaginary *and* offers a constraint that is lacking in fanaticism. In substituting a "purely negative exhibition" for a positive representation, it guards against the lure of representation *and* against the lure of the ineffable.

Here it is a matter not of an "evacuation" of content, but of a constraint, a constraining of the imagination that removes its sensual support or "prop" and obliges it to encounter what I am calling the lack in the Other. Indeed, Kant might even be read as addressing in the *Critique of Judgment* the very problem MacCannell identifies in the formulation of the categorical imperative, as if acknowledging the importance of a formal barrier or constraint (a constraint that is in this sense "external" to the subject, and not merely the "inner and intellectual constraint" of duty) as an aid to the disabling of the sensible (or of prescriptive content) that prevents it from veering into fanaticism. The *Critique of Judgment* could in this sense be read as correcting or amending the presentation of the categorical imperative in the *Critique of Practical Reason* by stressing the difference between a "negative exhibition" and a formal "emptiness" or void. The third critique develops a dimension of the moral law that is not particularly foregrounded in the second: the relationship between the self-constrained character of reason in the categorical imperative and the aesthetic function of the written constraint in dynamically sublime aesthetic judgments.

In the second critique, Kant defines the will as the power of rational beings "to determine their causality by the presentation of rules," and thus as a capacity to "perform actions according to principles" (*Practical Reason* 47). In the judgments human beings make about the lawfulness of their actions, he specifies that "their reason, incorruptible and self-constrained, . . . always holds the will's maxim in an action up to the pure will, i.e., to itself inasmuch as it regards itself as practical a priori" (46–47). The moral feeling of duty is therefore linked to the exercise of an "inner but intellectual constraint" (48), and not to a submissive posture with respect to a superior authority.

While the second critique emphasizes the *self*-constraint of reason (an argument that may indeed be subject to the problems Arendt and

MacCannell identify, inasmuch as nothing really guarantees that this constraint will be constraining), the third critique links the constraint to the function of writing as a limit.[12] It complements and completes the argument of the second critique by emphasizing that the "self-constraint" of reason is enabled by—if not indeed dependent upon—an "external" constraint, the written commandment whose "negative exhibition of the infinite" constrains the imagination, prevents it from rising to the level of "fanaticism," and thereby enables the imagination to do another kind of work. In short, it foregrounds the aesthetic dimension of the moral law.

Kant's analysis of the commandment distinguishes between the imaginary dimension of law as a representation of an authority or an existing state of affairs and its properly symbolic dimension, the structural function of the written law as constraint. In the process, he shows the constraint dimension of the written law to be indispensable in sustaining the very thing that is often opposed to it in contemporary discussions of politics: will. "Will" for Kant is not antinomial to written constraints, since the two are really inseparable. He links the exercise of the will to the cultivation of what might be called a "practice of the letter," which is quite different from respect for the authority of law or adherence to the rule it transmits.

In the last chapter, I cited a passage from the Babylonian Talmud in which Rabbi Eliezer, finding himself on the opposite side of the majority in a dispute over the interpretation of a cleanliness law, calls upon the Heavenly Voice to intervene on his behalf and so provide an authoritative resolution to the dispute. But when the Heavenly Voice promptly obliges by booming down from on high in support of his interpretation, the other assembled rabbis immediately respond that "we pay no attention to a Heavenly Voice, because Thou has lost since written in the Torah at Mount Sinai, *After the majority one must incline* [Exodus 23:2]."[13] Recourse to the written law thus allows the rabbis to forgo divine authority, politely inviting the Almighty God to butt out of their deliberations. MacCannell's reading of Eichmann allows us to develop further the stakes of the written law in this tradition, suggesting that it does not simply render obsolete the authority of the voice but explicitly defends against its status as the fantasmatic "principle behind the law." In the same way, when Rashi suggests that the voice of God took the form of a single, terrifying utterance, so unbearable that the people of Israel begged Moses to shield them from God's voice by reading the commandments for them, he suggests that the effect of the written law is to mediate and protect against its awesome force.[14]

Recourse to the written law does not actually eliminate the imaginary and real dimensions of the law, which in these examples are still very much in play: God is there palpably hovering over the scene in a very imaginary guise, his terrifyingly real voice reverberating in the ears (or at least the minds) of the assembled. The real for Lacan is not the "beyond" of speech, but one of its dimensions: hence his definition of the voice as the "product and object fallen from the organ of speech." But while the symbolic character of the written law does not replace or disable its imaginary and real dimensions, it does have the effect of putting them at a distance, and thereby diluting their force. In the same way, God as a might is not a fantasy or an illusion for Kant, but neither does his existence as a fearsome might diminish or overtake the symbolic sphere opened up by the voluntary submission to constraints in a sublime aesthetic judgment. God considered as a might is sublime—an object of sublimation—inasmuch as it calls on us to resist it, and therefore to exercise our humanity. Kant specifies that fearful manifestations of natural might can become "attractive," can be judged aesthetically, "provided we are in a safe place."[15] It follows that a sublime aesthetic judgment supposes a *distance* between the subject and the might he contemplates. This distance is not to be equated narrowly with the *physical* distance that separates the observer from the erupting volcano, however, since it is also sustained by recourse to the written law in its function as constraint.

When Freud identifies the Mosaic law with the possibility of sublimation, he suggests that the law obliges the Israelites to relinquish the fantasy object that gives consistency to the Other's "will" or demand (the voice as object a) and to confront the lack in the Other by traversing the negative space opened up by the commandments. For Lacan sublimation differs from the fantasy in providing a direct satisfaction of the drive through "objects that are socially valorized, objects of which the group approves, insofar as they are objects of public utility."[16] He suggests that the process of sublimation is concerned not merely with the construction of a new object that the collectivity finds to be of value, but with the fall of the imaginary object or ideal ego and the emptiness it exposes: "in every form of sublimation, emptiness is determinative" (*Ethics* 130). Religious forms of social organization are generally at odds with sublimation, since "religion in all its forms consists of avoiding this emptiness. We can illustrate that in forcing the note of Freudian analysis, for the good reason that Freud emphasized the obsessional traits of religious behavior" (130). Nevertheless, the Mosaic religion reveals that in some instances, religious practice can actually establish the conditions under which sublimation becomes possible. In its case, says Lacan, "a phrase like 'respecting this emptiness' perhaps goes further . . . the emptiness remains in the center, and that is precisely why sublimation is involved" (130).

With the institution of the Jewish law, I have argued that Moses creates a structure or a space in which the subject can encounter and explore the lack in the Other in a creative manner, without being so consumed by his anxiety that he violently rejects and represses it. The law is a structure that allows for a work on the absent Other, and in this respect functions as a sublimation for the age, and indeed for subsequent ages, as Kant attests: the sublimation functions not only for members of the Mosaic religion, but potentially for anyone who takes up this object.

The "dynamically sublime contemplation of might" is linked to the psychic function of sublimation in being concerned with an object (what Kant calls the "indelible idea of morality") that does not properly speaking "exist," that is not available to sense perception or the imagination, but that may nonetheless be explored by means of the commandment. The law is an instrument of sublimation that allows for the presentation of this object without refusing its negative character or seeking to recover it in the real: it substitutes a "purely negative exhibition" for a positive representation, facilitating the subject's "expansion of his soul" rather than erecting barriers against it.

This is the essence of Kant's distinction between "superstition" and "religion." Superstition entails the abdication of the subject's freedom to a superior might, while religion implies a process of transcendence in which the reasoning faculty, in the experience of the sublime, finds within itself an attitude commensurate with God's sublimity that precludes any such prostration. What superstition establishes in the mind is not a reverence for the sublime, but "fear and dread of that being of superior might to whose will the terrified person finds himself subjected but without holding him in esteem; and this can obviously give rise to nothing but ingratiation and fawning, never to a religion based on good conduct" (*Judgment* 123). In true religion there is thus a *distance* between the subject and God, who ceases to be the fearful enforcing presence that we see in superstition. It follows that the *truly* religious person can forgo God altogether, since God's sublimity is merely the occasion for the exercise of his own sublimity (making God less an arbiter or authority than a kind of thought experiment).[17] What Kant calls "religion" is thus a form of *work*, the free exercise of the reasoning faculty, while superstition is a passive abdication of the activity of the mind.

Badiou gives voice to a widely held diagnosis when he charges that Kant closes philosophy with his "legalism," and that a philosophy of limits can only be antithetical to revolutionary action. "A return to Kant," he complains, "is always a sign of closed and morbid times."[18] I would respond that both Badiou and MacCannell fail to appreciate the ally Kant is in the quest for a truly free account of will, something Walter Benjamin understood fully and that the recent work of Robert Kaufman has also affirmed in arguing that materialism cannot—and should not—do without Kant.[19] His critical project demonstrates that constraints work to disable fanaticism by constraining the imagination, or what MacCannell calls the "imaginary" dimension of the fantasy that seeks to identify with the "source" of the law, its "beyond." In the process, it shows that something more than representation is at stake in Arendt's call for written law. At issue is not a simple opposition of law or negation to the freedom of the act, but an enactment of constraints that actually facilitate the subject's freedom.

Badiou's critique of legalism notwithstanding, he does recognize the importance of literal constraints for subjective and political emancipation, and even draws selectively upon Kant as a precursor in this domain. In his work, however, these constraints tend to be identified almost exclusively with the practice of mathematics. In the essay "Mathematics and

Philosophy," published in 2004, Badiou proclaims that "mathematics is the necessary exercise through which is forged a subject adequate to the transformations he will be forced to undergo."[20] To pursue truth through mathematics, he suggests, is to forgo the representations, intuitions, and other imaginary supports that function as crutches to reason, and so diminish its true capacities and freedom. In Spinoza's *Ethics*, for example, mathematics "governs the historial destiny of knowledge, and hence the economy of freedom, or beatitude" (8). Badiou finds a further example in none other than Kant himself, who in his first critique emphasizes the subjective act at the origin of mathematics and the self-constrained nature of the method to which it gave rise. What Kant affirms in mathematics is not its timeless ideality or pure intelligibility, but its subject: the subject from whose desire it originated, and the subject whose freedom it enables.

> A new light flashed upon the mind of the first man (be he Thales or some other) who first demonstrated the properties of the isosceles triangle. The true method, so he found, was not to inspect what he discerned either in the figure, or in the bare concept of it, . . . but to bring out what was necessarily implied in the concepts that he himself formed a priori and had put into the figure in the construction by which he presented it to himself.[21]

Both examples attest to what Badiou calls the "concrete universalism of a trajectory of thought" (9), a trajectory sustained by the cold rigor of "iron rules" (11) that enable and sustain the subject in its struggle against subjugating forms of representation that limit reason or will to what can be imagined, and hence to the ontotheology of the image.

This argument might be construed as the affirmation of a certain kind of constraint, as in Georg Cantor's famous definition of mathematics as a practice of "freedom realized through constraints." Yet Badiou's own argument tends to drop the specific emphasis on constraints, and in particular any understanding of constraint that might be expanded to include the field of language or law. (This is especially true of *writing* as constraint, which is as essential to Cantor's own understanding of mathematics as it is to

Lacan's psychoanalytic take on mathematical formalization[22] or to Derrida's account of theoretical mathematics as an exemplary instance of "grammatology."[23]) As his disparaging comment about Kant's "morbidity" suggests, Badiou seems to distinguish the "good" Kant of mathematical reasoning from the "bad" Kant of limits, law, and aesthetics. I would argue that Kant's reflections on aesthetics and the moral law are not at odds with this affirmation of mathematics, however, but absolutely of a piece with it; his exaltation of mathematics should be understood as revealing something about his understanding of law, rather than pointing to an alternative trajectory. The enabling function of constraints is arguably Kant's fundamental question, which he explores in different ways across the three critiques.

What, then, accounts for this blanket repudiation of law on Badiou's part? In chapter 5 I noted that Badiou's work appears to leave no room for an understanding of *law* as constraint, which is almost invariably reduced to the imaginary function of representing the "situation" or "world" where the event intervenes. It tends to reinforce an understanding of the law as nothing more than the "dead letter," a normative representation of a "situation" that can be decisively transformed only through the intervention of an explosive event. "The field of law," he argues, "is always a concrete world or a concrete situation; but the event has a negative relationship to the laws of the world."[24]

Badiou, of course, is interested not in the constitutional liberalism with which Kant's thought tends to be identified, but in a revolutionary politics concerned with bringing forth what cannot be represented, foreseen, or even imagined: hence his affirmation of the "general will" as an evental force opposed to law. Badiou embraces Rousseau's account of the general will as an important precursor to his own theory of the event, and even describes his own thought as a "Rousseauism of the infinite."[25] In Peter Hallward's gloss, Badiou reads Rousseau as making a "decisive contribution to egalitarian politics" for recognizing

> that the political as such is inaugurated in a revolutionary event, rather than grounded in a structure or social norm. . . . Rather than emerge from any sort of social bond, politics begins with an inaugural intervention, a

voluntary association or contract through which a collective subject constitutes itself: what Rousseau calls "contract" is the "evental form that we
must presume if we want to think the truth of this aleatory being that is
the body politic."[26] General will is the practice—the "fidelity," or "opera-
tor of faithful connection"—that sustains the "co-belonging of the people
to itself"; as such, it is "intrinsically egalitarian," rigorously indiscernible
or generic, and subtracted from all representation, i.e. withdrawn from all
mediation through the state.[27]

If Badiou's definition of the general will does not exactly coincide with
Rousseau's own, Hallward writes, it is because Rousseau's "preoccupation
with sovereign legitimacy" means he is "not yet able to dissociate political willing from the quasi-parliamentarian practice of majority vote, and is
thereby drawn back into the logic of representation: he is not yet in a position to anticipate, via the transitional work of proletarian dictatorship, the
withering away of the state as such."[28]

Badiou's "Rousseauism of the infinite" should thus be understood as
an attempt to purge Rousseau's thought of a residual finitude, understood
not coincidentally as a failure of imagination. But is this really a failure on
Rousseau's part, or does he rather affirm as essential something Badiou
rejects: the interdependence of something like "will" and "contract"? That
is, can the "general will" really be dissociated from the legal dimensions of
the social contract, as Badiou proposes? Or are they logically inseparable?
Rousseau understands the general will as in a necessary relation to the social
contract, which is not its "representation" so much as the constrained field
of its manifestation; while the state may indeed recede, the constraining
character of the social contract does not. Rousseau does not repudiate law
altogether, therefore, but famously enjoins his readers in the opening lines
of *The Social Contract* to "take men as they are, and the laws as they might
be."[29] Conversely, it is not clear that Badiou has any notion of the "laws as
they might be," laws that would not be reducible to the function of representing or defining the boundaries of an existing situation. His inadequate
and overly reductive understanding of law as representation fails to see that
there is a dimension of law that is pure constraint, and has nothing to do

with representation. This distinction is crucial to the work of Walter Benjamin, who like Badiou was a partisan of revolutionary anarchistic violence. As we saw in the last chapter, his "Critique of Violence" offers an excoriating critique of law in its function as representation or sign of power. But he also distinguishes it from the function of the commandment as constraint, which serves as a "guideline" that men must "wrestle with in solitude," and thus as an instrument of what he calls "divine justice," itself radically opposed to any rote legalism.

I believe that the true legacy of Kant's critical project is to be found not in a conservative, status quo–bound philosophy of boundaries and restraints, much less in the rote obedience of an Eichmann; rather, it is found in the kinds of constrained practices we see not only in Arendt's and MacCannell's analyses, but in the constrained writing procedures of the Oulipo and the experience of psychoanalysis: two "literal practices" that might be understood as derivative of Kant's aesthetics in locating the emergence of the subject and its freedom in the struggle with constraints, and that ought to be central to any renewed reflection on will.

CONSTRAINT DEGREE ZERO: THE LITERAL PRACTICE OF THE OULIPO

In 1960, Raymond Queneau and François Le Lionnais founded in Paris the experimental literary collective called Oulipo, whose name stands for the *Ouvroir de littérature potentielle*, or Workroom in Potential Literature. The Oulipo, which today numbers more than thirty members worldwide (and whose ranks have included such figures as Georges Perec, Marcel Duchamp, and Italo Calvino), is dedicated to a textual practice defined by voluntary submission to formal constraints. These constraints may take any number of forms, including traditional fixed poetic forms like the sonnet or haiku, the mathematical constraints involved in the production of algorithms or combinatories, and the literal constraints implied in written forms such as metagrams, palindromes, and lipograms, which involve the reordering, substitution, or elimination of letters, the best known of which is Georges Perec's lipogrammatic novel *La Disparition* (The Disappearance, translated into English as *A Void*), published in 1969, a work of more than three hundred pages written without the letter "e."

The Oulipians embrace the hypothesis implied in Kant's aesthetics, that the subject's freedom, understood as the free exercise of its will, may actually depend upon laws and constraints. But they also develop another dimension of the constraint, by identifying it with a literal practice that has nothing to do with the domain of law in any traditional sense. The Oulipians are therefore concerned not merely with elaborating a new writing practice; they actually aspire to something like a *regeneration of the symbolic* through voluntary submission to constraints. In this, they also allow us to think about the aesthetic dimension of psychoanalytic technique.

The Oulipian Marcel Bénabou describes the constraint as a way of "passing from language to writing."[30] It allows us to access what he describes as the "functional modes of language and writing," which come into relief when language is "treated as an object in itself, considered in its materiality, and thus freed from its subservience to its significatory obligation" (*Oulipo* 41). It is not a matter merely of freeing language from its instrumental use as a tool of signification, however. The Oulipo's very Kantian claim is that constraints actually set *us* free. Perec writes of the "liberating potential of rigorous formal constraint," advancing that "the suppression of the letter, of the typographical sign, of the basic prop, is a purer, more objective, more decisive operation, something like *constraint degree zero*, after which everything becomes possible" (*Oulipo* 13). At stake are not only new literary possibilities, therefore, but latent possibilities within the writer as a subject. In Bénabou's words, "it is not only the virtualities of language that are revealed by constraint, but also the virtualities of [he] who accepts to submit himself to constraint" (*Oulipo* 43). The constraint gives rise not only to a poetics of the literary text, therefore, but to what might be termed a poetics of subjectivity. It supports the emergence of a virtual subject, a subject solicited and sustained by the struggle with the creative constraints implied in a practice of the letter.

The function of formal, written constraints in the work of Oulipo resonates powerfully with psychoanalysis, where "the subject who accepts to submit himself to constraint" actually offers a very precise definition of the analysand under transference. This subject is "virtual" in that the subject of the unconscious is a pure hypothesis that cannot be verified empirically. It is witnessed only in speech, in those discontinuities and slips of the tongue that interrupt the discourse of the ego. The subject of psychoanalysis is a subject that can be known or constructed only on the condition that it be called forth under the constraint of the transference and constrained to a construction.

In advancing that writing is a constraint that enables the emergence of the subject, the Oulipo allows us to understand something crucial about the role of constraints in psychoanalysis, and also about the unconscious as a scene of writing. What Perec and other Oulipians call "writing" is not merely the production of texts, but a specific modality of language that involves an encounter with an obstacle, limit, or empty space that interrupts another relation to language, as spontaneous conversation or as the communication of presence. It thus coincides quite precisely with what Lacan names the symbolic, that register of language in which the subject's desire is correlated to a lack in the Other, or that "constraint degree zero" that Perec makes the condition of possibility of the literary text and of subjective freedom alike. Yet these examples also draw out a dimension of the symbolic that is often overlooked, what I am calling its aesthetic dimension. The symbolic is something other than the loss of natural satisfaction to the signifier, which is an unavoidable necessity for the speaking being. It is a creative support for the subject of desire. In an early definition proposed by the group, Oulipians are "rats who must build the labyrinth from which they propose to escape" (*Oulipo* 22). The constraint offers a way of molding and shaping the subject's subjection to the signifier, making a potential prison a provocation to creative freedom.

The Oulipo's most important contribution to the field of aesthetics is the demonstration that constraints enable freedom by defending against *inspiration*. Queneau proposes that the group's task is to elaborate "a whole arsenal in which the poet may pick and choose, whenever he wishes to escape from that which is called inspiration" (*Oulipo* 10). But why would anyone need to escape inspiration? And what is the relationship between escaping a labyrinth that one builds and escaping inspiration? In Queneau's words, "the inspiration that consists in blind obedience to every impulse is in reality a sort of slavery. The classical playwright who writes his tragedy observing a certain number of familiar rules is freer than the poet who writes that which comes into his head and who is the slave of other rules of which he is ignorant" (*Oulipo* 18).[31]

The stakes of this claim can be understood by contrast with Surrealism, whose understanding of freedom it specifically rejects. In his first "Manifesto of Surrealism," for example, André Breton gives voice to a very traditional and widespread view, according to which freedom is necessarily freedom *from* the law, freedom from constraints of all kinds: social norms and conventions, moral inhibitions, and even the rules and conventions of genre, all of which are conceived as inhibiting the free reign of the imagination. Strikingly, however, this "freedom from" goes hand in hand with a marginalization of the subject, and in particular of the subject's volition or will. The poet is understood as nothing more than the passive receptacle of an inspiration that breaks in on his consciousness, in the form of gratuitous phrases that come "knocking at the window."[32] The manifesto ultimately relies upon a very classical notion of inspiration, according to which the human being is an inert vessel "animated" by a divine creator or spirit. Breton defines a "surreal" image as a "fortuitous juxtaposition of two terms" (37) in which the mind plays no role.[33] It follows, he writes, that the poet should make "no effort whatsoever to filter," but instead should aspire to be a "simple receptacle" of the echoes he transcribes, a "modest recording instrument" who "serves a nobler cause" (28). But what cause, or whose cause, is it? Breton writes: "It is true of Surrealist images as it is of opium images that man does not evoke them: rather they 'come to him spontaneously, despotically. He cannot chase them away: for the will is powerless now and no longer controls the faculties' (Baudelaire)" (36).

To the involuntary or "automatic" submission to inspiration, the writers of the Oulipo oppose the voluntary submission to constraint as enabling a

FREEDOM THROUGH CONSTRAINTS

different relation to freedom, not as a freedom *from* obstacles or limits but as a freedom *to* that foregrounds the activity of the will. If for Breton writing is secondary with respect to the "voice" of inspiration, the mere record or transcript of the poet's surrender to a superior force, for the Oulipians it is writing—and above all the constraint that structures its practice— that comes first, enabling the exercise of a freedom inseparable from this practice. Queneau maintains that "the poet is never inspired, if by that one means that inspiration is a function of humor, of temperature, of political circumstances, of subjective chance, or of the subconscious. The poet is never inspired, because he is the master of that which appears to others as inspiration . . . the powers of poetry are always at his disposition, subjected to his will, submissive to his own activity" (*Oulipo* 43). And in a celebration of the "liberating virtue of form," François Le Lionnais writes, "Nine or ten centuries ago, when a potential writer proposed the sonnet form, he left, through certain mechanical processes, the possibility of a choice" (cited in *Oulipo* 9).

These comments point to a profound structural analogy between the Oulipo's practice of writing under constraint and the technique of psychoanalysis. In inventing the unconscious and calling upon it to construct a knowledge under the constraint of the transference, Freud creates a mechanism that allows the analysand to traverse the fantasy, making it the object of a possible choice rather than a deterministic inevitability.

Admittedly, the equation between written constraints and the technique of psychoanalysis is potentially problematic on at least two counts: because of the Oulipo's emphasis on volition and will, which seems far removed from the concerns of psychoanalysis, and because of the Oulipians' repudiation of any aesthetic practice founded on the exploration of the "subconscious" as antithetical to free choice. Queneau, for example, insists on the voluntary, conscious dimension of artistic practice, and consistently and vigorously opposes any aesthetic practice that relies upon involuntary or automatic processes or submission to chance, all of which he identifies with the unconscious, or more precisely the subconscious (*subconscient*).[34] But this is because Queneau takes from Breton a reductive understanding of the unconscious as a wholly alien province of the mind, or as that deep, dark repository of unbridled impulses that Freud identifies with the id.[35] When he charges that the poet who impulsively writes whatever comes into his head is the "slave of other rules of which he is ignorant," Queneau is actually equating these "other rules" with the rules of the unconscious, understood in Breton's terms as a "fortuitous juxtaposition of terms" that does not answer to constraints of any kind.

I would counter that these "other rules" are not the laws of the unconscious as Freud understands it, however, but of the fantasy and its imaginary staging. Queneau confirms as much when, in answer to the question of whether Oulipo is "in favor of literary madmen," he states that "the only literature is voluntary literature" (*Oulipo* 6). In asserting that the writer subject to a delusion or fantasy is the slave of his supposed "freedom," Queneau is saying nothing that we do not also find in Freud. While Queneau's references to "reason" and to "will" may seem far removed from the domain of psychoanalysis, the preceding discussion of written constraints allows us to appreciate that the unconscious under constraints is an eminently rational mechanism. Reason for Freud is not an attribute of the *conscious* mind, but of the mind as such (whether conscious or unconscious). He shows us that reason and the unconscious are not opposed, and that the unconscious is necessarily a rational unconscious.[36]

When Warren Motte describes the Oulipian enterprise as "a sustained attack on the aleatory in literature, a crusade for the maximal motivation of the literary sign" (*Oulipo* 17), he might well be speaking of the unconscious itself. Contrary to Breton's reading, there is nothing "fortuitous" or accidental about the Freudian unconscious, whose implacable logic is eminently rational and formally excludes any notion of chance. Crucially, the unconscious is not the opposite of consciousness. Nor is it distinct from the mind. It is a symbolic mechanism that allows for a formal construction, under constraints, of a mental object, and that therefore sustains desire as a capacity for transcendence.

This claim may seem counterintuitive. Does the constraint not violate the cardinal rule of psychoanalysis, the law of free association according to which no restrictions whatsoever may be placed on the associative stream of thoughts, words, and images? To identify the technique of free association with the free reign of the imagination, as Breton does,[37] is to propagate a widespread misunderstanding of the unconscious for which Surrealism—as the first, unfortunate foray into the relation between psychoanalysis and literary production—bears much responsibility.[38] It ignores that free association is simultaneously *unrestricted* and *constrained*. In the clinic of the dream, for example, the seemingly endless associations to which its elements give rise inevitably butt up against the "navel" of the dream, the "hole" to which free association leads, the unrepresentable kernel around which it turns. The point is that association in language is "free" precisely to the extent that these substitutions revolve around an absent center. Under the constraint of the transference, free association leads to this "lack in the Other" that for Lacan conditions the symbolic, constraining the subject to confront it in order to "traverse" the seduction fantasy and experience the falling away of the imaginary Other it supposes: the Other of demand, love, or even "inspiration." Breton's understanding of the "Other" as source of inspiration emphasizes the imaginary Other to the exclusion of the symbolic or lacking Other, the finite language whose capacity for free play is a direct consequence of the lack at its center.[39] Put another way, his conception of the unconscious is one from which the function of *writing* is excluded.

In its critique of this exclusion, the Oulipo exposes the fallacy of a certain conception of the unconscious and of writing as a "writing of the Other," and allows us to locate with much more precision the stakes of the symbolic, the Other, and writing in psychoanalysis. At issue is what it means to consider the subject of psychoanalysis as a subject subjected to language, to the Other: on the one hand, a deterministic understanding of the subject as programmed or ventriloquized by a voice that subverts its agency; and on the other, a properly psychoanalytic account of the subject as assuming its desire—and therefore its freedom—through the creative assumption of the lack in (and of) the Other. Perec shows that "everything becomes possible" only when lack is assumed, when the "missing center" is accepted as the condition of language.

In view of what I have just said, Queneau's insistence on the agency of the will and the "mastery" of the imagination by consciousness may itself give pause, especially to psychoanalytically inclined readers. Is an affirmation of "will," "consciousness" or "mastery" not inherently at odds with the supposition that lack is the necessary condition of the subject's desire or freedom? After all, to adhere to a particular rhyme scheme or to suppress a letter from a text is quite different from affirming that there is a fundamental, structural, and insurmountable lack in language; to voluntarily constrain the composition of a text by rendering certain linguistic possibilities off-limits could even be interpreted as a refusal of the lack in the Other, a lack that is not a matter of choice but a structural inevitability for the speaking being. In affirming the "mastery" of the will, Queneau might even be understood as radically rejecting the very notion of the Other, and not only in its imaginary guise as the animating "spirit" of inspiration. Queneau's conception of the will is not a naïve intentionalism, however; it is closely tied to his understanding of writing as a constrained activity. A constrained system is not a system from which lack is excluded, as one might potentially infer from his affirmation of "voluntary" literature as an exclusion of the aleatory. While it may be opposed to "inspiration" and to the submissive or subservient posture toward the Other it implies, a constrained writing is not a writing that eliminates the Other altogether. It engages the lack in the Other, the symbolic Other that is not a source of "inspiration" or "spirit," but the absent center of a finite language that itself gives rise to a multitude of substitutions and permutations.

The Oulipo's treatment of constraint brings out a dimension of psychoanalysis that is not obvious: that despite its emphasis on the determinant character of unconscious fantasy, psychoanalysis takes the subject's freedom as its end point. Like the Oulipo, it supposes that freedom or free choice is made possible by a particular kind of work, the struggle with constraints; it supposes a *practice* of freedom, or an understanding of freedom as the result of a particular kind of work, rather than an ontological conception of freedom as an inborn attribute of the living being that can only be compromised by the application of external constraints or restrictions. As in Kant's aesthetics, this work has something to do with the exercise of the will and with reason, and is powerfully opposed to any evocation of "the Other" as a kind of dictatorial agency. The transference is a tool to defend against what the Oulipians call "inspiration," or the submission to an imaginary Other that Kant identifies with "fanaticism." It is the foundation of an ethics of emancipation, an ethics that supposes a practice of constraints.

THE SYMBOLIC AND THE SOCIAL LINK

Each of these examples demonstrates in a very modest way that even if traditional symbolic laws are no longer "compelling fictions," a practice of written constraints can provide many of the symbolic supports associated with law without any recourse to law in the traditional, patriarchal sense. For Bénabou, the Oulipo "seeks to *formulate problems* and eventually to *offer solutions* that allow any and everybody to construct, letter by letter, word by word, a text." More than that, he proposes that the "Oulipian act par excellence" is to "create a structure, . . . to propose an as yet undiscovered mode of organization for linguistic objects" (*Oulipo* 46). But while the structures Bénabou has in mind are primarily textual, François Le Lionnais, in his "Second Manifesto" of the Oulipo, is more ambitious: he proposes that the Oulipo aims to generate "artificial structures" that might "take root in the cultural tissue of a society," producing "leaf, flower, and fruit" (*Oulipo* 8). I submit that this is really the essence of the symbolic: to create new practices or mechanisms that sustain the subject in the exercise of its desire or freedom.

The Oulipians make a distinction between what they call "experimental" and "normative" uses of constraint (*Oulipo* 4). For the first poets who elaborated and developed the sonnet form, its constraints were experimental; but with the gradual codification of the form, those constraints became normative. If traditional laws belong to the order of "normative" constraints, the constrained writing of the Oulipo, the practice of psychoanalysis, and sublime aesthetic judgments belong to the "experimental." Each of these "new structures" advances a dynamic understanding of the symbolic, not as a reified set of inherited rules, norms, or traditions, but as a creative process of devising "compelling fictions." Kant could be read as trying to renew the experimental dimension of the Decalogue, which risks being received as nothing more than a "normative" constraint whose capacity to call forth reason in the experience of the sublime is no longer appreciated. When the Ten Commandments descend through familiarity to the status of normative constraints, we no longer experience them as sublime because they seem merely to uphold a morality, and not to provide an opportunity for the exercise of free will in the formulation of the categorical imperative. His argument can in turn be read as elevating the kind of experience the Oulipians are describing by suggesting that the kinds of structures they invent might be understood as taking the place or taking on the function that religions used to have, that of creating a space in which a certain kind of transcendence becomes possible.

"Experimental" implies an *experience*, something the subject undergoes. There is a practice of the letter, an engagement with language in its literality that is also a form of *work*, one that exalts the will. The point is that in the absence of such work, the will does not have the opportunity to exercise itself. This experimental register necessarily involves the individual subject, while the "normative" is more broad. But each of the examples I have discussed suggests that where the normative exists to the exclusion of the "experimental," a constraint risks becoming nothing more than a rule, and thereby losing its properly symbolic force.

NOTES

INTRODUCTION

1. Georg Cantor, "Foundations of a General Theory of Manifolds: A Mathematico-Philosophical Investigation into the Theory of the Infinite," in *From Kant to Hilbert: A Source Book in the Foundations of Mathematics*, ed. William Brag Ewald (Oxford: Clarendon, 1996), 2:878–920.

2. Immanuel Kant, *Critique of Practical Reason*, trans. Werner S. Pluhar (Indianapolis: Hackett, 2002), 47.

3. Warren Motte, ed. and trans., *Oulipo: A Primer of Potential Literature* (Champaign: Dalkey Archive, 1986), 13.

4. Ibid.

5. Ibid., 18.

6. André Breton, *Manifestoes of Surrealism*, trans. Richard Seaver and Helen R. Lane (Ann Arbor: University of Michigan Press, 1969, 1972), 21.

7. Badiou, "Mathematics and Philosophy: The Grand Style and the Little Style," in *Theoretical Writings*, ed. and trans. Ray Brassier and Alberto Toscano (London: Continuum, 2004), 14.

8. *Critique of Pure Reason*, cited by Badiou, *Theoretical Writings*, 9.

9. Badiou, *Theoretical Writings*, 8.

10. Ibid., 9.

11. See, in particular, Judith Butler, *Antigone's Claim: Kinship Between Life and Death* (New York: Columbia University Press, 2000); Daniel Borrillo, Éric Fassin, and Marcela Iacub, eds., *Au-delà du PACS: l'expertise familiale à l'épreuve de l'homosexualité* (Paris: Presses Universitaires de France, 2001); and Camille Robcis, *The Law of Kinship: Anthropology, Psychoanalysis, and the Family in France* (Ithaca: Cornell University Press, 2013).

12. Žižek, "The Big Other Doesn't Exist," *Journal of European Psychoanalysis* (Spring-Fall 1997).

13. Foucault, "Panopticism," in *Discipline and Punish: The Birth of the Prison*, trans. Alan Sheridan (New York: Vintage, 1979), 195–228.

14. Tim Dean argues that Žižek's tendency to give too concrete a form to the real functions rhetorically to conflate the Lacanian real with historical and cultural manifestations of the real. In Dean's analysis, this conflation in turn motivates a gender studies position (here identified with Judith Butler) where the real is identified with what is excluded, and must therefore be claimed as the material of a new identity. Dean, "Art as Symptom: Žižek and the Ethics of Psychoanalytic Criticism," *Diacritics* 32, no. 2 (Summer 2002): 21–41.

15. This vector has been developed in detail by Adrian Johnston, *Badiou, Žižek, and Political Transformations: The Cadence of Change* (Evanston, Ill.: Northwestern University Press, 2009). See, in particular, chapter 2, "One Must Have Confidence That the Other Does Not Exist: Select Preconditions for Events and Acts in Contemporary Circumstances."

16. Deleuze, "How Do We Recognize Structuralism?," in *Desert Islands, and Other Texts* (Los Angeles: Semiotext(e), 2004), 173.

17. Lacan, *Le séminaire livre XXIV: l'insu que sait de l'une-bévue, s'aile à mourre*, 1976–1977, January 18, 1977.

18. MacCannell, "Facing Fascism: A Feminine Politics of Jouissance," in *Lacan, Politics, Aesthetics*, ed. Willy Apollon and Richard Feldstein (Albany: SUNY Press, 1996), 67.

19. MacCannell, "Death Drive in Venice," *(a): the journal of culture and the unconscious* 11, no. 1 (winter-spring 2002), 71.

20. MacCannell, "Facing Fascism," 67.

21. Lacan, *The Seminar of Jacques Lacan, Book VII: The Ethics of Psychoanalysis*, ed. Jacques-Alain Miller, trans. Dennis Porter (New York: Norton, 1992), 174, 69.

22. Lucie Cantin, "La féminité: d'une complicité à la perversion à une éthique de l'impossible," *Savoir* 2, nos. 1–2 (May 1995), 77. Subsequent citations from the text will be given as page numbers in parentheses.

23. Michel de Certeau, *The Possession at Loudun*, trans. Michael B. Smith (Chicago: University of Chicago Press, 2000).

24. In Teresa's words, "It sometimes happens that I am seized so suddenly seized by this rapture and this elevation of the spirit that I cannot resist it. . . . At other times I am taken with impetuous movements, accompanied by an annihilation in God that I cannot control" (cited in Cantin 81).

25. Rancière, *Disagreement*, trans. Julie Rose (Minneapolis: University of Minnesota Press, 1995, 1999), 36. Subsequent citations from the text will be given as page numbers in parentheses.

26. Wikipedia, "Secessio plebis." Sources are "The Growth of Plebeian Privilege in Rome," *English Historical Review* 2 (April 1886); and G. Forsythe, *A Critical History of Early Rome* (Berkeley: University of California Press, 2005).

27. Ballanche, "Formule générale de tous les peuples appliquée à l'histoire du peuple romain," cited in Rancière 23.

28. Ballanche's restaging hinges upon a detail that has confounded historians: Was Menenius a patrician, or a pleb? Whose side was he really on? Although Livy asserts that Menenius

was "dear to the plebeians as one of themselves," his role as a consul and representative of the Senate suggests he could only have been a patrician.

29. Wikipedia.

30. This argument shows how Lacan's well-known dictum that "Woman does not exist" (*La femme n'existe pas*) might lend itself to a political reading of the type Rancière elaborates, by understanding "woman" as a political stance taken up within and in opposition to the language that bestows existence upon some but not others.

31. Hallward, "Staging Equality: On Rancière's Theotrocracy," *New Left Review* 37 (January–February 2006), 125–26.

32. MacCannell, "Death Drive in Venice" 70.

33. MacCannell, "Making Room: Woman and the City to Come," published in German translation as "Raum schaffen: Woman und die künftige Stadt," in *Bauarten von Sexualität, Körper, Phantasmen: Architektur und Psychoanalyse*, ed. Olaf Knellessen and Insa Härtel (Scheidegger and Spiess, 2012). Citations are from the original English-language manuscript, provided by the author.

34. Sophie Calle, *L'EROUV de Jérusalem* (Arles: Actes Sud, 1996).

35. Benslama, "Politiques des lieux," in *La démocratie à venir* (Paris: Galilée, 2004). Forthcoming in English in *Umbr(a): The Journal of the Unconscious*.

36. These and other images can be viewed on Banksy's official website, www.banksy.co.uk.

37. David Fieni, "What a Wall Wants, or How Graffiti Thinks: Nomad Grammatology in the French Banlieue," *diacritics* 40, no. 2 (Summer 2012): 72–93.

38. Gilles Deleuze and Félix Guattari, *A Thousand Plateaus*, trans. Brian Massumi (Minneapolis: Minnesota University Press, 1987).

39. Or for that matter commercial interests. Very often graffiti or street art is in a polemical relation to advertising, another form of "writing" that overruns the public space, but so as to capture it for a specific commercial purpose or to advance an ideology or agenda.

1. INVENTIONS OF THE SYMBOLIC

1. Jacques Lacan, *Le séminare livre XXIV: l'insu que sait de l'une-bévue, s'aile à mourre, 1976–1977*, ed. Jacques-Alain Miller; seminar of December 14, 1976; unpublished draft translation by Dan Collins.

2. *Seminar XXIV*, seminar of March 8 1977.

3. See, in particular, "The Passing of the Oedipus Complex" (1924), "Some Psychological Consequences of the Anatomical Distinction Between the Sexes" (1925), and "Femininity" (1933).

4. Lacan, *Écrits*, trans. Bruce Fink (New York: Norton, 2006), 203. Subsequent citations from the text will be given as page numbers in parentheses.

5. Among the most useful of these are Philippe Julien, *Jacques Lacan's Return to Freud: The Real, the Symbolic, and the Imaginary*, trans. Devra Beck Simiu (New York: NYU Press, 1994); and Richard Feldstein, ed., *Reading Seminars I & II: Lacan's Return to Freud* (Albany: SUNY Press, 1996).

6. Lévi-Strauss, *Elementary Structures of Kinship*, trans. James Harle Bell and John Richard von Sturmer (Boston: Beacon, 1969), 8–9.

7. Freud, *Three Essays on the Theory of Sexuality*, trans. James Strachey (New York: Basic Books, 1962), 34.

8. Freud, "Femininity," *New Introductory Lectures in Psychoanalysis*, trans. James Strachey (New York: Norton, 1965).

9. Apollon, "A Lasting Heresy, the Failure of Political Desire," in *Lacan, Politics, Aesthetics*, ed. Willy Apollon and Richard Feldstein (Albany: SUNY Press, 1996), 35ff.; see also Apollon, "Féminité dites-vous?," *Savoir* 2, nos. 1–2 (May 1995): 15–44.

10. Danielle Bergeron, "Femininity," in *Feminism and Psychoanalysis: A Critical Dictionary*, ed. Elizabeth Wright (Oxford: Blackwell, 1992), 93.

11. The father of the Oedipus complex is an agent of frustration, the representative of the law or prohibition who forbids access to the object of enjoyment. In its imaginary guise, however, the father's law not only debars the mother as a possible object of enjoyment, but also supports the fantasy that there is an object that would satisfy desire if only the subject could gain access to it. The father is not merely an agent of frustration, therefore, but—in the form of the paternal imago—the support for the ideal ego upon which the son attempts to model himself. Hence the importance of the relationship between the paternal function and the totemic myth, where the primal father—as the "one exception to the rule of castration"— supports the fantasy that there is one who enjoys, and that it is therefore possible to accede to this site of exceptional jouissance. The Oedipus complex and the totemic myth both stage the tension between the jouissance that language renders impossible (the primacy of lack) and the possibility of obtaining it by acceding to the place of the "exception" to the law.

12. Lacan, *The Seminar of Jacques Lacan Book XVII: The Other Side of Psychoanalysis*, ed. Jacques-Alain Miller, trans. Russell Grigg (New York: Norton, 2007), 99.

13. For Lacan the real is "impossible to write, that is, it does not stop not being written"; in contrast, the symptom is defined by "not ceasing to be written." *Seminar XXIV*, sessions of March 8 and April 19, 1977.

14. Dylan Evans, *An Introductory Dictionary of Lacanian Psychoanalysis* (London: Routledge, 1996), 211.

15. Sigmund Freud, *Dora: An Analysis of a Case of Hysteria*, ed. Philip Rieff (New York: Simon and Schuster, 1963), 106–7 (my emphases). Subsequent citations from the text will be given as page numbers in parentheses.

16. Evans, *An Introductory Dictionary*, 213.

17. Lacan, *Seminar XI: The Four Fundamental Concepts of Psycho-Analysis*, ed. Jacques-Alain Miller, trans. Alan Sheridan (New York: Norton, 1978), 146, my emphases. Subsequent citations from the text will be given as page numbers in parentheses.

18. Apollon, "Psychoanalysis and the Freudian Rupture," unpublished manuscript. My discussion of the Lacanian metapsychology is deeply indebted to this essay.

19. Freud, "Psychoanalytic Notes Upon an Autobiographical Account of Paranoia," in *Three Case Histories*, ed. Philip Rieff (New York: Simon and Schuster, 1963), 88–89, 94–95.

20. Freud, *Beyond the Pleasure Principle*, trans. James Strachey (New York: Norton, 1961).

21. Freud, *New Introductory Lectures in Psychoanalysis*, 95.
22. Apollon, "Psychoanalysis and the Freudian Rupture."
23. Lacan, *Seminar XI*, 232.
24. Freud's most extended meditation on the fantasy of seduction occurs in his essay "A Child Is Being Beaten" from 1919.
25. "I believe, however, that transference always has the same meaning of indicating the moments where the analyst goes astray and takes anew his bearings, and the same value of reminding us of our role: that of a positive nonaction aiming at the ortho-dramatization of the patient's subjectivity" (*Écrits* 184).
26. "If the unconscious has taught us anything, it is firstly this, that *somewhere, in the Other, it knows [ça sait].*" Lacan, *The Seminar of Jacques Lacan Book XX: On Feminine Sexuality, the Limits of Love and Knowledge, 1972–1973*, ed. Jacques-Alain Miller, trans. Bruce Fink (New York: Norton, 1998), 87–88, translation modified.
27. According to Lacan's "formulation of intersubjective communication," the "sender . . . receives from the receiver his own message in an inverted form" (*Écrits* 30).
28. This will be elaborated in Lacan's *Seminar VII: The Ethics of Psychoanalysis* from 1956, which formulates the ethics of psychoanalysis through the imperative "not to give up on one's desire," *ne pas céder sur son désir.*
29. Lacan, *Seminar XXIV*, session of 8 March 1977.
30. Lyne Rouleau, "La manœuvre du sujet, la manœuvre de l'analyste, position de l'analysant," unpublished manuscript.
31. Sigmund Freud, "History of an Infantile Neurosis," in *Three Case Histories*, 234.
32. Ibid., 234.
33. "A signifier is what represents the subject to another signifier. This latter signifier is therefore the signifier to which all the other signifiers represent the subject—which means that if this signifier is missing, all the other signifiers represent nothing. For something is only represented to" (*Écrits* 694).
34. This (-1) occurs whenever a proper name is pronounced, since as opposed to the "proper name from which I am absent, *I am* in the place of jouissance" (694).
35. Freud, *Moses and Monotheism*, trans. Katherine Jones (New York: Vintage, 1967), 103.
36. Ibid., 39–48. This point will be developed at length in the next chapter.
37. Lacan, *The Seminar of Jacques Lacan, Book VII: The Ethics of Psychoanalysis*, ed. Jacques-Alain Miller, trans. Dennis Porter (New York: Norton, 1992), 174.
38. Julia Lupton and Ken Reinhard, "Lacan and the Ten Commandments," *diacritics* 33, no. 2 (Summer 2003): 83.

2. DEMANDING THE IMPOSSIBLE

1. Freud describes Marxism as a revelatory discourse that joins with religion in attempting to "solve all the problems of our existence uniformly on the basis of one overriding hypothesis." He adds: "Any critical examination of Marxist theory is forbidden, doubts of

its correctness are punished in the same way as heresy was once punished by the Catholic Church. The writings of Marx have taken the place of the Bible and the Koran as a source of revelation, though they would seem to be no more free from contradictions and obscurities than those older sacred books." Freud, *New Introductory Lectures on Psycho-Analysis*, trans. James Strachey (New York: Norton, 1965), 195, 222–23.

2. Lacan, Jacques Lacan, *The Seminar of Jacques Lacan Book XVII: The Other Side of Psychoanalysis*, trans. Russell Grigg (New York: Norton, 2007), 207.

3. Lacan, *Écrits*, trans. Bruce Fink (New York: Norton, 2006), 237–68. Subsequent citations from the text will be given as page numbers in parentheses.

4. Hallward, "What's the Point? First Notes Towards a Philosophy of Determination," in *Material Worlds: Proceedings of the Conference Held at Glasgow University*, ed. Rachel Moffat and Eugene de Klerk (Cambridge: Cambridge Scholars, 2007), 154.

5. "Matters of Will," lecture presented at Cornell University, April 2007.

6. Lacan, *The Seminar of Jacques Lacan Book VII: The Ethics of Psychoanalysis*, ed. Jacques-Alain Miller, trans. Dennis Porter (New York: Norton, 1992), 319.

7. "The point concerns the *world*, and not a part or portion of the world. The world is the whole world. What matters is to change it, all of it. That is the material point. If we get the point, what matters is to transform the world, the whole world. If we get the point, the world is a scandal that demands deliberate and universal change." Hallward, "What's the Point?," 148.

8. Apollon, "Psychoanalysis and the Freudian Rupture," unpublished manuscript.

9. In the run-up to the presidential elections in 2008 I came across an interesting variant of this question in a poll conducted by the evangelical publication *Relevant Magazine*, which asked its readers, "Who would Jesus vote for?" Barack Obama was the winner and came out 27 percentage points ahead of his nearest rival. (The poll was cited in Nicholas D. Kristof, "Who Is More Electable?," *New York Times*, February 7, 2008.) The example is surprising if you consider the conservative tendencies of American evangelicals. One can imagine how different the result might have been if the question were "how does your faith tell you to vote?"; recent history suggests that the answer would have necessarily been "Republican."

10. Kidder, *Mountains Beyond Mountains: The Quest of Dr. Paul Farmer, the Man Who Would Cure the World* (New York: Random House, 1994).

11. Freud, *Group Psychology and the Analysis of the Ego*, trans. James Strachey (New York: Norton, 1959), 38. Subsequent citations from the text will be given as page numbers in parentheses.

12. Lacan, *Television: A Challenge to the Psychoanalytic Establishment*, ed. Joan Copjec, trans. Jeffrey Mehlman (New York: Norton, 1990), 82. Subsequent citations from the text will be given as page numbers in parentheses.

13. *Écrits* 576.

14. This castration really takes two forms: that there is no object that would satisfy the subject's desire, and that the subject cannot be the object of the Other's desire.

15. *Écrits* 75–81.

16. Apollon, "Psychoanalysis and the Freudian Rupture."

17. For a clinical discussion of the role of the analyst's desire in maintaining the transference, see Willy Apollon, Danielle Bergeron, and Lucie Cantin, "The Treatment of Psychosis," trans. Tracy McNulty, in *The Subject of Lacan: A Lacanian Reader for Psychologists*, ed. Stephen Friedlander and Kareen Malone (Albany: SUNY Press, 2000), 214–15. This essay will be discussed in more detail. Subsequent citations from the text will be given as page numbers in parentheses.

18. This lack in knowledge relates to the fact that there is no signifier for jouissance. It therefore corresponds to a structural lack in the Other (of language), which Willy Apollon writes as SSS . . . -1: the signifying chain elaborated under transference leads to a real that cannot be symbolized, or what Freud calls the "navel" of the dream. The fantasy attempts to compensate for this lack by providing a staging to account for the real of the drive, a staging that determines the structure of the subject's symptoms.

19. "Analysis shows us that *the ideational material has undergone displacements and substitutions, whereas the affects have remained unaltered.* It is small wonder that the ideational material, which has been changed by dream-distortion, should no longer be compatible with the affect, which is retained unmodified; nor is there anything left to be surprised at after analysis has put the right material back into its former position. In the case of a psychical complex which has come under the influence of the censorship imposed by resistance, the *affects* are the constituent which is least influenced and which alone can give us a pointer as to how we should fill in the missing thoughts." Freud, *The Interpretation of Dreams*, trans. James Strachey (New York: Avon, 1965), 497–98.

20. In Freud's words, "anxiety-dreams only occur if the censorship has been wholly or partly overpowered; and, on the other hand, the over-powering of the censorship is facilitated if anxiety has already been produced as an immediate sensation arising from somatic sources. We can thus plainly see the purpose for which the censorship exercises its office and brings about the distortion of dreams; it does so *in order to prevent the generation of anxiety or other forms of distressing affect.*" Ibid., 301.

21. Lacan, *Ethics*, 94; see Freud, *Three Essays on the Theory of Sexuality*, trans. James Strachey (New York: Basic Books, 1962), 44–45, 60, 72, 98, 104–5.

22. Freud, *Leonardo da Vinci and a Memory of His Childhood*, trans. James Strachey (New York: Norton, 1964), 26, 29–31, 82–84, 94–99.

23. Freud, *Moses and Monotheism*, trans. Katherine Jones (New York: Vintage, 1967), 63. Subsequent citations from the text will be given as page numbers in parentheses.

24. Although the Isaac story precedes the Mosaic period in the order of narrative, it is composed at a later moment in history and is marked by the Mosaic legacy.

25. *Television* 90.

26. Charles Shepherdson, "Translations of Emotion: Pity, Fear, and Anxiety from Aristotle and Kant to Freud and Lacan," lecture presented at Cornell University, March 16, 2005.

27. Lacan, *Le séminaire livre X: l'angoisse*, ed. Jacques-Alain Miller (Paris: Seuil, 2004), 321.

28. This passage really supposes an entire genealogy, one that alternately converges with and departs from Freud's analysis in *Moses and Monotheism*. It supposes three distinct mo-

2. DEMANDING THE IMPOSSIBLE

ments or epochs, articulated by a series of repressions and reelaborations. First, the pagan worship of local *elohim* (or what Lacan identifies under the heading of "metaphysico-sexual rites"); second, the institution of Hebraic law and the gap it interposes between desire and jouissance; and third, the return, in Christianity, both of the celebration of God's jouissance and of the superegoic logics of demand and sacrifice. In the way he emphasizes the logical articulation of these three moments, Lacan is really zeroing in on a different interpretation of the Hebraic moment, one that is overlooked both by Freud and by most other commentators, who tend to characterize Judaism as the religion of the superego, subject to an oppressive law that is impossible to fulfill. In contrast, Lacan suggests that the Israelites' real dilemma is not that they are subject to the capricious demands of the Deity, but that they are not able to surrender to the Other those objects that cause them anxiety.

29. Martin Buber, *Moses: The Revelation and the Covenant* (New York: Harper and Row, 1958), 125–26.

30. One might say that Moses is an analyst on the model of the early Freud, that is, he evacuates the illusory Imaginary Other, but doesn't allow the subject to arrive at the fall of the seduction fantasy himself, and as a result repression and resistance triumph.

31. This position is in fact central to many forms of analytic psychotherapy, which are predicated upon the idea that the analyst is the screen on which the patient projects his relations with his parents or the good or bad object of the fantasy; the conception of the analyst's function is thus explicitly imaginary.

32. This turn to psychosis probably requires a few words of justification, since psychosis is a very specific structure that departs from the neurotic framework supposed by the previous section (where the subject appeals to the ideal ego as a support for the unified body image that represses castration). In pioneering the psychoanalytic treatment of psychosis that for Lacan remained only a goal, Apollon, Bergeron, and Cantin have gone further than all other contemporary psychoanalysts not only in exploring the specific logic of psychosis, but in distinguishing between neurosis, psychosis, and perversion on the basis of structure, and not according to the phenomenology of symptoms or the "seriousness" of one pathology compared to another. In underscoring the analogies between the three psychic structures in and beyond their singular features, they have done much to overcome the historic tendency to conflate the features of neurosis with the human as such. They emphasize that the neurotic seduction fantasy, the psychotic delusion, and the perverse demonstration all work to repress castration through the invocation of an Imaginary Other, even if the form and function of this Other differ from one structure to the next. If the structure of psychosis is of special significance for them, as it is for Lacan, it is because it lays bare the function of the imaginary in a way that may be easier to miss in the case of the neurotic, even if it is no less significant. This is because the neurotic appeals to social reality (a "reality" that is really nothing more than a collective myth and thus itself a kind of "delusion") to facilitate his repression of the unconscious. The crux of Lacan's critique of ego psychology is that the analyst's own acceptance of or dependence upon this "reality" tends to facilitate the analysand's repression, precluding any access to the unconscious. See, in particular, Apollon, Bergeron, and Cantin, *Traiter la psychose* (Quebec: Gifric, 1990).

33. Freud, *Three Case Histories*, ed. Philip Rieff (New York: Collier, 1963), 100. Subsequent citations from the text will be given as page numbers in parentheses.

34. Lacan, *Seminar XVII*, 52.

35. This passage is what allows the analyst to enter into the "minimal social link" at stake in the transference without falling into what Freud called "counter-transference," or the resistance to the subject's unconscious that results from the analyst's failure to traverse the fantasy of seduction in his own analysis.

36. Rigorously speaking, such a subjective analysis must necessarily remain speculative in the case of Jesus. While I believe one can distinguish the remnants of something like an actual subjective position from the idealized portrait of Jesus, it is not possible to isolate the historical kernel of the legend as in the case of Freud's analysis of Moses (which draws upon, among other sources, the chronicles of the Egyptian pharaohs, the history of the Aton religion, and the ritual significance of circumcision in ancient Egypt).

37. As a kind of cinematic shorthand, the Jesus I am talking about is not the amiable camp counselor Jesus played by Willem Defoe in *The Last Temptation of Christ*, but the slender, effeminate, and at the same time slightly terrifying figure of Pasolini's masterpiece *The Gospel According to St. Matthew*, as anxiety-provoking as he is inspiring. This is the same Jesus who inspires Nietzsche's Zarathustra, a Jesus who wages war on the transcendent illusion of the eternal self in the name of a transformative desire liberated by the death of God.

38. After the arrest of Jesus, the Gospel of Matthew records that "Jesus stood before the governor [Pontius Pilate]; and the governor asked him, 'Are you the King of the Jews?' Jesus said, 'You say so.' But when he was accused by the chief priests and elders, he did not answer. Then Pilate said to him, 'Do you now hear how many accusations they make against you?' But he gave him no answer, not even to a single charge, so that the governor was greatly amazed" (Matthew 27:11–14).

39. Blaise Pascal, *Pensées*, trans. A. J. Krailsheimer (New York: Penguin, 1995), fragment 919, p. 313.

40. A resurrection whose stakes, I think, are more profoundly revealed by Nietzsche's reading than by Badiou's: it is about the resurrection of the ego, life after death, the refusal of castration. There's no "resurrection" in Jesus, and this is crucial to the difference between him and Paul.

41. Badiou, *Saint Paul: The Foundation of Universalism*, trans. Ray Brassier (Stanford: Stanford University Press, 2003). Badiou is quite right to insist on the discontinuity between Jesus and Paul, and to credit the latter with having conceived the doctrine of the resurrection. Without this distinction, it is impossible to appreciate the singularity of either figure.

42. Indeed, at no point does Jesus ever attempt to found a group of any kind: what he tells the disciples is that if you want to "follow me," you have to take up the cross and lose your life.

43. Lacan, *Le séminaire livre VIII: le transfert* (Paris: Seuil, 1991), 14, my translation.

44. This object cannot, however, take the form merely of a theory or an interpretation. As Hallward suggests in his citation of Marx, it is not a matter of understanding or describing the world in different terms, but of intervening in the world in a different way. This is why a psychoanalytically inflected ideology critique could never rise to the challenge presented by Freud's desire. An analytic act cannot consist merely in applying an interpretive grid or

in considering unconscious factors, and thereby staying ahead of the usual problems that plague social or political undertakings. The problem with this purely intellectual use of psychoanalysis is that it does not involve a confrontation with desire or anxiety. The clinical experience of analysis pushes toward the necessity of an act: an act in the world, the act of becoming an analyst, the act that sustains the transference. This constant confrontation with the necessity of an act and the anxiety it provokes is an important part of the ongoing experience of analysis. But the theoretical application of psychoanalysis does not suppose such a necessity, and even acts as a defense against it.

3. WRESTLING WITH THE ANGEL

1. Pierre Legendre, "The Masters of Law: A Study of the Dogmatic Function," in *Law and the Unconscious: A Legendre Reader*, ed. Peter Goodrich, trans. Peter Goodrich with Alain Pottage and Anton Schütz (London: St. Martin's, 1997), 110. Subsequent citations from the text will be given as page numbers in parentheses.

2. Compare Jacques Derrida's celebrated reading of the theme of the "book of nature," a "natural writing" or "writing in the heart" opposed to the "fallen" writing of pure exteriority. Derrida, *Of Grammatology*, trans. Gayatri Chakravorty Spivak (Baltimore: Johns Hopkins University Press, 1976), 15–18.

3. Legendre, "'Les juifs se livrent à des interprétations insensées': expertise d'un texte," in *La Psychanalyse est-elle une histoire juive?* Colloque de Montpeller, 1980, ed. Adélie et Jean-Jacques Rassial (Paris: Seuil, 1981), 112.

4. Peter Goodrich, "Translating Legendre, or the Poetical Sermon of a Contemporary Jurist," in *Law and the Postmodern Mind*, ed. Goodrich and Gray Carlson (Ann Arbor: University of Michigan Press, 1998), 229–30.

5. Alain Badiou, *Saint Paul: The Foundation of Universalism*, trans. Ray Brassier (Stanford: Stanford University Press, 2003).

6. Legendre, "Masters of Law," 110–11.

7. Jacob Taubès, Daniel Boyarin, Alain Badiou, Giorgio Agamben, Slavoj Žižek, and Ken Reinhard, to name only a few of the most important recent contributors to Paul scholarship, have all developed facets of his work that would complicate, if not outright contradict, this canonical reception of Paul's letters within the political-theological traditions of Roman and Western jurisprudence.

8. Ken Reinhard suggested to me that Paul's "moral maxim" might be stated as follows: "Act 'as if' there were no law."

9. Badiou, *Saint Paul*, 18.

10. Emmanuel Lévinas, "The Pact," in *The Lévinas Reader*, ed. Sean Hand (Oxford: Basil Blackwell, 1989), 218. Subsequent citations from the text will be given as page numbers in parentheses.

11. Matthew 22:37–40.

12. "The same night he [Jacob] got up and took his two wives, his two maids, and his eleven children, and crossed the ford of the Jabbok. He took them and sent them across the

stream, and likewise everything that he had. Jacob was left alone; and a man wrestled with him until daybreak. When the man saw that he did not prevail against Jacob, he struck him on the hip socket; and Jacob's hip was put out of joint as he wrestled with him. Then he said, 'Let me go, for the day is breaking.' But Jacob said, 'I will not let you go, unless you bless me.' So he said to him, 'What is your name?' And he said, 'Jacob.' Then the man said, 'You shall no longer be called Jacob, but Israel, for you have striven with God and with humans, and have prevailed.' Then Jacob asked him, 'Please tell me your name.' But he said, 'Why is it that you ask my name?' And there he blessed him. So Jacob called the place Peniel, saying, 'For I have seen God face to face, and yet my life is preserved' " (Genesis 32:25–30). This passage will be discussed in more detail in chapter 6.

13. Jean-François Lyotard, *The Hyphen: Between Judaism and Christianity*, trans. Pascale-Anne Brault and Michael Nass (New York: Prometheus, 1999), 15. Subsequent citations from the text will be given as page numbers in parentheses.

14. Hannah Arendt, *Eichmann in Jerusalem: A Report on the Banality of Evil* (Harmondsworth: Penguin, 1963), 136. Subsequent citations from the text will be given as page numbers in parentheses.

15. Mladen Dolar, *A Voice and Nothing More* (Cambridge: MIT Press, 2006), 98. Subsequent citations from the text will be given as page numbers in parentheses.

16. Jacques Lacan, *Écrits*, trans. Bruce Fink (New York: Norton, 2006), 572–73; cited by *A Voice* 99.

17. Arendt, *Eichmann in Jerusalem*. Arendt's reading of Eichmann will be discussed in more detail in chapter 7.

18. Juliet Flower MacCannell, "Facing Fascism: A Feminine Politics of Jouissance," in *Lacan, Politics, Aesthetics*, ed. Willy Apollon and Richard Feldstein (Albany: SUNY, 1996), 73, 70. Subsequent citations from the text will be given as page numbers in parentheses.

19. Jacques Lacan, *Television: A Challenge to the Psychoanalytic Establishment*, ed. Joan Copjec, trans. Jeffrey Mehlman (New York: Norton, 1990), 87. Subsequent citations from the text will be given as page numbers in parentheses.

20. Lacan, *The Seminar of Jacques Lacan Book I: Freud's Papers on Technique, 1953–1954*, ed. Jacques-Alain Miller, trans. John Forrester (New York: Norton, 1988), 102, translation modified.

21. Lacan, *Le séminaire livre X: l'angoisse*, text established by Jacques-Alain Miller (Paris: Seuil, 2004), 287, my translation. Subsequent citations from the text will be given as page numbers in parentheses.

22. In Dolar's related formulation, "The voice of enunciation circumscribed a certain locus of the moral law without giving it any positive substance or content, while the voice of the superego obfuscates this locus, fills it with its vocality, thus seemingly presenting the awesome figure of "the Other of the Other," the Other without a lack, the horrendous Other—not merely the Other of law, but at the same time the Other of its transgression. For the excess of the voice here functions precisely as transgression of the law, and the admonishments that this voice issues cannot be turned into 'principles giving universal law' but, rather, diverge from universality" (*A Voice* 100).

23. This lack is represented in Talmudic tradition by the lack of the voice itself, the voice whose

inscription ancient Hebrew—as a nonphonetic language—does not allow, and whose absence from the letter of the text makes the task of interpretation all the more necessary. Precisely because they cannot "hear" the voice in the text, the members of the community are obliged to voice it themselves.

24. Moses Maimonides, glossing the same verse, suggests that God's speech lacked distinct phonemes. Cited by S. Y. Agnon, *Present at Sinai: The Giving of the Law*, trans. Michael Swirsky (Philadelphia: Jewish Publication Society, 1994), 260.

25. "Rashi explains that first all the commandments were uttered by God in a single instant. Then, God repeated the first two commandments word for word. Following that, the people were afraid that they could no longer endure the awesome holiness of God's voice and they asked that Moses repeat the remaining eight commandments to them." *Aseres Hadibros, The Ten Commandments: A New Translation with a Commentary Anthologized from Talmudic, Midrashic, and Rabbinic Sources*, ed. Rabbis Nosson Scherman and Meir Zlotowitz (Brooklyn: Artscroll Mesorah, 1981), 23.

26. Lacan, *Écrits*, 572–73.

27. Lacan, *The Seminar of Jacques Lacan Book VII: The Ethics of Psychoanalysis, 1959–1960*, ed. Jacques-Alain Miller, trans. Dennis Porter (New York: Norton, 1992), 69.

28. See, in particular, Žižek, *The Puppet and the Dwarf: The Perverse Core of Christianity* (Cambridge.: MIT Press, 2003).

29. Jacques Lacan, *Le séminaire livre XX: encore*, ed. Jacques-Alain Miller (Paris: Seuil, 1982), 70.

30. Frank Vande Veire, "Christus starb für dich! Über den sakrifiziellen Kern des Christentums," in *Wieder Religion? Christentum in zeitgenössischen kritischen Denken (Lacan, Zizek, Badiou u.a.)*, ed. Marc De Kesel and Dominiek Hoens (Wenen: Turia + Kant, 2005), 40–65.

31. In a way, this demonic manifestation is not unrelated to the appearance of the Voice in Paul: it is conceived as something that must be guarded against, not welcomed; but the same notion of jouissance is at stake in each case. Even in the blood sacrifice at the heart of the Passover ritual, it is striking that the lamb's blood painted on the lintel of the house serves not to exalt the Israelites over the Egyptians or to shield them from their might, but to protect the members of the household from YHWH himself.

32. Lacan, *Seminar VII*, 81–82.

33. In chapter 6 we will see that Walter Benjamin understands the sanction against lying as the essence of what he calls "mythic violence," and identifies the possibility of the lie with the function of language as an exclusion of violence.

34. See Freud's discussion of Schreber's autobiography in Freud, "Psychoanalytic Notes Upon an Autobiographical Account of a Case of Paranoia," *Three Case Histories*, ed. Philip Rieff (New York: Simon and Schuster, 1963).

35. Badiou, *Saint Paul*, 23.

36. For Lévinas's own analysis of the problem of "digestion" as a mode of relation to the other, see the first chapter of *Totality and Infinity*, entitled "Metaphysics and Transcendence." Lévinas, *Totality and Infinity: An Essay on Exteriority*, trans. Alphonso Lingis (Pittsburgh: Duquesne University Press, 1969).

37. Although it is customary to read the Jacob story as an allegory of castration, what is not always appreciated is that it is not only Jacob who is castrated, but God as well: the result of the contest is a mutual checking, a mutual castration.

38. Badiou's remarkable reading of Paul's letters has perhaps gone further than any other in demonstrating that Paul can in no way be reduced to the dogmatic authority canonized by Western jurisprudence. Yet this revolutionary reading also coexists quite comfortably with a celebration of the antisymbolic (and even anti-Semitic) side of Paul in a way that is not really acknowledged, and whose larger consequences are often contradictory (I develop this argument in more detail in chapter 5).

39. This false etymology, which recurs in many of Augustine's typological readings of the Hebrew Bible, is interesting in that it replaces "striving" with "seeing," struggle with vision.

40. Saint Augustine, *City of God*, trans. Henry Bettenson (London: Penguin, 1972, 1984), bk. 16, chap. 39.

41. For my own reading of Sarah's laughter, see the chapter entitled "Israel, Divine Hostess" in *The Hostess: Hospitality, Femininity, and the Expropriation of Identity* (Minneapolis: University of Minnesota Press, 2006).

42. According to Jean-François Lyotard, Abraham's and Sarah's laughter underscores the possible misrecognition that always presides over the transmission of the divine signifier: "The pure signifier, the tetragram . . . can always turn out to be lacking, to signify something other than what the chosen one believed it to say. It is this failure, this breakdown, that provokes laughter" (*The Hyphen* 10).

4. THE GAP IN THE WRITTEN LAW AND THE UNWRITABLE ACT OF DECISION

1. Carl Schmitt, *Political Theology: Four Chapters on the Concept of Sovereignty*, trans. George Schwab (Cambridge: MIT Press, 1985), 12. Subsequent citations from the text will be given as page numbers in parentheses.

2. The destruction of the norm does not imply the destruction of the legal order, however. For Schmitt, "the exception remains . . . accessible to jurisprudence because both elements, the norm as well as the decision, remain within the framework of the juristic" (12).

3. Giorgio Agamben translates Schmitt's definition of sovereignty with the formula "ecstasy-belonging," which captures very well its theological overtones. Agamben, *State of Exception*, trans. Kevin Attell (Chicago: University of Chicago Press, 2005), 35.

4. What Paul calls "sin" is really the problem internal to language as representation. This is essentially the Platonic argument according to which a linguistic or pictorial representation is merely a copy of a copy, an empty simulacrum with no "internal resemblance" to the truth.

5. This amounts to a foreclosure of anything like revolution or civil disobedience, the acts through which subjects claim for themselves a space in the political order.

6. Walter Benjamin, "On the Concept of History," trans. Harry Zohn, in *Selected Writings*,

vol. 4, *1938–1940*, ed. Howard Eiland and Michael W. Jennings (Cambridge: Harvard University Press, 2003), 392.

7. Agamben summarizes the stakes of Benjamin's critique in the following terms: "Germany found itself technically in a situation of sovereign dictatorship, which should have led to the definitive abolition of the Weimar Constitution and the establishment of a new constitution, whose fundamental characteristics Schmitt strove to define in a series of articles between 1933 and 1936. But what Schmitt could in no way accept was that the state of exception be wholly confused with the rule. In *Dictatorship*, he had already stated that arriving at a correct concept of dictatorship is impossible as long as every legal order is seen 'only as a latent and intermittent dictatorship.' To be sure, *Political Theology* unequivocally acknowledged the primacy of the exception, insofar as it makes the constitution of the normal sphere possible; but if, in this sense, the rule 'lives only by the exception,' what then happens when exception and rule become undecidable? From Schmitt's perspective, the functioning of the juridical order ultimately rests on an apparatus—the state of exception—whose purpose is to make the norm applicable by temporarily suspending its efficacy. When the exception becomes the rule, the machine can no longer function. In this sense, the undecidability of norm and exception formulated in the eighth thesis puts Schmitt's theory in check. Sovereign decision is no longer capable of performing the task that *Political Theology* assigned it: the rule, which now coincides with what it lives by, devours itself." Agamben, *State of Exception*, 58.

8. Paul shows how what Benjamin calls the "state of exception become the rule" is implicit in the political theology that grounds Schmitt's account of the exception, and belies Schmitt's claims that the suspension of the constitution can be merely temporary. In wondering about a state of exception that becomes the rule, Benjamin is really zeroing in on something that is laid bare by Paul, but passed over by Schmitt: the fundamental and irreparable antinomy between the spirit and the letter of the law, or between the sovereign exception and the constitutional order. While Schmitt cannot imagine a conflation of the state of exception with the rule, Paul makes clear that one can access the Good only if the "state of exception becomes the rule," if the Good is accessed through the suspension of the law.

9. Agamben explains that "Schmitt, in his tenacious critique of the legal state, gives the name 'fictitious' to a state of exception that would be regulated by law, with the aim of guaranteeing some degree of individual rights and liberties. Consequently, he forcefully denounces the Weimar jurists' inability to distinguish between the merely factual action of the president of the Reich under Article 48 and a procedure regulated by law. Benjamin once again reformulates the opposition in order to turn it back against Schmitt. Now that any possibility of a fictitious state of exception—in which exception and normal conditions are temporally and locally distinct—has collapsed, the state of exception 'in which we live' is real and absolutely cannot be distinguished from the rule. Every fiction of a nexus between violence and law disappears here: there is nothing but a zone of anomie, in which *violence works without juridical clothing of any kind.* The attempt of state power to annex anomie through the state of exception is unmasked by Benjamin for what it is: a *fictio iuris*

par excellence, which claims to maintain the law in its very suspension as force-of-law."
Agamben, *State of Exception*, 59, translation modified.

10. In his book on the Trauerspiel, Benjamin writes that "Spirit manifests itself as a capacity to
exercise dictatorship": the dismantling of the law introduces the possibility of a "dictatorship of spirit," a "force of law" that operates without regard for law, without limit. Benjamin, *The Origin of German Tragic Drama*, trans. George Steiner (London: Verso, 1998), 98.

11. Lacan, *The Seminar of Jacques Lacan Book VII: The Ethics of Psychoanalysis*, ed. Jacques-Alain
Miller, trans. Dennis Porter (New York: Norton, 1992), 70. Subsequent citations from the
text will be given as page numbers in parentheses.

12. "Freud is telling us the same thing as Saint Paul, namely, that what governs us on the path
of our pleasure is no Sovereign Good, and that moreover, beyond a certain limit, we are in
a thoroughly enigmatic position relative to that which lies within *das Ding*, because there
is no ethical rule which acts as a mediator between our pleasure and its real rule." *Ethics* 96.

13. Clinically, the elaboration of the signifying chain under transference offers some respite
from the drive by partially binding this unbound energy, lowering the tension associated
with the insistence of the real.

14. It is not surprising, therefore, that states of exception are so often marked by the resurgence
of the real, the violent or predatory practices that under "normal" circumstances are prohib-
ited by law: illegal detention and surveillance, torture and killing by the police or military,
"ethnic cleansing" and rape as means of population control, and so forth.

15. By means of condensation (metaphor) or displacement (metonymy).

16. The clinic of the dream reveals that the logic of "lying about evil" characterizes the action
of the signifier as such, which transforms disturbing psychic content through condensation
and displacement and so allows it to be represented; this representation in turn functions
to bind the drive energy. The example concerns the status of representation as a signifier,
and not as an image.

17. In this respect Lacan's account of the law as "lying about evil" also accords with Benjamin's
invocation of the "juridical clothing" of the letter of the law as a necessary obstacle to the
"state of exception become the rule." If, as Schmitt maintains, the law were simply the
representation of an authority that is not based on law (the sovereign decision, the transcendent "Law of God"), then it would not be necessary. But the notion of "juridical clothing" supposes another understanding of the law's function: to separate or erect a boundary
between exception and rule, between spirit and letter.

18. Kenneth Reinhard and Julia Reinhard Lupton, "The Subject of Religion: Lacan and the
Ten Commandments," *diacritics* 33, no. 2 (Summer 2003): 83.

19. Ibid.

20. One effect of this shift is that while spatiality and distance are of primary importance in
Judaism, the spatial configurations of Jewish worship are gradually displaced in Christianity in favor of transcendent or temporal configurations: the "Jerusalem above" versus the
"present Jerusalem," the spatially unspecific "brotherhood," the body as a "temple of the
holy spirit" in which the divine is fully present, and so forth.

21. The sign of this replacement is that the commandments of the first tablet essentially disappear in Christian observance, beginning with the commandment against making idols. Not only is it now possible to represent God, but images come to occupy a central place in Christian iconography. This shift is in turn intimately linked to the theory of sovereignty. Where the logic of the commandments specifically precludes the law being "embodied" or given form, Schmitt's decisionism—like Paul's account of the fulfillment of the law—gives pride of place to the imaginary incarnation of the law, and suggests that the word may indeed be "made flesh."

22. See, in particular, Freud, *Civilization and Its Discontents*, trans. James Strachey (New York: Norton, 1961), chap. 5, pp. 64–74.

23. This gap is understood not only as the place where the norms do not apply (or where representation does not function), but as a place where "something is missing," a space of negation.

24. Brad Zukovic has analyzed this passage as an example of the rhetorical-topological figure he calls "temporal synecdoche." Zukovic, "Four Ways Into a Vortex: Metaphor and Machine Logic," *(a): The Journal of Culture and the Unconscious* 6, no. 1 (Spring 2006): 19–27.

5. THE EVENT OF THE LETTER

1. Bruno Bosteels, Adrian Johnston, and Ed Pluth have all developed this side of Badiou's work, notably in relation to his *Theory of the Subject*. See Bruno Bosteels, *Badiou and Politics* (Durham: Duke University Press, 2010); Adrian Johnston, *Badiou, Žižek, and Political Transformations: The Cadence of Change* (Evanston, Ill.: Northwestern University Press, 2009); and Ed Pluth, *Badiou: A Philosophy of the New* (Cambridge: Polity, 2010).

2. As Peter Hallward has argued, this is even more true of Badiou's treatment of institutions. Hallward, "Consequences of Abstraction," introduction to *Think Again: Alain Badiou and the Future of Philosophy*, ed. Peter Hallward (London: Continuum, 2004), 1–20.

3. Badiou, "The Three Negations," *Cardozo Law Review* 29, no. 5 (April 2008): 1877–83.

4. Badiou, closing remarks at the symposium "Law and Event," Cardozo Law School, New York City, October 2007.

5. Alain Badiou, *Saint Paul: The Foundation of Universalism*, trans. Ray Brassier (Stanford: Stanford University Press, 2003), 56. Subsequent citations from the text will be given as page numbers in parentheses.

6. See, in particular, the Eric Marty, "Alain Badiou: the Future of a Negation (à Propos of *Circonstances 3*)," *Les Temps Modernes* 635-636 (December 2005-January 2006); and Badiou's response: Badiou, "The Word 'Jew' and the Sycophant," in *Polemics*, trans. Steve Corcoran (London: Verso, 2006), 230–47.

7. Badiou, *Polemics*, 158–59, translation modified; the French original was published as *Circonstances, 3: portées du mot "juif"* (Paris: Lignes & Manifestes, 2005), 9–10.

8. Peter Goodrich, opening remarks at the symposium "Alain Badiou: Law and Event," Cardozo Law School, November 11–12, 2007, unpublished.

9. Pierre Legendre, "The Masters of Law," in *Law and the Unconscious: A Legendre Reader*, ed. Peter Goodrich, trans. Peter Goodrich with Alain Pottage and Anton Schütz (London: St. Martin's, 1997), 68. Subsequent citations from the text will be given as page numbers in parentheses, preceded by "Masters."

10. Ernst Kantorowicz, *The King's Two Bodies: A Study in Mediaeval Political Theology* (Princeton: Princeton University Press, 1957).

11. Pierre Legendre, "'Les juifs se livrent à des interprétations insensées': expertise d'un texte," in *La Psychanalyse est-elle une histoire juive?* Colloque de Montpeller, 1980, ed. Adélie et Jean-Jacques Rassial (Paris: Seuil, 1981), 100. Subsequent citations from the text will be given as page numbers in parentheses, preceded by "Jews."

12. In this respect Jewish legal practice departs even from such deliberative models as Supreme Court arbitration, which certainly recognizes that the letter of the law is ambiguous and subject to varying interpretations, but ultimately sets itself the task of deciding.

13. Legendre's source is Gratian, whose compilations provided the basis for the scholastic foundations of modern juridicism.

14. Or as Paul puts it in his gloss of the Genesis passage where God promises to keep the covenant with Abraham and his offspring: "Now the promises were made to Abraham and to his offspring. It does not say 'And to offsprings,' referring to many; but, referring to one, 'And to your offspring,' which is Christ" (Galatians 3:16).

15. Legendre sees the same tension at stake in the quarrel between Jung and Freud. Freud's analysis of the dreamwork elucidates the function of the symbolic by demonstrating that the signifying chain elaborated under transference follows in the tracks of a primordial inscription linked to castration. Jung, on the other hand, offers a "spiritualized" translation of the dream image that now functions as an allegorical "type" or figure that belongs to a universal symbolism (the dream dictionary) and that is interpretable by a single authority (Jung himself as analyst).

16. The tension in Judaism between the nonspiritual letter and the spiritual law could be equated psychoanalytically with the distinction between the signifier as it appears clinically (that is to say, hysterically) and the "imaginary" function of the law as prohibition. In *Totem and Taboo*, Freud shows that the law of the fraternal pact is merely an internalization of the father's law. It originates in an exceptional authority "outside" the law, and sustains the fantasy that one might oneself accede to this exceptional site of enjoyment through identification with the father. In the clinic of hysteria, on the other hand, there is no imaginary dimension to the law of the signifier.

17. In Legendre's words, "the first juridical text of the Latin Church, the first counsular document, is the minutes of the Jerusalem Council, which took place during the lifetime of the apostles and in which Saint Paul participated. It was convened to discuss the question of circumcision, and you will find its formulas in Acts of the Apostles 15 . . . as well as in the Epistle to the Romans 2 and 4, where Paul explains the difference between the Law of faith and the law of circumcision. It is here, in these two essential passages (Acts and Paul), that the Christian grammar was inaugurated, the Christian exegesis of the law" ("Jews" 111).

18. This false etymology recurs in many of Augustine's typological readings of the Hebrew Bible. For an explanation of its significance to my reading, see chapter 3, note 20.

19. Augustine, *City of God*, trans. Henry Bettenson (London: Penguin, 1984), bk. 16, chap. 39. Subsequent citations from the text will be given as page numbers in parentheses.

20. *Saint Paul* 23.

21. Alain Badiou, "Huit thèses sur l'universel," in Alain Badiou and Etienne Balibar, "Forum sur l'universel," organized by the Collège International de Philosophie in Paris, November 4 1998. Cited by Peter Hallward, *Badiou: A Subject to Truth* (Minneapolis: University of Minnesota Press, 2003), 250–51.

22. Indeed, the "address to all" that conditions Pauline universalism is for Badiou nothing more than a generalization of the "self-love" born of the resurrection event: "only the event authorizes the subject to be something other than a dead Self, impossible to love. The new law is thus the deployment of the power of self-love made possible by subjectivation (conviction), directed toward others and destined to all" (*Saint Paul* 90).

23. Moreover, it is important to remember that the late prophets of the diaspora are actually much more important for Christianity than for Judaism, and will form the basis of all typological readings of the New Testament, both in the Gospels of Jesus and in the writings of subsequent apostles and Church Fathers. In Jewish tradition, on the other hand, the prophets are understood as "judges" who denounce the idolatry or sinful behavior of Israel, and not as foreseers of the future or decipherers of divine will. This perspective only enters in with typological reading, which is a paradigm of interpretation that has no analogy in Judaism. We have an excellent example in the Augustine passage cited earlier, which invokes a "prophetic statement"—"they have limped away from their paths"—not as an indictment of Jewish behavior, as it is in context, but as an allegorical formula subject to typological interpretation. See Psalms 18, 45.

24. *The Eerdmans Analytical Concordance to the Revised Standard Version of the Bible*, ed. Richard E. Whitaker (Grand Rapids: Eerdmans, 1988).

25. Concluding comments to the symposium "Alain Badiou: Law and Event," Cardozo Law School, November 11–12, 2007, unpublished.

26. Inasmuch as it is tied to an interpretation, faith is arguably itself a kind of "particularism," a communal attribute.

27. Simon Critchley, "A Heroism of the Decision, a Politics of the Event," *London Review of Books*, September 20, 2007, 33–34.

28. Badiou, *Polemics*, 95.

29. Jacques Lacan, *The Ethics of Psychoanalysis, 1959–1960*, ed. Jacques-Alain Miller, trans. Dennis Porter (New York: Norton, 1992), 174, my emphases.

30. Sigmund Freud, *Moses and Monotheism*, trans. Katherine Jones (New York: Vintage, 1939), III.

31. Martin Buber, *Moses* (New York: Harper and Row, 1958), 126.

32. According to this reasoning, one could argue that Paul does not so much universalize what would otherwise be particular as misconstrue the stakes of the Mosaic event by considering it through the lens of particularity, as Badiou himself does.

33. With the notable exception of circumcision, these elements are not especially central in Judaism either, which has always admitted converts from other races and religious traditions.

6. THE COMMANDMENT AGAINST THE LAW

1. Rolf Tiedemann, editorial note, in Benjamin, *Gesammelte Schriften*, vol. 1, part 3, ed. Rolf Tiedemann and Hermann Schueppenhäuser (Frankfurt: Suhrkamp, 1977), 886. Cited in Giorgio Agamben, *State of Exception*, trans. Kevin Attell (Chicago: University of Chicago Press, 2005), 52.

2. I am thinking of Jacques Derrida's justifiably famous reading of Benjamin's essay in "Force of Law," which will be discussed in more detail.

3. Benjamin, "Critique of Violence," in *Selected Writings*, vol. 1, *1913–1926*, ed. Marcus Bullock and Michael W. Jennings (Cambridge: Belknap, 1996), 248. Subsequent citations from the text will be given as page numbers in parentheses. German text is from Benjamin, *Gesammelte Schriften*, vol. 2, part 1, 179–204.

4. Note that these boundary violations go both ways: the human who crosses a boundary is punished by the gods, who in turn breach the boundaries of the human in exacting retribution.

5. This understanding of the law as a threshold or step that must not be crossed is preserved in the French *pas*, which is at once the particle of negation that figures prominently in legal proscriptions and the word for "step."

6. Walter Benjamin, *The Origin of German Tragic Drama*, trans. George Steiner (London: Verso, 1998), 98.

7. Jacques Derrida, "Force of Law," in *Acts of Religion*, ed. Gil Anidjar (New York: Routledge, 2002), 280. Subsequent citations from the text will be given as page numbers in parentheses.

8. "However sacred man is (or however sacred that life in him which is identically present in earthly life, death, and afterlife), there is no sacredness in his condition, in his bodily life vulnerable to injury by his fellow men" (251). Derrida reads this argument as a reflection of the Judaic critique of vitalism or biologism: what is sacred in man's life is not his life, but the *justice* of his life; it is a matter of "life beyond life, life against life, but always in life and for life" (289).

9. Korah's defiance of Moses' authority could itself be interpreted as a kind of "strike," and yet God annihilates him in a way that appears to sanction Moses' status as a representative of divine authority. It is not surprising then that some critics (notably Derrida and Weber) have even claimed that the judgment of Korah is an unambiguous example of mythic violence.

10. Even the example of the general strike might be assimilated to such a logic, since it opposes an unjust law in the name of another understanding of justice. One might think here of how Martin Luther King Jr., in the context of the American civil rights movement, drew on Christian theology to oppose the unjust laws of segregation in the name of a higher law,

or of the affinity between Marxist revolutionary movements and liberation theology in the Latin American context. Even when divine authority or religious tradition is not invoked, revolutionary struggle often appeals to a "higher" law of just ends—fundamental human rights, racial equality, the workers' assertion of the intrinsic value of labor or claim to shared ownership of the means of production, and so on—to oppose what is unjust in the legal order.

11. "In the Fall, since the eternal purity of names was violated, the sterner purity of the judging word arose. For the essential composition of language, the Fall has a threefold significance (in addition to its other meanings). In stepping outside the purer language of name, man makes language a means (that is, a knowledge appropriate to him), and therefore also, in one part at any rate, a mere sign; and this later results in the plurality of languages. The second meaning is that from the Fall, in exchange for the immediacy of name that was damaged by it, a new immediacy arises: the magic of judgment, which no longer rests blissfully in itself. The third meaning that can perhaps be tentatively ventured is that the origin of abstraction, too, as a faculty of the spirit of language, is to be sought in the Fall. For good and evil, being unnameable and nameless, stand outside the language of names, which man leaves behind precisely in the abyss opened by this question. Name, however, with regard to existing language, offers only the ground in which its concrete elements are rooted. But the abstract elements of language—we may perhaps surmise—are rooted in the word of judgment. The immediacy (which, however, is the linguistic root) of the communicability of abstraction resides in judgment. This immediacy in the communication of abstraction came into being as judgment, when, in the Fall, man abandoned immediacy in the communication of the concrete—that is, name—and fell into the abyss of the mediateness of all communication, of the word as means, of the empty word, into the abyss of prattle. For—it must be said again—the question as to good and evil in the world after the Creation was empty prattle. The Tree of Knowledge stood in the garden of God not in order to provide knowledge of good and evil but as the symptomatic sign of judgment borne by he who questions. This immense irony is the sign by which the mythical origin of law is recognized." Benjamin, "On Language as Such and on the Language of Man," in *Selected Writings*, 1:73, translation modified.

12. "God is the name of the absolute metonymy, what it names by displacing the names, the substitution and what substitutes itself in the name of this substitution. Even before the name, as soon as the first name: 'divine violence, which is the sign and seal but never the means of sacred execution, can be called sovereign violence.' It can be called—sovereign. In secret. Sovereign in that it calls itself and it is called there where sovereignly it calls itself. It names itself. Sovereign is the violent power of this originary appellation. Absolute privilege, infinite prerogative. The prerogative gives the condition of all appellation. It says nothing else, it calls itself, therefore, in silence. Nothing resonates, then, but the name, the pure nomination of the name before the name. The pre-nomination of God—here is justice in its infinite power. It begins and ends at the signature" ("Force of Law" 293).

13. The divine signature would be an invisible inscription, a preinscription, and thus an "unwritten law," a law that would already bear all the marks of the mythic order.

14. Benjamin, "On Language as Such," 74.

15. This passage seems to anticipate by more than thirty years the argument of Heidegger's famous lecture "The Nature of Language," which holds that when we speak "about" something, we are no longer having an experience with language, since the referent (or the illusion of "communication") dominates. As distinct from communication or expression, "language" implies opacity, the loss of the referent: the "communication of the incommunicable," in Benjamin's terms.

16. "Only late and in a peculiar state of decay has [language] been penetrated by legal violence in the penalty placed on fraud. For whereas the legal system at its origin, trusting to its victorious power, is content to defeat lawbreaking wherever it happens to appear, and deception, having itself no trace of power about it, was . . . exempt from punishment in Roman and ancient Germanic law, the law of a later period, lacking confidence in its own violence, no longer felt itself a match for that of all others. Rather, fear of the latter and mistrust of itself indicate its declining vitality. It begins to set itself ends, with the intention of sparing law-preserving violence more taxing manifestations. It turns to fraud, therefore, not out of moral considerations but for fear of the violence that it might unleash in the defrauded party. Since such fear conflicts with the violent nature of law derived from its origins, such ends are inappropriate to the justified means of law. They reflect not only the decay of its own sphere but also a diminution of pure means. For in prohibiting fraud, law restricts the use of wholly nonviolent means because they could produce reactive violence" (244–45).

17. "Force of Law" 279–80.

18. Benjamin, *Origin of German Tragic Drama*, 98.

19. "Force of Law" 280.

20. For the transcript of this testimony and a remarkable analysis of Eichmann's appeal to the will of the Führer as the "principle behind the law," see Hannah Arendt, *Eichmann in Jerusalem: A Report on the Banality of Evil* (Harmondsworth, UK: Penguin, 1963).

21. Implicit in this argument is a more fundamental distinction between the imaginary and the symbolic, or between representation and language as pure limit.

22. Samuel Weber, "Deconstruction Before the Name: Some Preliminary Remarks on Deconstruction and Violence," *Cardozo Law Review* 13 (1991–1992): 1189.

23. Neither is it marked by the "spectral mixture" of the lawmaking and law-preserving functions that for Benjamin encapsulates the perniciousness of all mythic law.

24. The tension between the "mythic" and the "divine" is nowhere more obvious than in the infamous episode from the Book of Exodus described in chapter 3, where God, after having called Moses to be his prophet, suddenly decides to kill him (Exodus 4:24–26). As I argued there, this may be the passage that best expresses the stakes of the covenant in the Jewish tradition, as a barrier *against* the deity that is intimately related to the function of the commandment as a limit against the mythic "spirit" of the law.

25. Benjamin could have chosen any number of words with a more resolutely transcendent character, or that relate sovereignty to immutability or ipseity; for example, *Herrschermacht* or *Hoheitsgewalt* (a sovereign power, especially of a state or sovereign) or *Herrschaftsgewalt*

(state sovereignty, the sovereignty of parents over children, but also "innate" sovereignty or ipseity, sovereignty as immutability).

26. Emmanuel Lévinas, "The Pact," in *The Lévinas Reader*, ed. Sean Hand (Oxford: Basil Blackwell, 1989), 219.

27. *The Babylonian Talmud*, Seder Nezikin Volume 2: Baba Mezi'a, ed. Rabbi Dr. I. Epstein (London: Soncino, 1935), tractate 59b, 352–53, brackets and emphases in original.

28. Or even that the power of human reasoning is derived from God. It is interesting that Eliezer invokes the oral law, or *halachah*, not God, and yet invokes it in such a way as to confuse it with the laws of nature and with the Heavenly Voice.

29. Immanuel Kant, *Critique of Judgment*, trans. Werner S. Pluhar (Indianapolis: Hackett, 1987), 119.

30. Kant specifies that these fearful manifestations of natural might can become "attractive," can be judged aesthetically, "provided we are in a safe place." It follows that a sublime aesthetic judgment supposes a *distance* between the subject and the might he contemplates, the maintaining of which is one function of the recourse to the written law as constraint.

31. The experience of the dynamically sublime sheds light on Benjamin's account of divine violence as "pure power over all life for the sake of the living" by suggesting that it exalts the self-preservation engendered by reason over the preservation of "mere life." The subject's ability to resist is located not in the finite life of the mortal body, but in the infinite or transcendent life of the mind. The dynamically sublime contemplation of natural might could itself be understood as a kind of "bloodless expiation," since it is situated at the level of reason: it is not necessary to submit to the violence of the volcano to experience the exaltation that results from the contemplation of a might, or the affirmation of a life that transcends its power.

32. Compare Benjamin's comments about the mythic quality of the death penalty: "in the exercise of violence over life and death, more than in any other legal act, the law reaffirms itself. But in this very violence something rotten in the law is revealed, above all to a finer sensibility, because the latter knows itself to be infinitely remote from conditions in which fate might imperiously have shown itself in such a sentence" (242).

33. *Critique of Judgment* 135 (274–75 in universal pagination), emphases in original.

34. The two different guises of "natural might" in Kant's analytic may help to account for the relatively slim margin that separates "mythic" from "divine" violence in Benjamin's essay. On the one hand, there is a deadly might that overwhelms "mere life" and inspires fear, and whose mere manifestation has a lawmaking function; it establishes a boundary that must not be crossed (the "laws of nature"), asserting its "bloody power over mere life." On the other, there is the boundless expansion of the reasoning faculty in the dynamically sublime contemplation of natural might, which asserts a "pure power over all life in the name of the living." It institutes a very different kind of boundary or limit, in the form of the physical distance interposed between the subject and a deadly force or the distance of contemplation that separates an experience of the sublime from mere fear for one's life.

35. See, for example, Benjamin's critique "of the stubborn prevailing habit of conceiving those

just ends as ends of a possible law—that is, not only as generally valid (which follows analytically from the very nature of justice) but also as capable of generalization, which as could be shown, contradicts the nature of justice" (247).

36. *The Book of Legends, Sefer Ha-Aggadah: Legends from the Talmud and Midrash*, ed. Hayim Nahman Bialik and Yehoshua Hana Ravnitzky, trans. William G. Braude (New York: Schocken, 1992), 408.

37. Benjamin, Letter to Martin Buber, July 1916, in *The Correspondence of Walter Benjamin, 1910–1940*, ed. Gershom Scholem and Theodor W. Adorno, trans. Manfred R. Jacobson and Evelyn M. Jacobson (Chicago: University of Chicago Press, 1994), 79–80, emphases in original.

38. In other words, Benjamin's conception of struggle is dialectical, involving a confrontation with a limit and not just an annihilation, effacement, or wiping clean.

7. FREEDOM THROUGH CONSTRAINTS

1. Hallward, "Sujet et volonté dans la philosophie d'Alain Badiou," in *Autour d'Alain Badiou*, ed. Isabelle Vodoz and Fabien Tarby (Paris: Germina, 2011).

2. In other essays Hallward does leave open the possibility of a fundamental and essential link between will and constraint. In an essay on Frantz Fanon, for example, he observes that for Fanon "political will is practiced through struggle against an enemy, a difficulty or an injustice. By definition, there is no will in the absence of constraint or resistance." It is unclear, however, whether constraint should be understood here only in the sense of "dominance and oppression," as Hallward glosses it, or in a more enabling sense. Hallward, "Fanon and Political Will," *Cosmos and History: The Journal of Natural and Social Philosophy* 7, no. 1 (2011): 117.

3. Hallward, "Sujet et volonté dans la philosophie d'Alain Badiou."

4. Immanuel Kant, *Critique of Practical Reason*, trans. Werner S. Pluhar (Indianapolis: Hackett, 2002), 45. Subsequent citations from the text will be given as page numbers in parentheses.

5. Hannah Arendt, *Eichmann in Jerusalem: A Report on the Banality of Evil* (Harmondsworth: Penguin, 1963), 136. Subsequent citations from the text will be given as page numbers in parentheses.

6. In an essay on fascist discourse, Mladen Dolar asks: "But what does this exalting voice say exactly? We don't get to know by reading the fascist reports of fascist speeches. We find a flood of words on the impressions of the reporter . . . on the atmosphere of the public, dead silences, ovations, etc. In the long poetization by Goebbels on his first encounter with the Führer we find only three specific words that the Führer speaks . . . 'honor, work, flag.'" Dolar, "Prolégomènes à une théorie du discours fasciste," *Analytica* 33 (1983): 42.

7. Juliet Flower MacCannell, "Facing Fascism: A Feminine Politics of Jouissance," in *Lacan, Politics, Aesthetics*, ed. Willy Apollon and Richard Feldstein (Albany: SUNY Press, 1996), 75. Subsequent citations from the text will be given as page numbers in parentheses.

8. Jacques Lacan, *Television: A Challenge to the Psychoanalytic Establishment*, ed. Joan Copjec, trans. Jeffrey Mehlman (New York: Norton, 1990), 87.
9. Jacques Lacan, *Écrits*, trans. Bruce Fink (New York: Norton, 2006), 572–73.
10. Mladen Dolar, *A Voice and Nothing More* (Cambridge: MIT Press, 2006), 100–1.
11. Why did the United States and other prominent member nations take so long to sign? When the CPPCG was first ratified by a number of member states in 1951, France and China were the only members of the Security Council to become parties to the treaty. Although the Convention had already removed language that would have defined "political" and "social groups" (and not merely nations or ethnic groups) as possible objects of genocide (in a concession to the Soviet Union and Western allies who feared they might face charges of genocide in the wake of World War II for eliminating political dissidents and ordering the forcible removal of populations), the United States was the last Security Council member to become a party to the treaty in 1988. See Adam Jones, *Genocide: A Comprehensive Introduction* (London: Routledge, 2010), 137. Many analysts believe that this is out of a fear that the displacement and in many cases virtual annihilation of indigenous Native American populations might be ruled a genocide, or that American soldiers might be exposed to similar charges for actions undertaken in the context of a military campaign in a foreign territory. In 1951, a contingent of American blacks went to the United Nations to charge the United States with genocide for the detrimental effects on the black population of systematic racism.
12. Kant also clarifies the stakes of "rationality" in Freud's reading of Moses, which is a matter not merely of refusing superstition and mysticism in the name of a more scientific worldview (as one might infer from Freud's comment that the pharaoh Ahkenaton, in basing the doctrine of monotheism on the cult of the sun god, actually anticipates the scientific discovery that the sun is the source of all life), but of freeing oneself (from superstition, from the father imago, and ultimately from the superego) through the struggle with constraints. Kant shows that reason and writing go hand in hand, inasmuch as written constraints enable the free exercise of the will.
13. *The Babylonian Talmud*, trans. and ed. Rabbi Dr. I. Epstein (London: Soncino, 1938), tractate 59b, 352–52, brackets and emphases in original.
14. *Aseres Hadibros, The Ten Commandments: A New Translation with a Commentary Anthologized from Talmudic, Midrashic, and Rabbinic Sources*, ed. Rabbis Nosson Scherman and Meir Zlotowitz (Brooklyn: Artscroll Mesorah, 1981), 23.
15. Kant, *Critique of Judgment*, trans. Werner S. Pluhar (Indianapolis: Hackett, 1987), 120. Subsequent citations from the text will be given as page numbers in parentheses.
16. Lacan, *The Ethics of Psychoanalysis, 1959–1960*, ed. Jacques-Alain Miller, trans. Dennis Porter (New York: Norton, 1992), 94. Subsequent citations from the text will be given as page numbers in parentheses.
17. In Lacan's terms, we might say that for the one who grovels before God's might, this God is an imaginary Other; for the one who practices true "religion," there is something akin to the traversal of the space of the symbolic.

18. Quoted in Peter Hallward, *Badiou: A Subject to Truth* (Minneapolis: University of Minnesota Press, 2003), 256.

19. Robert Kaufman, "Red Kant, or the Persistence of the Third *Critique* in Adorno and Jameson," *Critical Inquiry* 16 (Summer 2000): 682–724.

20. Badiou, "Mathematics and Philosophy: The Grand Style and the Little Style," in *Theoretical Writings*, ed. and trans. Ray Brassier and Alberto Toscano (London: Continuum, 2004), 14.

21. *Critique of Pure Reason*, cited by ibid., 9.

22. Lacan, *The Seminar of Jacques Lacan Book XX: On Feminine Sexuality, the Limits of Love and Knowledge, 1972–1973*, ed. Jacques-Alain Miller, trans. Bruce Fink (New York: Norton, 1998), 128.

23. Derrida, *Of Grammatology*, trans. Gayatri Spivak (New York: Columbia University Press, 1974), 10.

24. Alain Badiou, "The Three Negations," *Cardozo Law Review* 29, no. 5 (April 2008): 1877–83.

25. Badiou, "Ma position est celle d'un Rousseauisme de l'infini," in *L'explication: conversation avec Aude Lancelin*, by Alain Badiou and Alain Finkielkraut (Paris: Lignes, 2010), 54; cited in Hallward, *Badiou: A Subject to Truth*, 5.

26. Badiou, *Being and Event*, trans. Oliver Feltham (London: Continuum, 2007), 345.

27. Hallward, *Badiou: A Subject to Truth*, 5–6.

28. Ibid., 6.

29. Jean-Jacques Rousseau, *The Social Contract*, trans. Maurice Cranston (London: Penguin Books, 1968).

30. Warren Motte, ed. and trans., *Oulipo: A Primer of Potential Literature* (Champaign: Dalkey Archive, 1986), 41. Subsequent citations from the text will be given as page numbers in parentheses.

31. In the same vein, Kant specifies that to "follow some impulse or inclination" is to succumb to the "heteronomy of the power of choice," to become dependent on some "other law," and therefore to lose one's freedom (*Practical Reason* 49).

32. André Breton, *Manifestoes of Surrealism*, trans. Richard Seaver and Helen R. Lane (Ann Arbor: University of Michigan Press, 1969), 21. Subsequent citations from the text will be given as page numbers in parentheses.

33. In Breton's words, "All that results from listening to oneself, from reading what one has written, is the suspension of the occult, that admirable help." Ibid., 33.

34. "Another entirely false idea in fashion nowadays is the equivalence which is established between inspiration, exploration of the subconscious, and liberation; between chance, automatism, and freedom" (*Oulipo* 18). In calling this "zone of exploration" the "subconscious," Queneau is actually putting his finger on a characteristic feature of Breton's appropriation of Freud, his tendency to substitute a topographical understanding of the unconscious as an alien province of the mind for a dynamic understanding of the unconscious as interpretation.

35. Freud argues that the "truly dynamic" understanding of the unconscious as a mechanism

of interpretation must be distinguished from the increasingly widespread use of the term "unconscious" to "denote a mental *province* rather than a quality of what is mental" (my emphases). He proposes that the impersonal pronoun "id" (*Es*, "it") be used to express "the main characteristic of this province of the mind—the fact of its being alien to the ego." In giving the three "realms" or "provinces" of the mental apparatus the names "ego," "superego," and "id," Freud's second topic seeks to preserve the unconscious as a dynamic mechanism from a topographical definition. Freud, *New Introductory Lectures in Psycho-analysis*, trans. James Strachey (New York: Norton, 1965), 89–90.

36. In the same way, the problem of the will is not antithetical to a psychoanalytic theory of the subject, but expresses something essential about the work of the unconscious under transference; where they intersect is in their respective recourses to constraint.

37. Thanks to Freud, he writes, "the imagination is perhaps on the point of reasserting itself, of reclaiming its rights" (*Manifestoes* 10).

38. To illustrate this fallacy we need only consider how Surrealist painters of the stripe Breton promotes make use of the dream. Salvador Dali, for example, paints "dream worlds," scenes that have the "look" of dreams. Such treatments tend to draw upon the visual aspect of the dream more than upon the dreamwork *as a language*, however. At most, there is a reflection on what Freud calls the "considerations of representability," or the plastic transformations through which latent dream thoughts are translated into images. There is no meditation on the logic of the dream, the operations of condensation and displacement that determine the logic of the substitutions, or the dream's status as an interpretation. The unconscious for Breton is a "depth" and not (as in Freud) a surface, a matter of language. Breton is really celebrating the id, therefore, and not the unconscious. In contrast, Freud is critical of the depth metaphor that holds the unconscious to be a "hidden reality" or repository of "dark forces," emphasizing instead the *profoundly superficial* character of the unconscious, which manifests itself as a discontinuity in speech, in slips of the tongue, and so forth. It would be interesting to contrast Dali's evocation of the "unconscious" with Magritte, who is much closer to Freud in emphasizing the function of the signifier, the way in which the uncon-scious appears as a discontinuity in the surface and not as a "hidden world" or "depth." In his *Ceci n'est pas une pipe*, for example, the signifier (the word "pipe," but also *ceci*, the painting itself) is not the object (a pipe), but neither is there any depth "behind" this sur-face. Importantly, the unconscious for Freud is not distinct from the mind. While Breton equates the "mind" with consciousness, Freud sees consciousness as only one dimension of mental life.

39. In the well-known words of Jacques Derrida, language is a field of "*freeplay*, a field of infinite substitutions only because it is finite, because there is something missing from it: a center that arrests and founds the freeplay of substitutions." Derrida, *Writing and Differ-ence*, trans. Alan Bass (Chicago: University of Chicago Press, 1978), 260.

INDEX

will *(continued)*
260–64, 289*n*2, 290*n*12; and desire, 88;
Eichmann as executor of, 245, 247; of
Führer, 137, 241–43; general, 255–56; to
jouissance, 11–12, 243; Kant on, 247, 249–55;
of the people, 239–40, 245–46; and social
contract, 255–56; unspoken, 241, 245
women, 14, 16, 26, 36, 38–39, 41–47; Freud on,
14, 47, 52, 57–58
writing, 19–20, 24; "absolute," 125, 129, 184–86,
190, 202; banalization of, 126–29, 185, 199;
body's relation to, 185; and castration, 184;
as constraint, 7, 175, 233–35, 254–55, 258–64;
of jouissance, 78; living or embodied, 125,
185, 190, 199; logical, 155–58; in psychoanal-

ysis, 259, 263; as limit to superego, 242–43;
and the unconscious, 263
written laws, 34–36, 128–29, 200, 225, 227,
253; Benjamin on, 206, 208, 220–22; as constraint, 127, 129, 222, 231–57; displacement
of, 129, 175, 187; against genocide, 243–47,
290*n*11; of Roman Republic, 34; refusal
of, 242; as distinct from unwritten laws,
209, 216, 220, 223, 244, 286*n*13; *see also* commandments; constitution; Decalogue
wrong, 28, 37, 39

Yahweh, 82, 201, 224–25

Žižek, Slavoj, 9–10, 143, 268*n*14

GPSR Authorized Representative: Easy Access System Europe, Mustamäe tee
50, 10621 Tallinn, Estonia, gpsr.requests@easproject.com

www.ingramcontent.com/pod-product-compliance
Lightning Source LLC
Chambersburg PA
CBHW022139020426
42334CB00015B/964